MULTIPLE INTELLIGENCES

in the Classroom

3rd Edition

ASCD MEMBER BOOK

Many ASCD members received this book as a
member benefit upon its initial release.

Learn more at: www.ascd.org/memberbooks

MULTIPLE INTELLIGENCES
in the Classroom

3rd Edition

Thomas Armstrong

Alexandria, Virginia USA

1703 N. Beauregard St. • Alexandria, VA 22311-1714 USA
Phone: 800-933-2723 or 703-578-9600 • Fax: 703-575-5400
Web site: www.ascd.org • E-mail: member@ascd.org
Author guidelines: www.ascd.org/write

Gene R. Carter, *Executive Director;* Nancy Modrak, *Publisher;* Julie Houtz, *Director of Book Editing & Production;* Ernesto Yermoli, *Project Manager;* Reece Quiñones, *Senior Graphic Designer;* Mike Kalyan, *Production Manager;* BMWW, *Typesetter;* Kyle Steichen, *Production Specialist*

ASCD Member Book, No. FY09-6 (May 2009, P). ASCD Member Books mail to Premium (P) and Comprehensive (C) members on this schedule: Jan., PC; Feb., P; Apr., PC; May, P; July, PC; Aug., P; Sept., PC; Nov., PC; Dec., P.

PAPERBACK ISBN: 978-1-4166-0789-2   ASCD product #109007
Also available as an e-book through ebrary, netLibrary, and many online booksellers (see Books in Print for the ISBNs).

Quantity discounts for the paperback edition only: 10–49 copies, 10%; 50+ copies, 15%; for 1,000 or more copies, call 800-933-2723, ext. 5634, or 703-575-5634. For desk copies: member@ascd.org.

Library of Congress Cataloging-in-Publication Data

Armstrong, Thomas.
    Multiple intelligences in the classroom / Thomas Armstrong. — 3rd ed.
       p. cm.
    Includes bibliographical references and index.
    ISBN 978-1-4166-0789-2 (pkb.: alk. paper)
    1. Teaching.   2. Cognitive styles.   3. Learning.   4. Multiple intelligences.   I. Association for Supervision and Curriculum Development.   II. Title.

    LB1025.3.A76 2009
    370.15'23—dc22

                                                                    2009000377

20 19 18 17 16 15 14 13 12 11 10 09   1 2 3 4 5 6 7 8 9 10 11 12

3rd Edition

MULTIPLE INTELLIGENCES
in the classroom

Acknowledgments

Many people have helped make this book possible. First, I thank Howard Gardner, whose generous support of my work over the years has helped fuel my continued involvement in MI theory. I also want to thank Mert Hanley, former director of the Teaching/Learning Center in the West Irondequoit School District in upstate New York, for encouraging me to write a book for teachers on multiple intelligences and for providing me with the opportunity to work with several school districts in the Rochester, New York, area. Over a period of four years in those districts, I tried out many of the ideas in this book. Thanks also to the following individuals who helped in different ways to give form to *Multiple Intelligences in the Classroom* in one or more of its three editions: Ron Brandt, Sue Teele, David Thornburg, Chris Kunkel, Branton Shearer, Tom Hoerr, Jo Gusman, Jean Simeone, Pat Kyle, DeLee Lanz, Peggy Buzanski, Dee Dickinson, and my wife, Barbara Turner. I also want to thank Nancy Modrak, Scott Willis, Carolyn Pool, Julie Houtz, and the rest of the staff at ASCD for making this 3rd edition of *Multiple Intelligences in the Classroom* possible. Working with the wonderful people in the ASCD book department has been one of the literary and educational joys of my life. I encourage other educators who feel that they have a book inside of them to consider publishing with ASCD—go to www.ascd.org for submission guidelines. Finally, my special appreciation goes out to the thousands of teachers, administrators, and students who responded to the ideas and strategies presented in these pages: This book has been created in recognition of the rich potential that exists in each of you.

Preface

In addition to my own writings, there are now a number of guides to the theory of multiple intelligences, written by my own associates at Harvard Project Zero and by colleagues in other parts of the country. Coming from a background in special education, Thomas Armstrong was one of the first educators to write about the theory. He has always stood out in my mind because of the accuracy of his accounts, the clarity of his prose, the broad range of his references, and the teacher-friendliness of his tone.

Now he has prepared the book that you hold in your hands for members of the Association for Supervision and Curriculum Development. Displaying the Armstrong virtues that I have come to expect, this volume is a reliable and readable account of my work, directed particularly to teachers, administrators, and other educators. Armstrong has also added some nice touches of his own: the notion of a "paralyzing experience," to complement Joseph Walters' and my concept of a "crystallizing experience"; the suggestion to

Howard Gardner is Hobbs Professor of Cognition and Education and codirector of Project Zero at the Harvard Graduate School of Education and adjunct professor of neurology at the Boston University School of Medicine. He is the author of *Frames of Mind: The Theory of Multiple Intelligences* (Basic Books, 1983/1993), *Multiple Intelligence: The Theory in Practice* (Basic Books, 1993), *Intelligence Reframed: Multiple Intelligences for the 21st Century* (Basic Books, 1999), and *Multiple Intelligences: New Horizons* (Basic Books, 2006).

attend to the way that youngsters misbehave as a clue to their intelligences; and some informal suggestions about how to involve youngsters in an examination of their own intelligences and how to manage one's classroom in an MI way. He has included several rough-and-ready tools that can allow one to assess one's own intellectual profile, to get a handle on the strengths and proclivities of youngsters under one's charge, and to involve youngsters in games built around MI ideas. He conveys a vivid idea of what MI classes, teaching moves, curricula, and assessments can be like. Each chapter concludes with a set of exercises to help one build on the ideas and practices that one has just read about.

As Armstrong points out in his introduction, I do not believe that there is a single royal road to an implementation of MI ideas in the classroom. I have been encouraged and edified by the wide variety of ways in which educators around the country have made use of my ideas, and I have no problem saying, "Let 100 MI schools bloom." From my perspective, the essence of the theory is respect for the many differences among people, the multiple variations in the ways that they learn, the several modes by which they can be assessed, and the almost infinite number of ways in which they can leave a mark on the world. Because Thomas Armstrong shares this vision, I am pleased that he has had the opportunity to present these ideas to you, and I hope that you in turn will be stimulated to extend them in ways that bear your own particular stamp.

Howard Gardner

Introduction
to the 3rd Edition

This book has emerged from my work over the past 23 years in applying Howard Gardner's theory of multiple intelligences to the nuts-and-bolts issues of classroom teaching. I was initially attracted to MI theory in 1985 when I saw that it provided a language for talking about the inner gifts of children, especially those students who have been given labels such as "LD" and "ADHD" during their school careers (Armstrong, 1987a, 1987b, 1988, 1997, 1999b). It was as a learning disabilities specialist during the late 1970s and early 1980s that I began to feel the need to disassociate myself from what I considered to be a deficit-oriented paradigm in special education. I wanted to forge a new model based on what I plainly saw were the many gifts of these so-called disabled children.

I didn't have to create a new model. Howard Gardner had already done it for me. In 1979, as a Harvard researcher, Gardner was asked by a Dutch philanthropic group, the Bernard Van Leer Foundation, to investigate human potential. This invitation led to the founding of Harvard Project Zero, which served as the institutional midwife for the theory of multiple intelligences. Although Gardner had been thinking about the notion of "many kinds of minds" since at least the mid-1970s (see Gardner, 1989, p. 96), the publication in 1983 of his book *Frames of Mind* marked the effective birthdate of

"MI" theory. Since that time, awareness among educators about the theory of multiple intelligences has continued to grow steadily. From a model that was originally popular mostly in the field of gifted education and among isolated schools and teachers around the United States in the mid- to late 1980s, MI theory has expanded its reach over the past 20 years to include thousands of school districts, tens of thousands of schools, and hundreds of thousands of teachers in the United States and numerous countries across the globe.

In this book, I present my own particular adaptation of Gardner's model for teachers and other educators. My hope is that people can use this book in several ways to help stimulate continued reforms in education:

- As a practical introduction to the theory of multiple intelligences for individuals new to the model;
- As a supplementary text for teachers in training in schools of education;
- As a study guide for groups of teachers and administrators working in schools that are implementing reforms; and
- As a resource book for teachers and other educators looking for new ideas to enhance their teaching experience.

Each chapter concludes with a section called "For Further Study" that can help readers integrate the material into their instructional practice. Several appendixes and a list of references alert readers to other materials related to MI theory that can enrich and extend their understanding of the model.

With the publication of the 2nd edition of *Multiple Intelligences in the Classroom* in 2000, two new features were added to the original work. First, the naturalist intelligence (integrated into MI theory by Howard Gardner in 1997) was incorporated into all the activities, charts, strategies, and other materials related to the first seven intelligences. Second, a new chapter (Chapter 14) was added focusing on the possibility of a ninth intelligence—the existential—which Gardner describes as the intelligence of concern with ultimate life issues such as the meaning of life, the problem of evil, and the aims of human endeavor (Gardner, 1999). As of this writing, the existential intelligence still has not been formally included as one of the intelligences in MI theory but, rather, exists on the periphery as a potential candidate.

Now, in this 3rd edition, two more chapters have been added. Chapter 15 focuses on criticisms that have been made about MI theory over the past 10 years. These criticisms have emerged in part because of the overwhelming success of the model (success tends to invite criticism), in part because of the more conservative nature of the times (a consequence of the U.S. federal government's No Child Left Behind law—see Armstrong, 2006), and in part because criticism of a theory is always an important component of its further development and improvement. In addition to providing critical arguments from a number of journalistic and academic sources against the validity of multiple intelligences, I've provided my own responses, which I hope will stimulate further critical conversations about MI theory. I've also added Chapter 16, which focuses on the spread of MI theory around the world. Even as MI theory has received increasing criticism in the United States, it has spread by leaps and bounds in many countries around the world. I provide a snapshot of some of these international developments, by chronicling the impact of MI theory at the policymaking level (MI has been incorporated into some countries' laws and federal initiatives), at the academic level (many new studies are coming out on MI theory covering populations from Hong Kong to Zimbabwe), at the community level (in Denmark, for example, a world-class interactive museum has been created based on multiple intelligences), and finally, at the school and classroom level. In addition to two new chapters, I have updated all of the references, resources, and technological developments so that they reflect the rapid expansion in the past eight years of new books, journal articles, software, and other materials that support MI theory.

Thomas Armstrong
Sonoma County, California
July 2008

1

The Foundations
of MI Theory

It is of the utmost importance that we recognize and nurture all of the varied human intelligences, and all of the combinations of intelligences. We are all so different largely because we all have different combinations of intelligences. If we recognize this, I think we will have at least a better chance of dealing appropriately with the many problems that we face in the world.

—Howard Gardner

In 1904, the minister of public instruction in Paris asked the French psychologist Alfred Binet and a group of colleagues to develop a means of determining which primary grade students were "at risk" for failure so these students could receive remedial attention. Out of their efforts came the first intelligence tests. Imported to the United States several years later, intelligence testing became widespread, as did the notion that there was something called "intelligence" that could be objectively measured and reduced to a single number or "IQ" score.

Almost 80 years after the first intelligence tests were developed, a Harvard psychologist named Howard Gardner challenged this commonly held belief. Saying that our culture had defined intelligence too narrowly, he proposed in the book *Frames of Mind* (Gardner, 1993a) the existence of at least seven basic intelligences. More recently, he has added an eighth and discussed the possibility of a ninth (Gardner, 1999). In his theory of multiple intelligences (MI theory), Gardner sought to broaden the scope of human potential beyond the confines of the IQ score. He seriously questioned the validity of determining intelligence through the practice of taking individuals out of their natural learning environment and asking them to do isolated tasks they'd never done before—and probably would never choose to do again. Instead, Gardner suggested that intelligence has more to do with the capacity for (1) solving problems and (2) fashioning products in a context-rich and naturalistic setting.

The Eight Intelligences Described

Once this broader and more pragmatic perspective was taken, the concept of intelligence began to lose its mystique and became a functional concept that could be seen working in people's lives in a variety of ways. Gardner provided a means of mapping the broad range of abilities that humans possess by grouping their capabilities into the following eight comprehensive categories or "intelligences":

Linguistic: The capacity to use words effectively, whether orally (e.g., as a storyteller, orator, or politician) or in writing (e.g., as a poet, playwright, editor, or journalist). This intelligence includes the ability to manipulate the syntax or structure of language, the phonology or sounds of language, the semantics or meanings of language, and the pragmatic dimensions or practical uses of language. Some of these uses include rhetoric (using language to convince others to take a specific course of action), mnemonics (using language to remember information), explanation (using language to inform), and metalanguage (using language to talk about itself).

Logical-mathematical: The capacity to use numbers effectively (e.g., as a mathematician, tax accountant, or statistician) and to reason well (e.g., as a scientist, computer programmer, or logician). This intelligence includes sensitivity to logical patterns and relationships, statements and propositions (if-then, cause-effect), functions, and other related abstractions. The kinds of processes used in the service of logical-mathematical intelligence include categorization, classification, inference, generalization, calculation, and hypothesis testing.

Spatial: The ability to perceive the visual-spatial world accurately (e.g., as a hunter, scout, or guide) and to perform transformations upon those perceptions (e.g., as an interior decorator, architect, artist, or inventor). This intelligence involves sensitivity to color, line, shape, form, space, and the relationships that exist between these elements. It includes the capacity to visualize, to graphically represent visual or spatial ideas, and to orient oneself appropriately in a spatial matrix.

Bodily-kinesthetic: Expertise in using one's whole body to express ideas and feelings (e.g., as an actor, a mime, an athlete, or a dancer) and facility in using one's hands to produce or transform things (e.g., as a craftsperson, sculptor, mechanic, or surgeon). This intelligence includes specific physical skills such as coordination, balance, dexterity, strength, flexibility, and speed, as well as proprioceptive, tactile, and haptic capacities.

Musical: The capacity to perceive (e.g., as a music aficionado), discriminate (e.g., as a music critic), transform (e.g., as a composer), and express (e.g., as a performer) musical forms. This intelligence includes sensitivity to the rhythm, pitch or melody, and timbre or tone color of a musical piece. One can have a figural or "top-down" understanding of music (global, intuitive), a formal or "bottom-up" understanding (analytic, technical), or both.

Interpersonal: The ability to perceive and make distinctions in the moods, intentions, motivations, and feelings of other people. This can include sensitivity to facial expressions, voice, and gestures; the capacity for discriminating among many different kinds of interpersonal cues; and the ability to respond effectively to those cues in some pragmatic way (e.g., to influence a group of people to follow a certain line of action).

Intrapersonal: Self-knowledge and the ability to act adaptively on the basis of that knowledge. This intelligence includes having an accurate picture of oneself (one's strengths and limitations); awareness of inner moods, intentions, motivations, temperaments, and desires; and the capacity for self-discipline, self-understanding, and self-esteem.

Naturalist: Expertise in the recognition and classification of the numerous species—the flora and fauna—of an individual's environment. This also includes sensitivity to other natural phenomena (e.g., cloud formations, mountains, etc.) and, in the case of those growing up in an urban environment, the capacity to discriminate among inanimate objects such as cars, sneakers, and CD covers.

The Theoretical Basis for MI Theory

Many people look at the above categories—particularly musical, spatial, and bodily-kinesthetic—and wonder why Howard Gardner insists on calling them intelligences rather than *talents* or *aptitudes*. Gardner realized that people are used to hearing expressions like "He's not very intelligent, but he has a wonderful aptitude for music"; thus, he was quite conscious of his use of the word *intelligence* to describe each category. He said in an interview, "I'm deliberately being somewhat provocative. If I'd said that there's seven kinds of competencies, people would yawn and say 'Yeah, yeah.' But by calling them 'intelligences,' I'm saying that we've tended to put on a pedestal one variety called intelligence, and there's actually a plurality of them, and some are things we've never thought about as being 'intelligence' at all" (Weinreich-Haste, 1985, p. 48). To provide a sound theoretical foundation for his claims, Gardner set up certain basic "tests" that each intelligence had to meet to be considered a full-fledged intelligence and not simply a talent, skill, or aptitude. The criteria he used include the following eight factors:

1. Potential isolation by brain damage
2. The existence of savants, prodigies, and other exceptional individuals
3. A distinctive developmental history and a definable set of expert "end-state" performances
4. An evolutionary history and evolutionary plausibility
5. Support from psychometric findings
6. Support from experimental psychological tasks
7. An identifiable core operation or set of operations
8. Susceptibility to encoding in a symbol system

Potential Isolation by Brain Damage

At the Boston Veterans Administration, Gardner worked with individuals who had suffered accidents or illnesses that affected specific areas of the brain. In several cases, brain lesions seemed to have selectively impaired one intelligence while leaving all the other intelligences intact. For example, a person with a lesion in Broca's area (left frontal lobe) might have a substantial portion of his linguistic intelligence damaged and thus experience great difficulty speaking, reading, and writing. Yet he might still be able to sing, do math, dance, reflect on feelings, and relate to others. A person with a lesion in the temporal lobe of the right hemisphere might have her musical capacities selectively impaired, while frontal lobe lesions might primarily affect the personal intelligences.

Gardner, then, is arguing for the existence of eight relatively autonomous brain systems—a more sophisticated and updated version of the "right-brain/left-brain" model of learning that was popular in the 1970s. Figure 1.1 shows the brain structures for each intelligence.

The Existence of Savants, Prodigies, and Other Exceptional Individuals

Gardner suggests that in some people we can see single intelligences operating at high levels, much like huge mountains rising up against the backdrop of a flat horizon. Savants are individuals who demonstrate superior abilities in part of one intelligence while one or more of their other intelligences function at a low level. They seem to exist for each of the eight intelligences. For instance, in the movie *Rain Man* (which is based on a true story), Dustin Hoffman plays the role of Raymond, a logical-mathematical autistic savant. Raymond rapidly calculates multidigit numbers in his head and does other amazing mathematical feats, yet he has poor peer relationships, low language functioning, and a lack of insight into his own life. There are also savants who draw exceptionally well, savants who have amazing musical memories (e.g., playing a composition after hearing it only one time), savants who read complex material yet don't comprehend what they're reading (hyperlexics), and savants who have exceptional sensitivity to nature or animals (see Grandin & Johnson, 2006, and Sacks, 1995).

A Distinctive Developmental History and a Definable Set of Expert "End-State" Performances

Gardner suggests that intelligences are galvanized by participation in some kind of culturally valued activity and that the individual's growth in such an activity follows a developmental pattern. Each intelligence-based activity has its own developmental trajectory; that is, each activity has its own time of arising in early childhood, its own time of peaking during one's lifetime, and its own pattern of either rapidly or gradually declining as one gets older. Musical composition, for example, seems to be among the earliest culturally valued activities to develop to a high level of proficiency: Mozart

1.1
MI Theory Summary Chart

Intelligence	Core Components	Symbol Systems	High End-States	Neurological Systems (Primary Areas)	Developmental Factors	Ways that Cultures Value	Evolutionary Origins	Presence in Other Species	Historical Factors (Relative to Current U.S. Status)
Linguistic	Sensitivity to the sounds, structure, meanings, and functions of words and language	Phonetic languages (e.g., English)	Writer, orator (e.g., Virginia Woolf, Martin Luther King Jr.)	Left temporal and frontal lobes (e.g., Broca's/ Wernicke's areas)	"Explodes" in early childhood; remains robust until old age	Oral histories, storytelling, literature	Written notations found dating to 30,000 years ago	Apes' ability to name	Oral transmission more important before printing press
Logical-Mathematical	Sensitivity to, and capacity to discern, logical or numerical patterns; ability to handle long chains of reasoning	Computer languages (e.g., Basic)	Scientist, mathematician (e.g., Madame Curie, Blaise Pascal)	Left frontal and right parietal lobes	Peaks in adolescence and early adulthood; higher math insights decline after age 40	Scientific discoveries, mathematical theories, counting and classification systems	Early number systems and calendars found	Bees calculate distances through their dances	More important with influence of computers
Spatial	Capacity to perceive the visual-spatial world accurately and to perform transformations on one's initial perceptions	Ideographic languages (e.g., Chinese)	Artist, architect (e.g., Frida Kahlo, I. M. Pei)	Posterior regions of right hemisphere	Topological thinking in early childhood gives way to Euclidean paradigm around age 9–10; artistic eye stays robust into old age	Artistic works, navigational systems, architectural designs, inventions	Cave drawings	Territorial instinct of several species	More important with advent of video and other visual technologies
Bodily-Kinesthetic	Ability to control one's body movements and to handle objects skillfully	Sign languages, Braille*	Athlete, dancer, sculptor (e.g., Martha Graham, Auguste Rodin)	Cerebellum, basal ganglia, motor cortex	Varies depending upon component (strength, flexibility) or domain (gymnastics, baseball, mime)	Crafts, athletic performances, dramatic works, dance forms, sculpture	Evidence of early tool use	Tool use of primates, anteaters, and other species	Was more important in agrarian period

Intelligence	Core Components	Symbol Systems	High End-States	Neurological Systems	Developmental Factors	Ways That Cultures Value	Evolutionary Origins	Presence in Other Species	Historical Factors
Musical	Ability to produce and appreciate rhythm, pitch, and timbre; appreciation of the forms of musical expressiveness	Musical notational systems, Morse Code	Composer, performer (e.g., Stevie Wonder, Midori)	Right temporal lobe	Earliest intelligence to develop; prodigies often go through developmental crisis	Musical compositions, performances, recordings	Evidence of musical instruments back to Stone Age	Bird song	Was more important during oral culture, when communication was more musical in nature
Interpersonal	Capacity to discern and respond appropriately to the moods, temperaments, motivations, and desires of other people	Social cues (e.g., gestures and facial expressions)	Counselor, political leader (e.g., Carl Rogers, Nelson Mandela)	Frontal lobes, temporal lobe (especially right hemisphere), limbic system	Attachment/bonding during first 3 years critical	Political documents, social institutions	Communal living groups required for hunting/gathering	Maternal bonding observed in primates and other species	More important with increase in service economy
Intrapersonal	Access to one's own "feeling" life and the ability to discriminate among one's emotions; knowledge of one's own strengths and weaknesses	Symbols of the self (e.g., in dreams and artwork)	Psychotherapist, religious leader (e.g., Sigmund Freud, the Buddha)	Frontal lobes, parietal lobes, limbic system	Formation of boundary between "self" and "other" during first 3 years critical	Religious systems, psychological theories, rites of passage	Early evidence of religious life	Chimpanzees can locate self in mirror; apes experience fear	Continues to be important with increasingly complex society requiring choice-making
Naturalist	Expertise in distinguishing among members of a species; recognizing the existence of other neighboring species; and charting out the relations, formally or informally, among several species	Species classification systems (e.g., Linnaeus); habitat maps	Naturalist, biologist, animal activist (e.g., Charles Darwin, E. O. Wilson, Jane Goodall)	Areas of left parietal lobe important for discriminating "living" from "nonliving" things	Shows up dramatically in some young children; schooling or experience increases formal or informal expertise	Folk taxonomies, herbal lore, hunting rituals, animal spirit mythologies	Early hunting tools reveal understanding of other species	Hunting instinct in innumerable species to discriminate between prey and nonprey	Was more important during agrarian period; then fell out of favor during industrial expansion; now "earth-smarts" are more important than ever to preserve endangered ecosystems

*Recent research suggests that many sign languages, such as American Sign Language, have a strongly linguistic basis as well (see, for example, Sacks, 1990).

was only 4 years old when he began to compose. Numerous composers and performers have been active well into their 80s and 90s, so expertise in musical composition also seems to remain relatively robust into old age.

Higher mathematical expertise appears to have a somewhat different trajectory. It doesn't emerge as early as music composition ability (4-year-olds do not create new logical principles), but it does *peak* relatively early in life. Many great mathematical and scientific ideas were developed by teenagers such as Blaise Pascal and Karl Friedrich Gauss. In fact, a review of the history of mathematical ideas suggests that few original mathematical insights come to people past the age of 40. Once people reach this age, they're considered over the hill as higher mathematicians! Most of us can breathe a sigh of relief, however, because this decline generally does not seem to affect more pragmatic skills such as balancing a checkbook.

One can become a successful novelist at age 40, 50, or even later. Nobel Prize–winner in literature Toni Morrison didn't publish her first novel until she was 39. One can even be over 75 and choose to become a painter: Grandma Moses did. Gardner points out that we need to use several different developmental maps in order to understand the eight intelligences. Piaget provides a comprehensive map for logical-mathematical intelligence, but we may need to go to Erik Erikson for a map of the development of the personal intelligences, and to Noam Chomsky or Lev Vygotsky for developmental models of linguistic intelligence. Figure 1.1 includes a summary of developmental trajectories for each intelligence.

Gardner (1993b) points out that we can best see the intelligences working at their zenith by studying the "end-states" of intelligences in the lives of truly exceptional individuals. For example, we can see musical intelligence at work by studying Beethoven's *Eroica Symphony*, the naturalist intelligence through Darwin's theory of evolution, or spatial intelligence via Michelangelo's Sistine Chapel paintings. Figure 1.1 includes examples of end-states for each intelligence.

An Evolutionary History and Evolutionary Plausibility

Gardner concludes that each of the eight intelligences meets the test of having its roots deeply embedded in the evolution of human beings and, even earlier, in the evolution of other species. So, for example, spatial intelligence can be studied in the cave drawings of Lascaux, as well as in the way certain insects orient themselves in space while tracking flowers. Similarly, musical intelligence can be traced back to archaeological evidence of early musical instruments, as well as through the wide variety of bird songs. Figure 1.1 includes notes on the evolutionary origins of the intelligences.

MI theory also has a historical context. Certain intelligences seem to have been more important in earlier times than they are today. Naturalist and bodily-kinesthetic intelligence, for example, were probably valued more 100 years ago in the United States, when a majority of the population lived in rural settings and the ability to hunt, harvest grain, and build silos had strong social approbation. Similarly, certain intelligences may become more important in the future. As more and more people receive their information from films, television, DVDs, and online sources, the value placed on having a strong spatial intelligence may increase. Similarly, there is now a growing need for individuals who have expertise in the naturalist intelligence to help protect endangered ecosystems. Figure 1.1 notes some of the historical factors that have influenced the perceived value of each intelligence.

Support from Psychometric Findings

Standardized measures of human ability provide the "test" that most theories of intelligence (as well as many learning-style theories) use to ascertain the validity of a model. Although Gardner is no champion of standardized tests, and in fact has been an ardent supporter of alternatives to formal testing (see Chapter 10), he suggests that we can look at many existing standardized tests for support of the theory of multiple intelligences (although Gardner would point out that standardized tests assess multiple intelligences in a strikingly decontextualized fashion). For example, the Wechsler Intelligence Scale for Children includes subtests that require linguistic intelligence (e.g., information, vocabulary), logical-mathematical intelligence (e.g., arithmetic), spatial intelligence (e.g., picture arrangement), and to a lesser extent bodily-kinesthetic intelligence (e.g., object assembly). Still other assessments tap personal intelligences (e.g., the Vineland Society Maturity Scale and the Coopersmith Self-Esteem Inventory). Chapter 3 includes a survey of the types of formal tests associated with each of the eight intelligences.

Support from Experimental Psychological Tasks

Gardner suggests that by looking at specific psychological studies, we can witness intelligences working in isolation from one another. For example, in studies where subjects master a specific skill, such as reading, but fail to transfer that ability to another area, such as mathematics, we see the failure of linguistic ability to transfer to logical-mathematical intelligence. Similarly, in studies of cognitive abilities such as memory, perception, or attention, we can see evidence that individuals possess selective abilities. Certain individuals, for instance, may have a superior memory for words but not for faces; others may have acute perception of musical sounds but not verbal sounds. Each of these cognitive faculties, then, is intelligence-specific; that is, people can demonstrate different levels of proficiency across the eight intelligences in each cognitive area.

An Identifiable Core Operation or Set of Operations

Gardner says that much as a computer program requires a set of operations (e.g., DOS) in order for it to function, each intelligence has a set of core operations that serve to drive the various activities indigenous to that intelligence. In musical intelligence, for example, those components may include sensitivity to pitch or the ability to discriminate among various rhythmic structures. In bodily-kinesthetic intelligence, core operations may include the ability to imitate the physical movements of others or the capacity to master established fine-motor routines for building a structure. Gardner speculates that these core operations may someday be identified with such precision as to be simulated on a computer.

Susceptibility to Encoding in a Symbol System

According to Gardner, one of the best indicators of intelligent behavior is the ability to use symbols. The word "cat" that appears here on the page is simply a collection of marks printed in a specific way, yet it probably conjures up for you an entire range of associations, images, and memories. What has occurred is the bringing to the present ("re-present-ation") of something that is not actually here. Gardner suggests that the ability to symbolize is one of the most important factors separating humans from most other species. He notes that each of the eight intelligences in his theory meets the criterion of being able to be symbolized. Each intelligence, in fact, has its own unique symbol or notational systems. For linguistic intelligence, there are a number of spoken and written languages such as English, French, and Spanish. For spatial intelligence, there is a range of graphic languages used by architects, engineers, and designers, as well as certain partially ideographic languages such as Chinese. Figure 1.1 includes examples of symbol systems for all eight intelligences.

Key Points in MI Theory

Beyond the descriptions of the eight intelligences and their theoretical underpinnings, certain points of the MI model are important to remember:

Each person possesses all eight intelligences. MI theory is not a "type theory" for determining the *one* intelligence that fits. It is a theory of cognitive functioning, and it proposes that each person has capacities in all eight intelligences. Of course, the eight intelligences function together in ways unique to each person. Some people appear to possess extremely high levels of functioning in all or most of the eight intelligences—for example, German poet-statesman-scientist-naturalist-philosopher Johann Wolfgang von Goethe. Other people, such as certain severely impaired individuals in institutions for the developmentally disabled, appear to lack all but the most rudimentary aspects of the intelligences. Most of us fall somewhere in between these two poles—being highly developed in some intelligences, modestly developed in others, and relatively underdeveloped in the rest.

Most people can develop each intelligence to an adequate level of competency. Although individuals may bewail their deficiencies in a given area and consider their problems innate and intractable, Gardner suggests that virtually everyone has the capacity to develop all eight intelligences to a reasonably high level of performance if given the appropriate encouragement, enrichment, and instruction. He points to the Suzuki Talent Education Program as an example of how individuals of relatively modest biological musical endowment can achieve a sophisticated level of proficiency in playing the violin or piano through a combination of the right environmental influences (e.g., an involved parent, exposure from infancy to classical music, and early instruction). Such educational models can be found in other intelligences as well (see, for example, Edwards, 1989, for a method that improves one's spatial abilities through drawing).

Intelligences usually work together in complex ways. Gardner points out that each intelligence as described above is actually a "fiction"; that is, no intelligence exists by itself in life (except perhaps in very rare instances in savants and brain-injured individuals). Intelligences are always interacting with each other. To cook a meal, one must read the recipe (linguistic), perhaps double the recipe (logical-mathematical), develop a menu that satisfies all members of the family (interpersonal), and placate one's own appetite as well (intrapersonal). Similarly, when a child plays a game of kickball, she needs bodily-kinesthetic intelligence (to run, kick, and catch), spatial intelligence (to orient herself to the playing field and to anticipate the trajectories of flying balls), and linguistic and interpersonal intelligences (to successfully argue a point during a dispute in the game). The intelligences have been taken out of context in MI theory only for the purpose of examining their essential features and learning how to use them effectively. We must always remember to put them back into their specific culturally valued contexts when we are finished with their formal study.

There are many ways to be intelligent within each category. There is no standard set of attributes that one must have to be considered intelligent in a specific area. Consequently, a person may not be able to read, yet be highly linguistic because he can tell a terrific story or has a large oral vocabulary. Similarly, a person may be quite awkward on the playing field, yet possess superior bodily-kinesthetic intelligence when she weaves a carpet or creates an inlaid chess table. MI theory emphasizes the rich diversity of ways in which people show their gifts *within* intelligences as well as *between* intelligences. (See Chapter 3 for more information on the varieties of attributes in each intelligence.)

The Existence of Other Intelligences

Gardner points out that his model is a tentative formulation; after further research and investigation, some of the intelligences on his list may not meet certain of the eight criteria described above and therefore may no longer qualify as intelligences. However, we may identify *new* intelligences that do meet the various tests. In fact, Gardner has acted on this belief by adding a new intelligence—the naturalist—after deciding that it fits each of the eight criteria. His consideration of a ninth intelligence—the existential—is also based upon its meeting most of the criteria (see Chapter 14 for a detailed discussion of the existential intelligence). Other intelligences that have been proposed by individuals other than Gardner include spirituality, moral sensibility, humor, intuition, creativity, culinary (cooking) ability, olfactory perception (sense of smell), an ability to synthesize the other intelligences, and mechanical ability. It remains to be seen whether these proposed intelligences can, in fact, meet each of the eight tests described above.

The Relationship of MI Theory to Other Intelligence Theories

Gardner's theory of multiple intelligences is certainly not the first model to grapple with the notion of intelligence. There have been theories of intelligence since ancient times, when the mind was considered to reside somewhere in the heart, the liver, or the kidneys. In more recent times, theories of intelligence have emerged touting anywhere from 1 (Spearman's "g") to 150 (Guilford's Structure of the Intellect) types of intelligence.

A growing number of learning-style theories also deserve to be mentioned here. Gardner has sought to differentiate the theory of multiple intelligences from the concept of "learning style." He writes: "The concept of *style* designates a general approach that an individual can apply equally to every conceivable content. In contrast, an *intelligence* is a capacity, with its component processes, that is geared to a specific content in the world (such as musical sounds or spatial patterns)" (Gardner, 1995, pp. 202–203). There is no clear evidence yet, according to Gardner, that a person highly developed in spatial intelligence, for example, will show that capacity in every aspect of his or her life (e.g., washing the car spatially, reflecting on ideas spatially, socializing spatially, etc.). He suggests that this task remains to be empirically investigated. (For an example of an attempt in this direction, see Silver, Strong, & Perini, 1997.)

Still, it *is* tempting to want to relate MI theory to any of a number of learning-style theories that have gained prominence in the past two decades, since learners expand their knowledge base by linking new information (in this case, MI theory) to existing schemes or models (the learning-style model with which they're most familiar). This task is not so easy, however, partly because of what we've suggested above and partly because MI theory has a different type of underlying structure than do many of the most current learning-style theories. MI theory is a *cognitive* model that seeks to describe how individuals use their intelligences to solve problems and fashion products. Unlike other models that are primarily process oriented, Gardner's approach is particularly geared to how the human mind operates on the *contents* of the world (e.g., objects, persons, numerical patterns, etc.). A seemingly related theory, the Visual-Auditory-Kinesthetic model, is actually very different from MI theory, in that it is a *sensory-channel* model. (MI theory is not specifically tied to the senses; it is possible to be blind and have spatial intelligence or to be deaf and be quite musical—as is the case, for example, with the world-renowned percussionist Evelyn Glennie.) Another popular theory, the Myers-Briggs model, is actually a *personality* theory based on Carl Jung's theoretical formulation of different types of personalities. To attempt to correlate MI theory with models like these is akin to comparing apples with oranges. Although we can identify relationships and connections, our efforts may resemble those of the blind men and the elephant: each model touching upon a different aspect of the whole learner.

For Further Study

1. Form a study group on MI theory using Howard Gardner's seminal book *Frames of Mind: The Theory of Multiple Intelligences—10th Anniversary Edition* (1993a) as a text. Each member can be responsible for reading and reporting on a specific chapter. For an example of how a multiple intelligences school arose from such a study group, see Hoerr (2000).

2. Use Gardner's comprehensive bibliography on MI theory found in his books *Multiple Intelligences: New Horizons in Theory and Practice* (2006) and *Intelligence Reframed: Multiple Intelligences for the 21st Century* (1999) as a basis for reading more widely about the model.

3. Propose the existence of a new intelligence and apply Gardner's eight criteria to see if it qualifies for inclusion in MI theory.

4. Collect examples of symbol systems in each intelligence. Robert McKim's book *Experiences in Visual Thinking* (1980) contains examples of several spatial "languages" used by designers, architects, artists, and inventors,

and you can consult books on music history that provide examples of earlier systems of musical notation.

5. Read about savants in each intelligence. Some of the footnoted entries in Gardner's *Frames of Mind* identify sources of information on savants in logical-mathematical, spatial, musical, linguistic, and bodily-kinesthetic intelligences. In addition, the work of neurologist Oliver Sacks (1985, 1995) provides engagingly written case studies of savants and other individuals with specific brain damage that has affected their intelligences in intriguing ways.

6. Relate MI theory to a learning-style model (e.g., V-A-K-T, Myers-Briggs, Dunn and Dunn, etc.).

2

MI Theory and Personal Development

What kind of school plan you make is neither here nor there; what matters is what sort of a person you are.

—*Rudolf Steiner*

Before applying any model of learning in a classroom environment, we should first apply it to ourselves as educators and adult learners, for unless we have an experiential understanding of the theory and have personalized its content, we are unlikely to be committed to using it with students. Consequently, an important step in using the theory of multiple intelligences (after grasping the basic theoretical foundations presented in Chapter 1) is to determine the nature and quality of our *own* multiple intelligences and seek ways to develop them in our lives. As we begin to do this, it will become apparent how our particular fluency (or lack of fluency) in each of the eight intelligences affects our competence (or lack of competence) in the various roles we have as educators.

Identifying Your Multiple Intelligences

As you will see in the later chapters on student assessment (Chapters 3 and 10), developing a profile of a person's multiple intelligences is not a simple matter. No test can accurately determine the nature or quality of a person's intelligences. As Howard Gardner has repeatedly pointed out, standardized tests measure only a small part of the total spectrum of abilities. The best way to assess your own multiple intelligences, therefore, is through a realistic appraisal of your performance in the many kinds of tasks, activities, and experiences associated with each intelligence. Rather than perform several artificial learning tasks, look back over the kinds of real-life experiences you've already had involving these eight intelligences. The MI inventory in Figure 2.1 can assist you in doing this.

It's important to keep in mind that this inventory is *not* a test and that quantitative information (such as the number of checks for each intelligence) has no bearing on determining your intelligence or lack of intelligence in each category. The purpose of the inventory is to begin to connect you to your own life experiences with the eight intelligences. What sorts of memories, feelings, and ideas emerge from this process?

Tapping MI Resources

The theory of multiple intelligences is an especially good model for looking at teaching strengths as well as for examining areas needing improvement. Perhaps you avoid drawing pictures on the blackboard or stay away from using highly graphic materials in your presentations because spatial intelligence is not particularly well developed in your life. Or possibly you gravitate toward cooperative learning strategies or ecological activities because you are an interpersonal or naturalist sort of learner/teacher yourself. Use MI theory to survey your own teaching style, and see how it matches up with the eight intelligences. While you don't have to be a master in all eight intelligences, you probably should know how to tap resources in the intelligences you typically shy away from in the classroom. Here are some ways to do this:

Draw on colleagues' expertise. If you don't have ideas for bringing music into the classroom because your musical intelligence is undeveloped,

2.1
An MI Inventory for Adults

Check those statements that apply in each intelligence category. Space has been provided at the end of each intelligence for you to write additional information not specifically referred to in the inventory items.

Linguistic Intelligence

____ Books are very important to me.

____ I can hear words in my head before I read, speak, or write them down.

____ I get more out of listening to the radio or a spoken-word recording than I do from television or films.

____ I enjoy word games like Scrabble, Anagrams, or Password.

____ I enjoy entertaining myself or others with tongue twisters, nonsense rhymes, or puns.

____ Other people sometimes have to stop and ask me to explain the meaning of the words I use in my writing and speaking.

____ English, social studies, and history were easier for me in school than math and science.

____ Learning to speak or read another language (e.g., French, Spanish, German) has been relatively easy for me.

____ My conversation includes frequent references to things that I've read or heard.

____ I've written something recently that I was particularly proud of or that earned me recognition from others.

Other Linguistic Abilities:

Logical-Mathematical Intelligence

____ I can easily compute numbers in my head.

____ Math and/or science were among my favorite subjects in school.

____ I enjoy playing games or solving brainteasers that require logical thinking.

____ I like to set up little "what if" experiments (for example, "What if I double the amount of water I give to my rosebush each week?")

____ My mind searches for patterns, regularities, or logical sequences in things.

____ I'm interested in new developments in science.

____ I believe that almost everything has a rational explanation.

____ I sometimes think in clear, abstract, wordless, imageless concepts.

____ I like finding logical flaws in things that people say and do at home and work.

____ I feel more comfortable when something has been measured, categorized, analyzed, or quantified in some way.

Other Logical-Mathematical Abilities:

Spatial Intelligence

____ I often see clear visual images when I close my eyes.

____ I'm sensitive to color.

____ I frequently use a camera or camcorder to record what I see around me.

____ I enjoy doing jigsaw puzzles, mazes, and other visual puzzles.

____ I have vivid dreams at night.

____ I can generally find my way around unfamiliar territory.

____ I like to draw or doodle.

____ Geometry was easier for me than algebra in school.

____ I can comfortably imagine how something might appear if it were looked down on from directly above in a bird's-eye view.

____ I prefer looking at reading material that is heavily illustrated.

Other Spatial Abilities:

Bodily-Kinesthetic Intelligence

____ I engage in at least one sport or physical activity on a regular basis.

____ I find it difficult to sit still for long periods of time.

____ I like working with my hands at concrete activities such as sewing, weaving, carving, carpentry, or model building.

(continued)

2.1
An MI Inventory for Adults (continued)

____ My best ideas often come to me when I'm out for a long walk or a jog or when I'm engaging in some other kind of physical activity.

____ I often like to spend my free time outdoors.

____ I frequently use hand gestures or other forms of body language when conversing with someone.

____ I need to touch things in order to learn more about them.

____ I enjoy daredevil amusement rides or similar thrilling physical experiences.

____ I would describe myself as well coordinated.

____ I need to practice a new skill rather than simply reading about it or seeing a video that describes it.

Other Bodily-Kinesthetic Abilities:

Musical Intelligence

____ I have a pleasant singing voice.

____ I can tell when a musical note is off-key.

____ I frequently listen to music on radio, records, cassettes, or compact discs.

____ I play a musical instrument.

____ My life would be poorer if there were no music in it.

____ I sometimes catch myself walking down the street with a television jingle or other tune running through my mind.

____ I can easily keep time to a piece of music with a simple percussion instrument.

____ I know the tunes to many different songs or musical pieces.

____ If I hear a musical selection once or twice, I am usually able to sing it back fairly accurately.

____ I often make tapping sounds or sing little melodies while working, studying, or learning something new.

Other Musical Abilities:

Interpersonal Intelligence

___ I'm the sort of person that people come to for advice and counsel at work or in my neighborhood.

___ I prefer group sports like badminton, volleyball, or softball to solo sports such as swimming and jogging.

___ When I have a problem, I'm more likely to seek out another person for help than attempt to work it out on my own.

___ I have at least three close friends.

___ I favor social pastimes such as Monopoly or bridge over individual recreations such as video games and solitaire.

___ I enjoy the challenge of teaching another person, or groups of people, what I know how to do.

___ I consider myself a leader (or others have called me that).

___ I feel comfortable in the midst of a crowd.

___ I like to get involved in social activities connected with my work, church, or community.

___ I would rather spend my evenings at a lively party than stay at home alone.

Other Interpersonal Abilities:

Intrapersonal Intelligence

___ I regularly spend time alone meditating, reflecting, or thinking about important life questions.

___ I have attended counseling sessions or personal growth seminars to learn more about myself.

___ I am able to respond to setbacks with resilience.

___ I have a special hobby or interest that I keep pretty much to myself.

___ I have some important goals for my life that I think about on a regular basis.

___ I have a realistic view of my strengths and weaknesses (borne out by feedback from other sources).

___ I would prefer to spend a weekend alone in a cabin in the woods rather than at a fancy resort with lots of people around.

___ I consider myself to be strong willed or independent minded.

___ I keep a personal diary or journal to record the events of my inner life.

___ I am self-employed or have at least thought seriously about starting my own business.

Other Intrapersonal Abilities:

(continued)

2.1
An MI Inventory for Adults (continued)

Naturalist Intelligence

___ I like to spend time backpacking, hiking, or just walking in nature.

___ I belong to some kind of volunteer organization related to nature (e.g., Sierra Club), and I'm concerned about helping to save nature from further destruction.

___ I thrive on having animals around the house.

___ I'm involved in a hobby that involves nature in some way (e.g., bird watching).

___ I've enrolled in courses relating to nature at community centers or colleges (e.g., botany, zoology).

___ I'm quite good at telling the difference between different kinds of trees, dogs, birds, or other types of flora or fauna.

___ I like to read books and magazines or watch television shows or movies that feature nature in some way.

___ When on vacation, I prefer to go off to a natural setting (park, campground, hiking trail) rather than to a hotel/resort or city/cultural location.

___ I love to visit zoos, aquariums, or other places where the natural world is studied.

___ I have a garden and enjoy working regularly in it.

Other Naturalist Abilities:

---

consider getting help from the school's music teacher or a musically inclined colleague. The theory of multiple intelligences has broad implications for team teaching. In a school committed to developing students' multiple intelligences, the ideal teaching team or curriculum planning committee includes expertise in all eight intelligences; that is, each member possesses a high level of competence in a specific intelligence.

Ask students to help out. Students can often come up with strategies and demonstrate expertise in areas where your own knowledge may be deficient. For example, students may be able to do some picture drawing on the board, provide musical background for a learning activity, or share knowledge about lizards, insects, flowers, or other fauna or flora, if you don't feel comfortable or competent doing these things yourself.

Use available technology. Tap your school's technical resources to convey information you might not be able to provide through your own efforts. For instance, you can use tape recordings of music if you're not musical, videotapes if you're not picture-oriented, calculators and self-paced computer software to supplement your shortcomings in logical-mathematical areas, and so on.

The final way to come to grips with intelligences that seem to be "blind spots" in your life is through a process of careful cultivation or personal development of your intelligences. MI theory provides a model through which you can activate your neglected intelligences and balance your use of all the intelligences.

Developing Your Multiple Intelligences

I've been careful not to use the terms "strong intelligence" and "weak intelligence" in describing individual differences among a person's intelligences, because a person's "weak" intelligence may actually turn out to be her strongest intelligence, once it is given the chance to develop. As mentioned in Chapter 1, a key point in MI theory is that most people can develop all their intelligences to a relatively acceptable level of mastery. Whether an intelligence can develop depends upon three main factors:

1. *Biological endowment*—including hereditary or genetic factors and insults or injuries to the brain before, during, and after birth
2. *Personal life history*—including experiences with parents, teachers, peers, friends, and others who awaken intelligences, keep them from developing, or actively repress them
3. *Cultural and historical background*—including the time and place in which you were born and raised and the nature and state of cultural or historical developments in different domains

We can see the interaction of these factors in the life of Wolfgang Amadeus Mozart. Mozart undoubtedly came into life already possessing a strong biological endowment (a highly developed right temporal lobe, perhaps). And he was born into a family of musical individuals; in fact, his father, Leopold, was a composer who gave up his own career to support his son's musical development. Finally, Mozart was born at a time in Europe when the arts (including music) were flourishing and wealthy patrons supported composers and performers. Mozart's genius, therefore, arose through a confluence of biological, personal, and cultural/historical factors. What would have happened if Mozart had been born to tone-deaf parents in Puritan England, where most music was considered the devil's work? His musical gifts likely would never have developed to a high level because of the forces working against his biological endowment.

The interaction of the above factors is also evident in the musical proficiency of many of the children who have been enrolled in the Suzuki Talent Education Program. Although some Suzuki students may be born with a relatively modest genetic musical endowment, they are able to develop their musical intelligence to a high level through experiences in the program. MI theory is a model that values nurture as much as, and in some ways more than, nature in accounting for the development of intelligences.

Activators and Deactivators of Intelligences

Crystallizing experiences and *paralyzing experiences* are two key processes in the development of intelligences. Crystallizing experiences, a concept originating with David Feldman (1980) at Tufts University and further developed by Howard Gardner and his colleagues (Walters & Gardner, 1986), are the "turning points" in the development of a person's talents and abilities. Often these events occur in early childhood, although they can occur anytime during the life span. For instance, when Albert Einstein was 4 years old, his father showed him a magnetic compass. The adult Einstein later said this compass filled him with a desire to figure out the mysteries of the universe. Essentially, this experience activated his genius and started him on his journey toward discoveries that would make him one of the towering figures in 20th-century thought. Similarly, when Yehudi Menuhin was almost 4 years old, his parents took him to a concert by the San Francisco Symphony Orchestra. The experience so enthralled him that afterward he asked his parents for a violin as a birthday present, and he said he wanted the violin soloist they heard that evening to teach him to play it! Crystallizing experiences, then, are the sparks that light an intelligence and start its development toward maturity.

Conversely, I use the term *paralyzing experiences* to refer to experiences that "shut down" intelligences. Perhaps a teacher humiliated you in front of your classmates when you showed your drawing during art period, and that event marked the end of a good part of your artistic development. Possibly a parent yelled at you to "stop making a racket" on the piano, and you never went near a musical instrument after that. Or maybe you were punished for bringing your "messy" leaf collection into the house, without any acknowledgment of the spark of the naturalist that you might have displayed. Paralyzing experiences are often filled with shame, guilt, fear, anger, and other negative emotions that prevent our intelligences from growing and thriving (Miller, 1981).

The following environmental influences also promote or suppress the development of intelligences:

- *Access to resources or mentors*—If your family was so poor that you couldn't afford a violin, piano, or other instrument, your musical intelligence might well have remained undeveloped.
- *Historical-cultural factors*—If you were a student who demonstrated "proclivities" in mathematics at a time when math and science programs were highly funded, your logical-mathematical intelligence would likely have developed.
- *Geographic factors*—If you grew up on a farm, you might well have had more opportunity to develop certain aspects of the naturalist intelligence than if you were raised on the 62nd floor of a Manhattan apartment building.
- *Familial factors*—If you wanted to be an artist but your parents wanted you to be a lawyer, their influence might well have promoted the development of your linguistic intelligence at the expense of your spatial intelligence.
- *Situational factors*—If you had to help take care of a large family while you were growing up, and you now have a large family yourself, you may have had little time to develop in areas of promise—unless they were interpersonal in nature.

MI theory offers a model of personal development that can help educators understand how their own profile of intelligences affects their teaching approaches in the classroom. Further, it opens the gate to a broad range of activities that can help us develop neglected intelligences, activate underdeveloped or paralyzed intelligences, and bring well-developed intelligences to even higher levels of proficiency.

For Further Study

1. Fill out the inventory in this chapter. Talk with a friend or colleague about the results of the inventory. Make sure to share something about what you perceive as your most developed intelligences and your least developed intelligences. Avoid talking in terms of quantitative information (e.g., "I had only three checks in musical intelligence"). Speak instead in anecdotal terms (e.g., "I've never felt very musical in my life; my classmates used to laugh at me when I had to sing solo in music class").

Also, begin to reflect upon how your developed and undeveloped intelligences affect what you put into, or keep out of, your work as an educator. What kinds of teaching methods or materials do you avoid because they involve using your underdeveloped intelligences? What sorts of things are you especially good at doing because of one or more highly developed intelligences?

2. Select an intelligence that you would like to nurture. It may be an intelligence you showed particular promise in as a child but never had the opportunity to develop (the intelligence may have gone "underground" as you grew up). Perhaps it is an intelligence you have had great difficulty with or one in which you would like to experience more competence and confidence. Or, possibly, it's a highly developed intelligence that you want to take to an even higher level. Rolling out a piece of mural paper perhaps five or six feet in length, create a time line showing the development of that intelligence from early childhood to the present. Note significant events along the way, including crystallizing and paralyzing experiences, people who helped you develop the intelligence (or sought to suppress it), school influences, what happened to the intelligence as you became an adult, and so forth. Leave space on the time line to include information about the *future* development of the intelligence (see Study Item 4 below).

3. Create a curriculum planning team or other school group that consists of individuals representing each of the eight intelligences. Before beginning the planning work, take time to share your personal experiences of your most highly developed intelligence.

4. Select an intelligence that is not very highly developed in your life and create a plan for cultivating it. Look over suggestions for developing the intelligences in *7 Kinds of Smart* (Armstrong, 1999a), or create your own list of ways to nurture each intelligence. As you begin personally developing an intelligence, notice whether this process influences what you do in the classroom. Are you bringing more aspects of that intelligence into your professional work?

3

Describing Intelligences in Students

Hide not your talents
For use they were made.
What's a sundial in the shade!

— *Ben Franklin*

Although it's true that each child possesses all eight intelligences and can develop all eight to a reasonable level of competence, children begin showing what Howard Gardner calls "proclivities" (or inclinations) toward specific intelligences from a very early age. By the time children begin school, they have probably established ways of learning that run more along the lines of some intelligences than others. In this chapter, we will examine how you can begin to describe students' most developed intelligences so that more of their learning in school can take place through their preferred intelligences.

Figure 3.1 provides brief descriptions of the capacities of children who display proclivities in specific intelligences. Keep in mind, however, that most students have strengths in *several* areas, so you should avoid pigeonholing a child in only one intelligence. You will probably find each student pictured in two or more of these intelligence descriptions.

3.1 **Eight Ways of Learning**			
Children who are highly . . .	**Think . . .**	**Love . . .**	**Need . . .**
Linguistic	in words	reading, writing, telling stories, playing word games	books, tapes, writing tools, paper, diaries, dialogue, discussion, debate, stories
Logical-Mathematical	by reasoning	experimenting, questioning, figuring out logical puzzles, calculating	materials to experiment with, science materials, manipulatives, trips to planetariums and science museums
Spatial	in images and pictures	designing, drawing, visualizing, doodling	art, Legos, videos, movies, slides, imagination games, mazes, puzzles, illustrated books, trips to art museums
Bodily-Kinesthetic	through somatic sensations	dancing, running, jumping, building, touching, gesturing	role-play, drama, movement, building things, sports and physical games, tactile experiences, hands-on learning
Musical	via rhythms and melodies	singing, whistling, humming, tapping feet and hands, listening	sing-along time, trips to concerts, playing music at home and school, musical instruments
Interpersonal	by bouncing ideas off other people	leading, organizing, relating, manipulating, mediating, partying	friends, group games, social gatherings, community events, clubs, mentors/apprenticeships
Intrapersonal	in relation to their needs, feelings, and goals	setting goals, meditating, dreaming, planning, reflecting	secret places, time alone, self-paced projects, choices
Naturalist	through nature and natural forms	playing with pets, gardening, investigating nature, raising animals, caring for planet earth	access to nature, opportunities for interacting with animals, tools for investigating nature (e.g., magnifying glasses, binoculars)

Assessing Students' Multiple Intelligences

There is no "megatest" on the market that can provide a comprehensive survey of your students' multiple intelligences. If anyone should tell you they have a computer-scored test that in 15 minutes can provide a bar graph showing the eight "peaks" and "valleys" of each student in your class or school, I'd suggest that you be very skeptical. This isn't to say that formal testing can't provide some information about a student's intelligences; as I discuss later, it can provide clues to various intelligences. The single best tool for assessing students' multiple intelligences, however, is probably one readily available to all of us: simple observation.

I've often humorously suggested to teachers that one good way to identify students' most highly developed intelligences is to observe how they *misbehave* in class. The strongly linguistic student will be talking out of turn, the highly spatial student will be doodling and daydreaming, the interpersonally inclined student will be socializing, the bodily-kinesthetic student will be fidgeting, and the naturalistically engaged student might well bring an animal to class without permission! These students are metaphorically saying through their misbehaviors: "This is how I learn, teacher, and if you don't teach me in the way that I most naturally learn, guess what? I'm going to do it *anyway!*" These intelligence-specific misbehaviors, then, are sort of a cry for help—a diagnostic indicator of how students want to be taught.

Another good observational indicator of students' proclivities is how they spend their free time in school. In other words, what do they do when nobody is telling them what to do? If you have a "choice time" in class when students can choose from a number of activities, what activities do students pick? Highly linguistic students might gravitate toward books, social students toward group games and gossip, spatial students toward drawing, bodily-kinesthetic students toward hands-on building activities, and naturalistically inclined students toward the gerbil cage or aquarium. Observing kids in these student-initiated activities can tell a world about how they learn most effectively.

Every teacher should consider keeping a notebook, diary, or journal handy in a desk for recording observations of this kind. Of course, if you're working with 150 students a day at the middle or high school level, regularly recording observations for each student would hardly be possible. You might, however, single out the two or three most troublesome or puzzling students in class and focus your MI assessment upon them. Even if you have a class of 25 to 35 students, writing a couple of lines about each student each week may pay off in the long run. Writing two lines a week for 40 weeks yields 80 lines, or three to four pages of solid observational data for each student.

To help organize your observations of a student's multiple intelligences, you can use a checklist like the one in Figure 3.2. Keep in mind that this

3.2
Multiple Intelligences Checklist for Students

Name of Student: _____

Check items that apply.

Linguistic Intelligence

____ Writes better than average for age
____ Spins tall tales or tells jokes and stories
____ Has a good memory for names, places, dates, or trivia
____ Enjoys word games
____ Enjoys reading books
____ Spells words accurately (or if preschool, does developmental spelling that is advanced for age)
____ Appreciates nonsense rhymes, puns, tongue twisters
____ Enjoys listening to the spoken word (stories, commentary on the radio, talking books)
____ Has a good vocabulary for age
____ Communicates to others in a highly verbal way

Other Linguistic Abilities:

Logical-Mathematical Intelligence

____ Asks a lot of questions about how things work
____ Enjoys working or playing with numbers
____ Enjoys math class (or if preschool, enjoys counting and doing other things with numbers)
____ Finds math and computer games interesting (or if no exposure to computers, enjoys other math or science games)
____ Enjoys playing chess, checkers, or other strategy games
____ Enjoys working on logic puzzles or brainteasers (or if preschool, enjoys hearing logical nonsense)
____ Enjoys putting things in categories, hierarchies, or other logical patterns
____ Likes to do experiments in science class or in free play
____ Shows interest in science-related subjects
____ Does well on Piagetian-type assessments of logical thinking

Other Logical-Mathematical Abilities:

(continued)

3.2
Multiple Intelligences Checklist for Students (continued)

Spatial Intelligence
___ Reports clear visual images

___ Reads maps, charts, and diagrams more easily than text (or if preschool, enjoys looking at more than text)

___ Daydreams a lot

___ Enjoys art activities

___ Is good at drawings

___ Likes to view movies, slides, or other visual presentations

___ Enjoys doing puzzles, mazes, or similar visual activities

___ Builds interesting three-dimensional constructions (e.g., Lego buildings)

___ Gets more out of pictures than words while reading

___ Doodles on workbooks, worksheets, or other materials

Other Spatial Abilities:

Bodily-Kinesthetic Intelligence
___ Excels in one or more sports (or if preschool, shows physical prowess advanced for age)

___ Moves, twitches, taps, or fidgets while seated for a long time in one spot

___ Cleverly mimics other people's gestures or mannerisms

___ Loves to take things apart and put them back together again

___ Puts his/her hands all over something he/she's just seen

___ Enjoys running, jumping, wrestling, or similar activities (or if older, will show these interests in a more "restrained" way—e.g., running to class, jumping over a chair)

___ Shows skill in a craft (e.g., woodworking, sewing, mechanics) or good fine-motor coordination in other ways

___ Has a dramatic way of expressing herself/himself

___ Reports different physical sensations while thinking or working

___ Enjoys working with clay or other tactile experiences (e.g., finger painting)

Other Bodily-Kinesthetic Abilities:

Musical Intelligence

____Tells you when music sounds off-key or disturbing in some other way

____Remembers melodies of songs

____Has a good singing voice

____Plays a musical instrument or sings in a choir or other group (or if preschool, enjoys playing percussion instruments and/or singing in a group)

____Has a rhythmic way of speaking or moving

____Unconsciously hums to himself/herself

____Taps rhythmically on the table or desk as he/she works

____Is sensitive to environmental noises (e.g., rain on the roof)

____Responds favorably when a piece of music is put on

____Sings songs that he/she has learned outside of the classroom

Other Musical Abilities:

Interpersonal Intelligence

____Enjoys socializing with peers

____Seems to be a natural leader

____Gives advice to friends who have problems

____Seems to be street-smart

____Belongs to clubs, committees, organizations, or informal peer groups

____Enjoys informally teaching other kids

____Likes to play games with other kids

____Has two or more close friends

____Has a good sense of empathy or concern for others

____Is sought out for company by others

Other Interpersonal Abilities:

(continued)

3.2
Multiple Intelligences Checklist for Students (continued)

Intrapersonal Intelligence

____Displays a sense of independence or a strong will

____Has a realistic sense of his/her abilities and weaknesses

____Does well when left alone to play or study

____Marches to the beat of a different drummer in his/her style of living and learning

____Has an interest or hobby that he/she doesn't talk much about

____Has a good sense of self-direction

____Prefers working alone to working with others

____Accurately expresses how he/she is feeling

____Is able to learn from his/her failures and successes in life

____Has good self-esteem

Other Intrapersonal Abilities:

Naturalist Intelligence

____Talks a lot about favorite pets, or preferred spots in nature, during class sharing

____Likes field trips in nature, to the zoo, or to a natural history museum

____Shows sensitivity to natural formations (e.g., while walking outside with the class, will notice mountains, clouds; or if in an urban environment, may show this ability in sensitivity to popular culture "formations" such as sneakers or automobile styles)

____Likes to water and tend to the plants in the classroom

____Likes to hang around the gerbil cage, the aquarium, or the terrarium in class

____Gets excited when studying about ecology, nature, plants, or animals

____Speaks out in class for the rights of animals or the preservation of planet earth

____Enjoys doing nature projects, such as bird watching, collecting butterflies or insects, studying trees, or raising animals

____Brings to school bugs, flowers, leaves, or other natural things to share with classmates or teachers

____Does well in topics at school that involve living systems (e.g., biological topics in science, environmental issues in social studies)

Other Naturalist Abilities:

checklist is *not* a test—it has not been subjected to any protocols necessary to establish reliability and validity—and should only be used in conjunction with other sources of assessment information when describing students' multiple intelligences.

In addition to observation and checklists, there are several other excellent ways to get assessment information about students' multiple intelligences:

Collect documents. Anecdotal records are not the only way to document students' strongest intelligences. Teachers should consider having a digital camera available to snap pictures of students displaying evidence of their multiple intelligences. Photos are particularly useful for documenting products or experiences that might be gone in another 10 minutes, like giant Lego structures. If students show a particular capacity for telling stories or singing songs, record them and keep the recording as a document. If students have drawing or painting abilities, keep samples of their work or take photos of them. If students show their greatest assets during a football game or through a hands-on demonstration of how to fix a machine or plant a flower, capture their performance on videotape. Ultimately, MI assessment data will consist of several kinds of documents, including photos, sketches, samples of schoolwork, audio and video samples, color photocopies, and more. Creating computer files for these documents and putting them on CD or DVD can allow all of this information to be conveniently included on a single disc and reviewed by teachers, administrators, parents, and the students themselves. (For more on assessment through multiple intelligences, see Chapter 10.)

Look at school records. As two-dimensional and lifeless as they sometimes appear, cumulative records can provide important information about a student's multiple intelligences. Look at the student's grades over the years. Are grades in math and the hard sciences consistently higher than grades in literature and the social sciences? If so, this may be evidence of an inclination toward logical-mathematical rather than linguistic intelligence. High grades in art and graphic design may indicate well-developed spatial intelligence, while *A*s and *B*s in physical education and shop class may point toward bodily-kinesthetic abilities. Similarly, standardized test scores can sometimes provide differential information about a student's intelligences. On intelligence tests, for example, there are often subtests that tap linguistic intelligence (vocabulary and "information" categories), logical-mathematical intelligence (analogies, arithmetic), and spatial intelligence (picture arrangement, block design). A number of other tests may point toward specific intelligences. Here is a partial list of the kinds of tests that may relate to each intelligence:

- *Linguistic*—reading tests, language tests, the verbal sections of intelligence and achievement tests
- *Logical-mathematical*—Piagetian assessments, math achievement tests, the reasoning sections of intelligence tests
- *Spatial*—visual memory and visual-motor tests, art aptitude tests, some performance items on intelligence tests
- *Bodily-kinesthetic*—manual dexterity tests, some motor subtests in neuropsychological batteries, the President's Physical Fitness Test
- *Interpersonal*—social maturity scales, sociograms, interpersonal projective tests (e.g., Family Kinetic Drawing)
- *Intrapersonal*—self-concept assessments, projective tests, tests of emotional intelligence
- *Naturalist*—test items that include questions about animals, plants, or natural settings

School records may also contain valuable *anecdotal* information about a student's multiple intelligences. One of the most valuable sources, I've discovered, is the kindergarten teacher's report. Often, the kindergarten teacher is the only educator to see the child regularly using all eight intelligences. Consequently, comments like "loves finger painting," "moves gracefully during music and dance time," or "creates beautiful structures with blocks" can provide clues to a student's spatial, musical, or bodily-kinesthetic proclivities.

When reviewing a student's cumulative records, I've found it useful to photocopy the records (with permission from the school and parents, of course) and then take a highlighter and highlight all the positive information about that student, including the highest grades and test scores and the positive observations of others. I then type up each piece of highlighted information on a separate sheet of paper and organize the sheets according to intelligences. This practice provides me with solid information about a student's strongest intelligences that I can then communicate to parents, administrators, and the student's teachers. This approach allows you to begin conferences on a positive note, particularly with troubled and troublesome students (such as at IEP meetings), thus facilitating constructive solutions.

Talk with other teachers. If you have students only for English or math class, then you are usually not in a position to observe them displaying bodily-kinesthetic or musical gifts (unless, of course, you are regularly teaching through the multiple intelligences). Even if you work with students through all subject areas, you can often get additional information by contacting specialists who are working more specifically with one or two of the intelligences. Hence, the art teacher might be the best person to talk with about a student's spatial intelligence, the physical education teacher about certain bodily-kinesthetic abilities, and the school about the personal intelligences (although the counselor's ability to share information may be limited due to issues of confidentiality). Regard your colleagues as important sources of assessment information about students' multiple intelligences and meet with them periodically to compare notes. You may find that a child who appears quite low functioning in one class will be one of the stars in a class that requires a different set of intelligences.

Talk with parents. Parents are true experts on a child's multiple intelligences. They've had the opportunity to see the child learn and grow under a broad spectrum of circumstances encompassing all eight intelligences. Consequently, they ought to be enlisted in the effort to identify the child's strongest intelligences. During back-to-school night, parents should be introduced to the concept of multiple intelligences and be provided with specific ways through which they can observe and document their child's strengths at home, including the use of scrapbooks, audio and video samples, photos, stories, sketches, and artifacts that emerged from a child's special hobby or other interest. Then, parents can bring any information that may help teachers develop a broader understanding of the child's multiple intelligences to future parent-teacher conferences.

Many years ago, the phrase "the six-hour retarded child" was used to describe a student who showed little promise or potential in the classroom but was a real achiever outside of school, perhaps as the leader of a youth group, a jack-of-all-trades to whom neighbors came for all kinds of repairs, or a fledgling entrepreneur with a flourishing small business. Obtaining assessment information from the home is critical in discovering ways to transplant such successes from the home to the school.

Ask students. Students are the ultimate experts on their multiple intelligences, because they've lived with them 24 hours a day ever since they were born. After they have been introduced to the idea of multiple intelligences (see Chapter 4), you can sit down and interview them to discover what *they* consider to be their most highly developed intelligences. I've used the "MI Pizza" shown in Chapter 4 (Figure 4.1) as a record-keeping form for making notes while I ask students individually about their abilities in each area. You can also have students draw pictures of themselves doing things in their most developed intelligences (a spatial approach), rank from 1 to 7 their most developed to least developed intelligence on the MI Pizza (a logical-mathematical approach), or pantomime their most developed intelligences (a bodily-kinesthetic approach). Some of the activities in Chapter 4 can also be helpful in getting assessment data about students' multiple intelligences.

Set up special activities. If you regularly teach through the multiple intelligences, then you have frequent opportunities to assess through the multiple intelligences as well. So, for example, if you teach a lesson on fractions eight different ways, you can note how different children respond to each activity. The child who is almost falling asleep during the logical presentation may come alive when the bodily-kinesthetic approach begins, only to tune out again when a musical method is used. Seeing little light bulbs go on and off during the course of a day is both an affirmation of the existence of these intelligences as well as a record of the individual differences in your class. Similarly, setting up activity centers for each intelligence (see Chapter 7) provides opportunities for seeing how students function in each area or which areas students naturally gravitate toward when they are free to choose. Since the MI perspective on assessment (presented in Chapter 10) is based on a close connection between instruction and assessment, many of the activities in Chapters 5 and 6 can be used as diagnostic indicators as well as teaching activities.

For Further Study

1. Fill out the inventory in Figure 3.2 for each student in your classroom. Notice which items cannot be answered for lack of sufficient background

information about the student. Identify methods you can use to obtain information about these items (e.g., parent or child interview, experiential activities), and then use them to help complete the inventory. How does your view of individual children remain the same or change as a result of framing their lives in terms of MI theory? What implications do the inventory results have for your teaching? Alternatively, use one of the standardized measures that have been developed to assess students' multiple intelligences, such as Branton Shearer's Multiple Intelligence Developmental Assessment Scales (MIDAS) or Sue Teele's Teele Inventory for Multiple Intelligences (TIMI) (Shearer, 1994; Teele, 1992).

2. Keep a journal to record observations of students' multiple intelligences. If you observe students outside the classroom (e.g., as a recess or lunchroom monitor) notice how their behavior is the same as or different from their behavior in the classroom. What evidence for each student's multiple intelligences emerges from the anecdotal data?

3. Select one form of documenting students' learning activities that you haven't yet tried, such as audio, video, or photography. Experiment with it and notice how effective it may be in providing and communicating information about students' multiple intelligences.

4. Have students express to you their preferred intelligences through one or more of the following media: writing, drawing, pantomime, group discussion, and personal interview. Make sure they have first been introduced to MI theory through some of the activities described in Chapter 4.

5. During parent-teacher conferences, devote some time to acquiring information about a student's multiple intelligences at home.

6. Review selected students' cumulative files, focusing on data that suggest the presence of special proclivities in one or more of the eight intelligences. If possible, obtain copies of the file material so you can highlight strengths with a highlighter and then transcribe the highlighted items onto separate sheets of paper. Distribute these "strength profiles" at the next meeting called to discuss students' learning.

7. Confer with other teachers about students' multiple intelligences. Set aside special time so that teachers who are responsible for different intelligences in school (e.g., math, shop, art, literature, biology, and music teachers) can reflect upon students' performance in each learning context.

4

Teaching Students about MI Theory

Give me a fish and I eat for a day.
Teach me to fish and I eat for a lifetime.

—Proverb

One of the most useful features of MI theory is that it can be explained to a group of children as young as 1st graders in as little as 5 minutes in such a way that they can then use the MI vocabulary to talk about how they learn. While many other theories of learning contain terms and acronyms not easily understood by adults, let alone children (e.g., INFP in the Myers-Briggs typology, which refers to an "Introverted, Intuitive, Feeling, Judging" person) the eight intelligences of MI are linked to concrete things that young and old alike have had experience with: words, numbers, pictures, the body, music, people, the self, and nature.

Research in cognitive psychology applied to education has supported the notion that children benefit from instructional approaches that help them reflect upon their own learning processes (Marzano et al., 1988). When children engage in this kind of metacognitive activity, they can select appropriate strategies for problem solving. They can also serve as advocates for themselves when placed in new learning environments.

Five-Minute Introduction to MI Theory

How does a teacher present the theory of multiple intelligences to a group of students? Naturally, the answer to that question will depend in part on the size of the class, the developmental level of students, their background, and the kinds of instructional resources available. The most direct way to introduce MI theory to students is simply to explain it to them. When I go to a new classroom to demonstrate how to teach a multiple intelligence lesson, I always begin with a 5-minute explanation of the theory so students have a context for understanding what I am doing there. I usually begin by asking, "How many of you think you're intelligent?" I've discovered that there seems to be an inverse relationship between the number of hands that go up and the grade level that I'm teaching—that is, the lower the grade level, the more hands go up. This reminds me of NYU professor Neil Postman's remark that "children go into school as question marks and leave school as periods." What do we do in the intervening years to convince children that they're not intelligent?

Regardless of the number of hands that go up, I usually say, "All of you are intelligent—and not just in one way. Each of you is intelligent in at least eight different ways." I draw an "MI Pizza" (a circle divided into eight slices) on the blackboard and then begin to explain the model. "First, there is something called word smart." I use simple terms to describe the intelligences, since words like "linguistic" are a mouthful for many children. As shown in Figure 4.1, I also accompany each term with a graphic symbol to spatially reinforce it. Then I ask questions. "How many people here can speak?" Usually, I'll get a lot of hands with this question! "Well, in order to speak you have to use words, so all of you are word smart!" "How many people here can write? You're using words here also, so again, you're all word smart." Essentially, I ask questions that build inclusion. I steer clear of questions that might exclude lots of students, such as "How many of you have read 15 books in the past month?" This is a learning model not for deciding which exclusive group one is a member of, but for celebrating all of one's potentials for learning. Otherwise, teachers might be preparing the way for students to say, "I just learned in school today that I'm not linguistically intelligent," or "I don't have to read this book, because I'm really not word smart."

4.1
MI Pizza

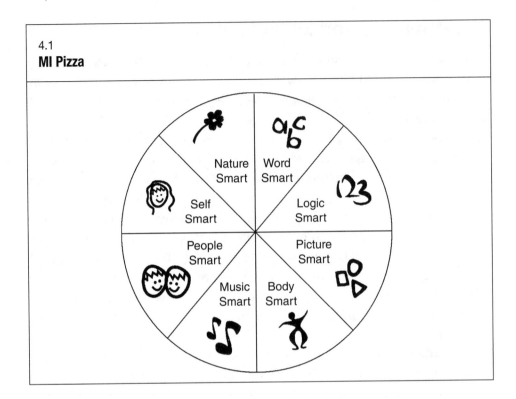

Here are the simple terms for each of the intelligences and some questions that I use in my presentations:

- *Linguistic*—Word Smart (see questions above)
- *Logical-mathematical*—Number Smart or Logic Smart: "How many of you can do math?" "How many people here have done a science experiment?"
- *Spatial*—Picture Smart: "How many of you draw?" "How many of you can see pictures in your heads when you close your eyes?" "How many of you enjoy watching television and films or playing video games?"
- *Bodily-kinesthetic*—Body Smart, Sports Smart, or Hand Smart (each term represents a different aspect of this intelligence): "How many of you like sports?" "How many of you enjoy making things with your hands, like models or Lego structures?"
- *Musical*—Music Smart: "How many of you enjoy listening to music?" "How many of you have ever played a musical instrument or sung a song?"

- *Interpersonal*—People Smart: "How many of you have at least one friend?" "How many of you enjoy working in groups at least part of the time here in school?"
- *Intrapersonal*—Self Smart: "How many of you have a secret or special place you go to when you want to get away from everybody and everything?" "How many of you like to spend at least part of the time working on your own here in class?"
- *Naturalist*—Nature Smart: "How many of you enjoy being out in nature?" "How many of you have ever had a butterfly collection, an insect collection, a collection of leaves from trees in your neighborhood, a collection of shells, or some other kind of collection of natural things?" "How many of you have pets or enjoy spending time with animals?"

You can develop your own questions to illustrate each intelligence. Just make sure they build in inclusion and give all children a chance to initially see themselves as intelligent. You can also give examples of what Howard Gardner calls the "end-states" of each intelligence—that is, people who have developed an intelligence to a high level of competence. These examples provide students with models to be inspired by and to aspire to. Pick famous figures and heroes from each student's own world. Examples might include

- Authors of children's literature that the class has been reading (Word Smart)
- Famous scientists students have studied in class (Number Smart or Logic Smart)
- Illustrators of children's literature, famous cartoonists, and filmmakers (Picture Smart)
- Famous sports heroes and actors (Body Smart)
- Famous rock stars, rappers, and other musicians (Music Smart)
- TV talk show hosts and politicians (People Smart)
- Famous entrepreneurs ("self-made" people) (Self Smart)
- Animal experts and nature explorers (Nature Smart)

Activities for Teaching MI Theory

Naturally, you'll want to go beyond a simple verbal explanation of the model, and you should strive to teach the model in all eight intelligences. There are a number of ways of introducing the model or of following up your five-minute introduction with reinforcing activities and supplementary experiences. Here are some examples:

Career Day: If you regularly bring members of your community into the classroom to talk about their jobs, begin to contextualize this activity within a multiple intelligence framework. Bring in an editor to talk about the kinds of "word smart" activities he uses, a tax accountant to speak about how being "number smart" helps her to help people, or an architect to explain the usefulness of being "picture smart" in her career. Other Career Day guests might include an athlete (body smart), a professional musician (music smart), a counselor (people smart), a person who has started a business (self smart), or a veterinarian (nature smart). Keep in mind that each career usually involves several intelligences and that you might want to discuss how each role brings together a combination of intelligences in a unique way. These presentations are extremely important in emphasizing to students that each of the intelligences plays a vital part in people's success in the world. You may want to speak beforehand with the guests about the model so they can work it into their presentations. Or you can simply follow up their appearances by relating what they said or did to one or more of the eight intelligences.

Field trips: Take students to places in the community where each of the intelligences is particularly valued and practiced. Destinations might include a library (word smart), a science lab (logic smart), a crafts factory (body smart), a radio station that plays music (music smart), a graphic design studio (picture smart), a public relations firm (people smart), a psychologist's office (self smart), and a zoo (nature smart). Again, seeing these intelligences in context gives students a more accurate "real-life" picture of MI theory than they could ever get in a classroom setting.

Biographies: Have students study the lives of well-known people proficient in one or more of the intelligences (see Gardner, 1993c). Subjects for study might include Toni Morrison (word smart), Marie Curie (logic smart), Vincent Van Gogh (picture smart), Roberto Clemente (body smart), Yo-Yo Ma (music smart), Martin Luther King Jr. (people smart), Sigmund Freud (self smart), and Jane Goodall (nature smart). Make sure the people studied are representative of your students' cultural, racial, gender, and ethnic backgrounds. (See Chapter 13 for more multicultural examples of famous people and Chapter 11 for examples of famous people in each intelligence who overcame specific disabilities.)

Lesson plans: Teach an eight-way lesson on a particular subject or in a specific skill area (see Chapter 5 for guidelines on creating MI lessons). Explain beforehand to students that you are going to teach this material using each of the eight intelligences and that they should pay particular attention to *how* each of the eight intelligences is covered. After the lesson, ask students to describe your use of each intelligence. This activity requires students to reflect upon the kinds of processes necessary for each intelligence and reinforces their metacognitive awareness. You may also want to ask them which particular method or methods they preferred. In this way, you help students begin to understand which strategies they prefer to use when learning something new.

Quick experiential activities: An experiential way of introducing MI theory is to have students complete eight activities, each of which draws primarily upon the use of one intelligence. For instance, you might have students do some writing ("write down a few lines from a poem that you know"), math ("tell me how long ago a million seconds ago was"), drawing ("draw a picture of an animal"), running ("go outside and run to the end of the block and back"), singing ("let's all sing 'Row, Row, Row Your Boat' together"), sharing ("turn to a partner and share something nice that happened to you this week"), self-reflecting ("close your eyes and think about the happiest moment in your life—you won't have to share it with anybody"), and observing nature ("look out the window and notice all the living things and natural formations you can see"). Adjust the activities to the ability level of your students, choosing activities that just about everyone can do and giving those who can't do them modified versions of the activities. You can use this approach either before or after explicitly describing the "eight kinds of smart." Make sure to ask students which activities they prefer, and remember to relate each activity to one (or more) of the eight intelligences.

Wall displays: Walk into a typical U.S. classroom and you'll often find a poster of Albert Einstein on the wall. Einstein is probably a good representative of multiple intelligences because he used several of them in his work, including spatial, bodily-kinesthetic, and logical-mathematical. Rather than just displaying this one poster, however, consider hanging eight posters on the wall, each representing a person especially proficient in one of the intelligences (see Gardner, 1993c, and the "Biographies" section in this chapter for suggested names). Or hang a banner reading "Eight Ways to Learn" or "This Is How We Learn in School" and display photos of students in the school using each of the intelligences.

Displays: Show products made by students in the school that required the use of each of the eight intelligences. Examples might include essays, stories, or poems (word smart); computer programs (logic smart); drawings and paintings (picture smart); musical scores (music smart); three-dimensional projects (body smart); cooperative projects (people smart); individual projects (self smart); and simulations of ecosystems (nature smart). The products could be displayed on a shelf, in a glass case, or on a table and rotated regularly so all students have a chance to display their achievements. Make sure each product is labeled with the intelligence or intelligences required to produce it.

Readings: For high school students, you can assign readings from any of the growing number of books and articles on the theory of multiple intelligences, including chapters from *Frames of Mind* (Gardner, 1993a) or *7 Kinds of Smart* (Armstrong, 1999a). Upper elementary and middle school students can read *You're Smarter Than You Think: A Kid's Guide to Multiple Intelligences* (Armstrong, 2003). Appendix B includes many more suggested readings.

MI tables: Set up eight tables in the classroom, each clearly labeled with a sign referring to one of the eight intelligences. On each table, place an activity card indicating what students are to do. At the word smart table, students can do a writing activity; at the number smart table, a math or science activity; at the picture smart table, a drawing activity; at the body smart table, a building activity; at the music smart table, a musical activity; at the people smart table, a cooperative activity; at the self smart table, an individualized activity; and at the nature smart table, an activity that involves observing an animal or plant. Divide the class equally into eight groups, assigning each group to a particular table. Have the groups work at the activity for a designated amount of time (perhaps five minutes), and then use a musical signal (e.g., a bell) to indicate that it's time to move to the next table (move clockwise). Continue until all students have been to each table and experienced each activity. Afterward, talk about students' preferences, relating each activity to its primary intelligence. (Chapter 7 deals more specifically with how to set up activity centers that reflect a multiple intelligence perspective.)

Human intelligence hunt: If you are introducing MI theory at the beginning of the school year, when students still don't know each other very well, a "human intelligence hunt" is a useful way to teach students experientially about the eight kinds of smart while helping them get to know one another better. It is based on the premise that each of us is a "treasure chest" filled with special gifts. These gifts are our intelligences. Sometimes, though, we're unaware of other people's gifts, so we have to go on a "treasure hunt"—in this case, an "intelligence hunt"—to discover each other's special talents. Each student receives a list of activities like those in Figure 4.2. On a signal such as a bell, students take the activity sheet along with a pen or pencil and find other students in the room who can do the activities listed. There are three basic rules:

1. Students must actually *perform* the activities listed, not simply say they can do them.
2. Once a student performs an activity to the "treasure hunter's" satisfaction, he or she should initial the blank space next to the appropriate activity on the "treasure hunter's" sheet.
3. "Treasure hunters" can ask a person to perform only one activity; therefore, to compete in the treasure hunt, a student must have eight different sets of initials.

You can modify the activities listed in Figure 4.2 to include activities geared to your students' aptitudes and abilities. For instance, if you're working with very young students, you may want to use the song "Old MacDonald Had a Farm" rather than Beethoven's Fifth Symphony. You can even create a hunt based entirely on pictures, which would involve students finding people in the class who particularly enjoy doing the kinds of activities depicted in each picture. After the activity, remember to link each task to a different intelligence and to talk about what students learned about one another's gifts or intelligences.

4.2
Human Intelligence Hunt

Find someone who can:
- Hum some of Beethoven's Fifth Symphony (Music Smart)
- Do a simple dance step (Body Smart)
- Recite four lines from a poem (Word Smart)
- Explain why the sky is blue (Logic Smart)
- Briefly share a recent dream (Self Smart)
- Draw a picture of a horse (Picture Smart)
- Honestly say she is relaxed and comfortable relating to other people during this exercise (People Smart)
- Name five different types of birds (or trees) that are found in the immediate area (Nature Smart)

Board games: You can create a homemade board game based on the eight intelligences. Get a manila file folder and a magic marker and create the common board game format of a winding roadway divided into many small squares. Assign each intelligence a color and then place an appropriately colored intelligence symbol on each square of the game board. You may use the symbols in Figure 4.1 or make up your own. Then create eight sets of two-by-three-inch game cards from eight colors of paper that match the colored symbols on the game board. On each set of game cards, type or write activities that involve using a specific intelligence. Here, for instance, are some activities for picture smart at the primary level:

- Draw a picture of a dog in less than 30 seconds.
- Find an object in the shape of a circle in the class.
- Tell us your favorite color.
- Describe four blue things you see in the room.
- Close you eyes and describe the pictures in your mind.

Make sure most of the activities are within the capabilities of your students. Then get a pair of dice and some miniature plastic figurines as game pieces, and start playing! Alternatively, there are commercially available games that include activities that cover most of the multiple intelligences (e.g., the board game Cranium).

MI stories, songs, or plays: Be creative and make up your own story, song, or play for teaching the idea of multiple intelligences (your students can help you). You might, for example, create a story about eight children, each an expert in a particular intelligence, who don't get along very well and who are forced into an adventure that requires them to travel to distant magical lands. In each part of the story they encounter challenges that require the unique intelligence of a particular child. For example, the children come to a land where, in order to be understood, people have to communicate through singing, so the musical child guides them through this land. In another land, they fall into a hole and get out through the body-smart child's expertise. At the end of the story, they are able to accomplish their task (perhaps to retrieve a golden jewel) because they have drawn upon the talents or intelligences of all eight children.

This story can then be used as a metaphor for classroom behavior: we need to respect and find ways of celebrating the unique talents and gifts of each student. A story like this one could be put on as a play, a puppet show, or a musical and performed for other students in the school.

There are undoubtedly many other activities that would help teach students about the theory of multiple intelligences. The development of such experiences should be an ongoing process throughout the year. After you have introduced a few activities, it may be helpful to prominently display a poster listing the eight intelligences, perhaps in the form of the MI Pizza. When something happens that seems to relate to one or more of the eight intelligences, you can then use the poster to help emphasize the relationship. For example, if several students express a strong desire to work together on a project, you can point out that they want to use their "people smarts." For a student who has created a particularly apt visual illustration for an assignment, you can suggest that she really employed her "picture smarts" in the work. By modeling the practical uses of MI theory frequently in the daily activities of the classroom, you will help students internalize the theory and you should begin to see them use its vocabulary to make sense out of their own learning processes.

For Further Study

1. Drawing upon the material in this chapter or activities of your own choosing, develop a way to introduce the theory of multiple intelligences to your students. Note their initial reactions. Follow this up with supplementary activities. How long does it take before students begin to use the terms themselves? Note two or three examples of how students used the theory to explain their learning processes.

2. Create a mini-unit or special course for students on "learning about learning" that includes instruction in the theory of multiple intelligences. Include readings, exercises, activities, and strategies designed to help students understand their thinking styles so that they can learn more effectively.

3. Design a special wall display, bulletin board, or exhibit area where the eight intelligences are honored and celebrated. Include posters of famous people, photos of students engaged in MI activities, examples of products made by students in each of the intelligences, or all of these things.

5

MI Theory and Curriculum Development

We do not see in our descriptions [of classroom activity] . . . much opportunity
for students to become engaged with knowledge so as to employ their full range of
intellectual abilities. And one wonders about the meaningfulness of whatever is
acquired by students who sit listening or performing relatively repetitive exercises,
year after year. Part of the brain, known as Magoun's brain, is stimulated by novelty.
It appears to me that students spending 12 years in the schools we studied would
be unlikely to experience much novelty. Does part of the brain just sleep, then?

—*John I. Goodlad*

MI theory makes its greatest contribution to education by suggesting that
teachers need to expand their repertoire of techniques, tools, and strategies
beyond the typical linguistic and logical ones predominantly used in American classrooms. According to John Goodlad's pioneering "A Study of Schooling" project, which involved researchers in observing over 1,000 classrooms
nationwide, nearly 70 percent of classroom time is consumed by "teacher"
talk—mainly teachers talking "at" students, such as by giving instructions
or lecturing. The next most widely observed activity was students doing written assignments, and according to Goodlad (2004), "much of this work was
in the form of responding to directives in workbooks or on worksheets"

(p. 230). Twenty-five years after Goodlad's study was originally published, the scenario has not changed much and may even, in fact, have become worse. The federal government's No Child Left Behind law has created a climate in which standardized tests, and standardized methods to prepare for them, have overwhelmed the landscape in schools across the United States (Wallis, 2008). In this context, the theory of multiple intelligences functions not only as a specific remedy to one-sidedness in teaching but also as a "metamodel" for organizing and synthesizing all the educational innovations that have sought to break out of this narrowly confined approach to learning. In doing so, MI theory provides a broad range of stimulating curricula to "awaken" the slumbering brains that Goodlad fears populate our nation's schools.

The Historical Background of Multimodal Teaching

Multiple intelligences as a philosophy guiding instruction is hardly a new concept. Even Plato (1952), in a manner of speaking, seemed aware of the importance of multimodal teaching when he wrote: ". . . do not use compulsion, but let early education be a sort of amusement; you will then be better able to find out the natural bent" (p. 399). More recently, virtually all the pioneers of modern education developed systems of teaching based upon more than verbal pedagogy. The 18th-century philosopher Jean Jacques Rousseau declared in his classic treatise on education, *Emile,* that the child must learn not through words but through experience, not through books but through "the book of life." The Swiss reformer Johann Heinrich Pestalozzi emphasized an integrated curriculum that regarded physical, moral, and intellectual training based solidly on concrete experiences. And the founder of the modern-day kindergarten, Friedrich Froebel, developed a curriculum consisting of hands-on experiences with manipulatives ("gifts"), in addition to playing games, singing songs, gardening, and caring for animals. In the 20th century, innovators like Maria Montessori and John Dewey evolved systems of instruction based upon MI-like techniques, including Montessori's tactile letters and other self-paced materials and Dewey's vision of the classroom as a microcosm of society.

By the same token, many recent alternative educational models essentially are multiple intelligence systems using different terminologies (and with varying levels of emphasis upon the different intelligences). Cooperative learning, for example, seems to place its greatest emphasis upon interpersonal intelligence, yet specific activities can involve students in each of the other intelligences as well. Similarly, whole language instruction has at its core the cultivation of linguistic intelligence, yet it uses music, hands-on activities, introspection (through journal keeping), and group work to carry out its fundamental goals.

MI theory essentially encompasses what good teachers have always done in their teaching: reaching beyond the text and the blackboard to awaken students' minds. Two exemplary movies about great teachers, *Stand and Deliver* (1987) and *Dead Poets Society* (1989), underline this point. In *Stand and Deliver,* Jaime Escalante (played by Edward James Olmos), a high school mathematics teacher, uses apples to introduce fractions, fingers to teach multiplication, and imagery and metaphor to clarify negative numbers (if one digs a hole in the ground, the hole represents negative numbers, the pile of dirt next to it signifies positive numbers). John Keating (played by Robin Williams), the prep school instructor in *Dead Poets Society,* has students reading literary passages while kicking soccer balls and listening to classical music. MI theory provides a way for *all* teachers to reflect upon their best teaching methods and to understand why these methods work (or why they work well for some students but not for others). It also helps teachers expand their current teaching repertoire to include a broader range of methods, materials, and techniques for reaching an ever wider and more diverse range of learners.

The MI Teacher

A teacher in an MI classroom contrasts sharply with a teacher in a traditional linguistic/logical-mathematical classroom. In the traditional classroom, the teacher lectures while standing at the front of the classroom, writes on the blackboard, asks students questions about the assigned reading or handouts, and waits while students finish their written work. In the MI classroom, while keeping her educational objective firmly in mind, the teacher continually shifts her method of presentation from linguistic to spatial to musical and so on, often combining intelligences in creative ways.

The MI teacher may spend part of the time lecturing and writing on the blackboard at the front of the room. This, after all, is a legitimate teaching technique. Teachers have simply been doing too much of it. The MI teacher, however, also draws pictures on the blackboard or shows a video clip to illustrate an idea. She often plays music at some time during the day, either to set the stage for an objective, to make a point about the objective, or to provide an environment for studying the objective. The MI teacher provides hands-on experiences, whether they involve getting students up and moving about, passing an artifact around to bring to life the material studied, or having students build something tangible to reveal their understanding. The MI teacher also has students interacting with each other in different ways (e.g., in pairs, small groups, or large groups); plans time for students to engage in self-reflection, undertake self-paced work, or link their personal experiences and feelings to the material being studied; and creates opportunities for learning to occur through living things.

Such characterizations of what the MI teacher does and does not do, however, should not serve to rigidify the instructional dimensions of MI theory. The theory can be implemented in a wide range of instructional contexts, from highly traditional settings where teachers spend much of their time directly teaching students to open environments where students regulate most of their own learning. Even traditional linguistic teaching can take place in a variety of ways designed to stimulate the eight intelligences. The teacher who lectures with rhythmic emphasis (musical), draws pictures on the board to illustrate points (spatial), makes dramatic gestures as she talks (bodily-kinesthetic), pauses to give students time to reflect (intrapersonal), asks questions that invite spirited interaction (interpersonal), and includes references to nature in her lectures (naturalist) is using MI principles within a traditional teacher-centered perspective.

Key Materials and Methods of MI Teaching

There are a number of teaching tools in MI theory that go far beyond the traditional teacher-as-lecturer mode of instruction. Figure 5.1 provides a quick summary of some MI teaching methods. The list on pp. 60–64 provides a broader, but still incomplete, survey of the techniques and materials that can be employed in teaching through the multiple intelligences. (Capitalized items in the list are discussed more fully in Chapter 6.)

5.1
Summary of the Eight Ways of Teaching

Intelligence	Teaching Activities (examples)	Teaching Materials (examples)	Instructional Strategies	Sample Educational Movement (primary intelligence)	Sample Teacher Presentation Skill	Sample Activity to Begin a Lesson
Linguistic	lectures, discussions, word games, storytelling, choral reading, journal writing	books, tape recorders, typewriters, stamp sets, books on tape	read about it, write about it, talk about it, listen to it	Critical Literacy	teaching through storytelling	long word on the blackboard
Logical-Mathematical	brainteasers, problem solving, science experiments, mental calculation, number games, critical thinking	calculators, math manipulatives, science equipment, math games	quantify it, think critically about it, put it in a logical framework, experiment with it	Critical Thinking	Socratic questioning	posing a logical paradox
Spatial	visual presentations, art activities, imagination games, mind-mapping, metaphor, visualization	graphs, maps, video, Lego sets, art materials, optical illusions, cameras, picture library	see it, draw it, visualize it, color it, mind-map it	Integrated Arts Instruction	drawing/ mind-mapping concepts	unusual picture on the overhead

Bodily-Kinesthetic	hands-on learning, drama, dance, sports that teach, tactile activities, relaxation exercises	building tools, clay, sports equipment, manipulatives, tactile learning resources	build it, act it out, touch it, get a "gut feeling" of it, dance it	Hands-On Learning	using gestures/dramatic expressions	mysterious artifact passed around the class
Musical	rhythmic learnings, rapping, using songs that teach	tape recorder, tape collection, musical instruments	sing it, rap it, listen to it	Orff Schulwerk	using voice rhythmically	piece of music played as students come into class
Interpersonal	cooperative learning, peer tutoring, community involvement, social gatherings, simulations	board games, party supplies, props for role-plays	teach it, collaborate on it, interact with respect to it	Cooperative Learning	dynamically interacting with students	"Turn to a neighbor and share . . ."
Intrapersonal	individualized instruction, independent study, options in course of study, self-esteem building	self-checking materials, journals, materials for projects	connect it to your personal life, make choices with regard to it, reflect on it	Individualized Instruction	bringing feeling into presentation	"Close your eyes and think of a time in your life when . . ."
Naturalist	nature study, ecological awareness, care of animals	plants, animals, naturalists' tools (e.g., binoculars), gardening tools	connect it to living things and natural phenomena	Ecological Studies	linking subject matter to natural phenomena	bring in an interesting plant or animal to spark discussion about topic

Linguistic

- Books
- BRAINSTORMING
- Choral reading
- Debates
- Extemporaneous speaking
- Individualized reading
- JOURNAL KEEPING
- Large- and small-group discussions
- Lectures
- Manuals
- Memorizing linguistic facts
- PUBLISHING (e.g., creating class newspapers)
- Reading to the class
- Sharing time
- STORYTELLING
- Student speeches
- Talking books
- TAPE RECORDING ONE'S WORDS
- Using word processing software
- Word games
- Worksheets
- Writing activities

Logical-Mathematical

- CLASSIFICATIONS AND CATEGORIZATIONS
- Computer programming languages
- Creating codes
- HEURISTICS
- Logic puzzles and games
- Logical problem-solving exercises
- Logical-sequential presentation of subject matter
- Mathematical problems on the board
- Piagetian cognitive exercises
- CALCULATIONS AND QUANTIFICATIONS
- SCIENCE THINKING

- Scientific demonstrations
- SOCRATIC QUESTIONING

Spatial

- 3-D construction kits
- Art appreciation
- Charts, graphs, diagrams, and maps
- COLOR CUES
- Computer graphics software
- Creative daydreaming
- Draw-and-paint/computer-assisted-design software
- GRAPHIC SYMBOLS
- IDEA SKETCHING
- Imaginative storytelling
- Mind-maps and other visual organizers
- Optical illusions
- Painting, collage, and other visual arts
- Photography
- Picture literacy experiences
- PICTURE METAPHORS
- Videos, slides, and movies
- Visual awareness activities
- Visual pattern seeking
- Visual puzzles and mazes
- Visual thinking exercises
- VISUALIZATION

Bodily-Kinesthetic

- BODY ANSWERS
- BODY MAPS
- CLASSROOM THEATER
- Competitive and cooperative games
- Cooking, gardening, and other "messy" activities
- Crafts
- Creative movement
- Field trips

- Hands-on activities of all kinds
- HANDS-ON THINKING
- KINESTHETIC CONCEPTS
- Manipulatives
- Mime
- Physical awareness exercises
- Physical education activities
- Physical relaxation exercises
- Tactile materials and experiences
- Use of kinesthetic imagery
- Using body language/hand signals to communicate
- Virtual reality software

Musical

- Creating new melodies for concepts
- DISCOGRAPHIES
- Group singing
- Linking old tunes with concepts
- Listening to inner musical imagery
- MOOD MUSIC
- Music appreciation
- Musical composition software
- MUSICAL CONCEPTS
- Playing live music on piano, guitar, or other instruments
- Playing percussion instruments
- Playing recorded music
- RHYTHMS, SONGS, RAPS, AND CHANTS
- Singing, humming, or whistling
- SUPERMEMORY MUSIC
- Using background music

Interpersonal

- Academic clubs
- Apprenticeships
- BOARD GAMES

- Community involvement
- Conflict mediation
- COOPERATIVE GROUPS
- Cross-age tutoring
- Group brainstorming sessions
- Interactive software or Internet platforms
- Interpersonal interaction
- Parties or social gatherings as context for learning
- PEER SHARING
- PEOPLE SCULPTURES
- SIMULATIONS

Intrapersonal

- CHOICE TIME
- Exposure to inspirational/motivational curricula
- FEELING-TONED MOMENTS
- GOAL-SETTING SESSIONS
- Independent study
- Individualized projects and games
- Interest centers
- ONE-MINUTE REFLECTION PERIODS
- Options for homework
- PERSONAL CONNECTIONS
- Private spaces for study
- Self-esteem activities
- Self-paced instruction
- Self-teaching programmed instruction

Naturalist

- Aquariums, terrariums, and other portable ecosystems
- Class weather station
- ECO-STUDY
- Gardening
- Nature-oriented software
- Nature study tools (binoculars, telescope, microscope)

- Nature videos, films, and movies
- NATURE WALKS
- PET-IN-THE-CLASSROOM
- PLANTS AS PROPS
- WINDOWS ONTO LEARNING

How to Create MI Lesson Plans

On one level, MI theory applied to the curriculum might best be represented by a loose and diverse collection of teaching strategies such as those listed above. In this sense, MI theory represents a model of instruction that has no distinct rules other than the demands imposed by the cognitive components of the intelligences themselves and the specific needs of the domain in which they are teaching (e.g., math, science, literature, etc.). Teachers can pick and choose from the above activities, implementing the theory in ways suited to their own unique teaching style and congruent with their educational philosophy (as long as that philosophy does not declare that all children learn in the exact same way).

On a deeper level, however, MI theory suggests a set of parameters within which educators can create new curricula. In fact, the theory provides a context within which educators can address any skill, content area, theme, or instructional objective and develop at least eight ways to teach it. Essentially, MI theory offers a means of building daily lesson plans, weekly units, year-long themes, and programs in such a way that all students can have their strongest intelligences addressed at least some of the time.

The best way to approach curriculum development using the theory of multiple intelligences is by thinking about how one can *translate* the material to be taught from one intelligence to another. In other words, how can we take a linguistic symbol system, such as the English language, and translate it not into other linguistic languages, such as Spanish or French, but into the languages of other intelligences, namely, pictures, physical or musical expressions, logical symbols or concepts, social interactions, intrapersonal connections, and naturalistic associations?

The following seven-step procedure suggests one way to create lesson plans or curriculum units using MI theory as an organizing framework:

1. Focus on a specific objective or topic. You might want to develop curricula on a large scale (e.g., for a year-long theme) or create a program for reaching a specific instructional objective (e.g., for a student's individualized education plan). Whether you have chosen "ecology" or "the schwa sound" as a focus, however, make sure you have clearly and concisely stated the objective. Place the objective or topic in the center of a sheet of paper, as shown in Figure 5.2.

2. Ask key MI questions. Figure 5.2 shows the kinds of questions to ask when developing a curriculum for a specific objective or topic. These questions can help prime the creative pump for the next steps.

3. Consider the possibilities. Look over the questions in Figure 5.2, the list of MI techniques and materials in Figure 5.1, and the descriptions of specific strategies in Chapter 6. Which of the methods and materials seem most appropriate? Think also of other possibilities not listed.

4. Brainstorm. Using an MI Planning Sheet like the one shown in Figure 5.3, begin listing as many teaching approaches as possible for each intelligence. You should end up with something like the sheet shown in Figure 5.4.

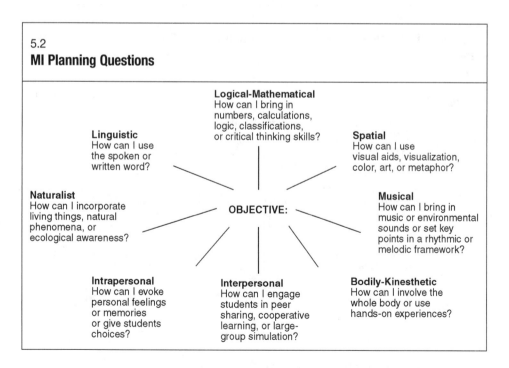

5.2
MI Planning Questions

Logical-Mathematical
How can I bring in numbers, calculations, logic, classifications, or critical thinking skills?

Linguistic
How can I use the spoken or written word?

Spatial
How can I use visual aids, visualization, color, art, or metaphor?

Naturalist
How can I incorporate living things, natural phenomena, or ecological awareness?

OBJECTIVE:

Musical
How can I bring in music or environmental sounds or set key points in a rhythmic or melodic framework?

Intrapersonal
How can I evoke personal feelings or memories or give students choices?

Interpersonal
How can I engage students in peer sharing, cooperative learning, or large-group simulation?

Bodily-Kinesthetic
How can I involve the whole body or use hands-on experiences?

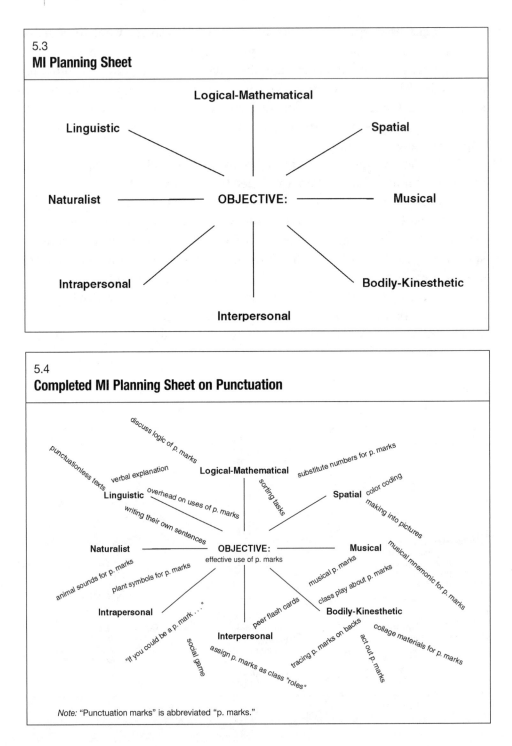

5.3
MI Planning Sheet

Logical-Mathematical

Linguistic

Spatial

Naturalist — OBJECTIVE: — Musical

Intrapersonal

Bodily-Kinesthetic

Interpersonal

5.4
Completed MI Planning Sheet on Punctuation

discuss logic of p. marks

punctuationless texts

verbal explanation

Logical-Mathematical

substitute numbers for p. marks

Linguistic

overhead on uses of p. marks

sorting tasks

Spatial color coding

writing their own sentences

making into pictures

Naturalist — OBJECTIVE: — Musical

effective use of p. marks

musical mnemonic for p. marks

animal sounds for p. marks

plant symbols for p. marks

musical p. marks

class play about p. marks

Intrapersonal

Bodily-Kinesthetic

"If you could be a p. mark . . ."

peer flash cards

tracing p. marks on backs

collage materials for p. marks

social game

Interpersonal

act out p. marks

assign p. marks as class "roles"

Note: "Punctuation marks" is abbreviated "p. marks."

When listing approaches, be specific about the topic you want to address (e.g., "video clip of rain forest" rather than simply "video clip"). The rule of thumb for brainstorming is "list *everything* that comes to mind." Aim for at least 20 or 30 ideas and at least two or three ideas for each intelligence. Brainstorming with colleagues may help stimulate your thinking.

5. Select appropriate activities. From the ideas on your completed planning sheet, circle the approaches that seem most workable in your educational setting.

6. Set up a sequential plan. Using the approaches you've selected, design a lesson plan or unit around the specific topic or objective chosen. Figure 5.5 shows what an eight-day lesson plan might look like when 35 to 40 minutes of class time each day are allotted to the objective.

7. Implement the plan. Gather the materials needed, select an appropriate time frame, and then carry out the lesson plan. Modify the lesson as needed to incorporate changes that occur during implementation (e.g., based on feedback from students).

Appendix C contains additional examples of MI lessons and programs.

MI and Thematic Instruction

More and more educators are recognizing the importance of teaching students from an interdisciplinary point of view. Although academic skill teaching or the teaching of isolated chunks of knowledge may provide students with competencies or background information that can prove useful to them in their further education, such instruction often fails to connect students to the real world—a world that they will have to function in as citizens a few years hence. Consequently, educators are turning toward models of instruction that more closely imitate or mirror life in some significant way. Such instruction is frequently *thematic* in nature. Themes cut through traditional curricular boundaries, weave together subjects and skills that are found naturally in life, and provide students with opportunities to use their multiple intelligences in practical ways. As Susan Kovalik (1993), developer of the Integrated Thematic Instruction model, puts it: "A key feature of *here and now* curriculum is that it is immediately recognized (by the student) as being relevant and meaningful. . . . Furthermore, it purports to teach our young about their world and the skills necessary to act within and upon it, thus

5.5
Sample Eight-Day MI Lesson Plan

Level: 4th grade

Subject: Language arts

Objective: To understand the function of, and differences between, four punctuation marks: the question mark, period, comma, and exclamation point.

Monday *(Linguistic Intelligence)*: Students listen to a verbal explanation of the function of punctuation marks, read sentences having examples of each mark, and complete a worksheet requiring them to fill in their own marks.

Tuesday *(Spatial Intelligence)*: The teacher draws on the board graphic images that correspond in meaning and form to each mark. Question mark = a hook, since questions "hook" us into requiring an answer; exclamation point = a staff that you pound on the floor when you want to exclaim something; a period = a point, since you've just made your point, plain and simple; and a comma = a brake pedal, since it requires you to temporarily stop in the middle of a sentence. Students can make up their own images and then place them as pictures in sentences (with different colors assigned to different marks).

Wednesday *(Bodily-Kinesthetic Intelligence)*: The teacher asks students to use their bodies to form the shapes of the different punctuation marks as she reads sentences requiring these marks (e.g., a curved body posture for question mark).

Thursday *(Musical Intelligence)*: Students make up different sounds for the punctuation marks (as Victor Borge did in his comedy routines) and then make these sounds in unison as different students read sample sentences requiring the use of the four marks.

Friday *(Logical-Mathematical Intelligence)*: Students form groups of four to six. Each group has a box divided into four compartments, each of which is assigned a punctuation mark. The groups sort sentence stubs with missing punctuation marks (one per sentence stub) into the four compartments according to the punctuation needed.

Monday *(Interpersonal Intelligence)*: Students form groups of four to six. Each student has four cards, and each card has a different punctuation mark written on it. The teacher places a sentence requiring a given punctuation mark on the overhead projector. As soon as students see the sentence, they toss the relevant card in the center of their group's circle. The first student in the group to throw in a correct card gets five points, the second four, and so on.

Tuesday *(Intrapersonal Intelligence)*: Students are asked to create their own sentences using each of the punctuation marks; the sentences should relate to their personal lives (e.g., a question they'd like somebody to answer, a statement they feel strongly about, a fact they know that they'd like others to know about).

Wednesday *(Naturalist Intelligence)*: Students are asked to assign an animal and its respective sound to each of the punctuation marks (e.g., a period might be a dog barking; a comma, a duck quacking; a question mark, a cat meowing; and an exclamation point, a lion roaring). As the teacher (or a student) reads a passage, the students make the animal sounds corresponding to each punctuation mark encountered.

preparing themselves for living the fast-paced changes of the [future]" (p. 5). Kovalik's thematic model is based in part on year-long themes (e.g., "What Makes It Tick?") that are themselves made up of month-long components (e.g., clocks/time, electrical power, transportation) and weekly topics (e.g., seasonal change and geologic time). Other curricular approaches focus on alternative time frames, such as semester units or three-month themes. Regardless of the time element involved, MI theory provides a context for structuring thematic curricula. It provides a way of making sure the activities selected for a theme will activate all eight intelligences and therefore draw upon every child's inner gifts.

Figure 5.6 outlines the kinds of activities that might be used for the theme "Inventions." It shows how activities can be structured to address traditional academic subjects as well as each of the eight intelligences. Significantly, this chart illustrates how science activities needn't focus only on logical-mathematical intelligence and how language activities (reading and writing) needn't focus only on linguistic intelligence. They can, in fact, span all eight intelligences.

Keep in mind that MI theory can be applied to the curriculum in a variety of ways. There are no standard guidelines to follow. The ideas in this chapter are suggestions only. I invite you to create other forms or formulas for lesson planning or thematic development and encourage you to incorporate other formats, including those developed by educators such as Kovalik (1993) and Hunter (see Gentile, 1988). Ultimately, you should be guided by your deepest and sincerest attempts to reach beyond the intelligences you may currently be teaching to, so that every child has the opportunity to succeed in school.

For Further Study

1. Look over the list of teaching strategies in this chapter. Circle the strategies you use or have used in your instruction. Place a yellow star next to the approaches that have worked best. Place a red flag next to the activities you think you use too much. Finally, place a blue arrow pointing upward next to new activities you would like to try. Over the next few weeks, eliminate or scale back your use of some of the red-flagged/overused techniques,

5.6

MI and Thematic Instruction
Sample Theme: Inventions

Intelligence	Math	Science	Reading	Writing	Social Studies
Linguistic	Read math problems involving inventions	Talk about the basic scientific principles involved in specific inventions	Read a general book about inventions	Write about what you'd like to invent	Write about the social conditions that gave rise to certain inventions
Logical-Mathematical	Learn a math formula that served as the basis for an invention	Create a hypothesis for the development of a new invention	Read a book about the logic and math behind inventions	Write a word problem based on a famous invention	Create a time line of famous inventions
Spatial	Sketch the geometry involved in specific inventions	Draw a new or existing invention showing all working parts	Read a book with lots of diagrams of the inner workings of inventions	Label the individual components of your drawing of an invention	Paint a mural showing inventions in social/historical context
Bodily-Kinesthetic	Create an invention to measure a specific physical activity	Build your own invention based on sound scientific principles	Read the instructions for putting together an existing invention	Write instructions for building your own invention from scrap materials	Put on a play about how a certain invention came to be
Musical	Study the math involved in the invention of musical instruments	Study the science behind the invention of electronic music	Read about the background to invention songs such as "John Henry"	Write the lyrics for a song promoting a new invention	Listen to music about inventions at different historical periods
Interpersonal	Be in a study group that looks at the mathematics involved in specific inventions	Form a discussion group to study the science behind inventions	Read about the cooperation necessary for developing an invention	Write a play about inventions that can be put on by the class	Hold a discussion group about how a certain invention came to be
Intrapersonal	Create your own word problems based on inventions	Develop a self-study program to examine the scientific basis for a specific invention	Read the biography of a famous inventor	Write your personal autobiography as a "famous inventor"	Think about this question: if you could invent a time machine, where would you go?
Naturalist	Investigate inventions used to measure positions of natural phenomena (e.g., astrolabe)	Study the scientific principles behind cloning and how a cloned human being may someday represent a biological "invention"	Read about "naturalist inventions" such as "wetware" (biological software) and genetically altered foods	Write an essay on your opinion of the use of animals in experiments to develop inventions	Design an invention that would contribute to the ecological welfare of the planet

increase the time you spend using the yellow-starred approaches, and add some of the blue-arrowed techniques to your teaching repertoire.

2. Select a specific skill or instructional objective that many of your students don't seem to be effectively learning. Apply the seven-step planning process described in this chapter to generate a multiple intelligence lesson or series of lessons, and then teach your students using the activities you've developed.

Afterward, reflect upon the lesson. Which parts were most successful? Which were least successful? Ask students to reflect upon the lesson in the same way. What have you learned from this experience that can help you regularly teach through multiple intelligences?

3. Select a theme to serve as a basis for a curriculum in your class. Use the seven-step lesson-planning process described in this chapter to generate a basic framework of activities that includes all eight intelligences and each academic subject area. (Refer to Figure 5.6 for guidance in developing activities.)

4. Focus on an intelligence that you usually don't touch upon in your teaching, create a lesson plan that includes it, and teach the lesson to your students. (See Appendix B for instructional resources in each intelligence.)

6

MI Theory and Teaching Strategies

If the only tool you have is a hammer, everything around you looks like a nail.

—Abraham Maslow

MI theory opens the door to a wide range of teaching strategies that can be easily implemented in the classroom. In many cases, they are strategies that have been used for decades by good teachers. In other cases, the theory of multiple intelligences offers teachers an opportunity to develop innovative teaching strategies that are relatively new to the educational scene. MI theory suggests that no one set of teaching strategies will work best for all students at all times. All children have different proclivities in the eight intelligences, so any particular strategy is likely to be highly successful with one group of students and less successful with other groups. For example, teachers who use the Rhythms, Songs, Raps, and Chants strategy discussed in this chapter as a pedagogical tool will probably find that musically inclined students respond while nonmusical students remain unmoved. Similarly, the use of pictures and images in teaching will reach students who are more spatially oriented but perhaps have a different effect on those who are more physically or verbally inclined.

Because of these individual differences among students, teachers are best advised to use a broad range of teaching strategies with their students. As long as instructors shift their intelligence emphasis from presentation to presentation, there will always be a time during the period or day when a student has his or her own most highly developed intelligence(s) actively involved in learning.

In this chapter, I present 40 teaching strategies, five for each of the eight intelligences. The strategies are designed to be general enough so you can apply them at any grade level, yet specific enough so that little guesswork is required to implement them. Keep in mind that these are only a few samples of some of the strategies available (see Chapter 5 for a list of more strategies). I encourage you to find additional strategies or to develop your own unique adaptations of existing strategies.

Teaching Strategies for Linguistic Intelligence

Linguistic intelligence is perhaps the easiest intelligence to develop strategies for, because so much attention has been given to its cultivation in the schools. I do not include the traditional linguistic strategies involving textbooks, worksheets, and lectures among the five strategies discussed here, however, simply because they have been overused. This is not to say that textbooks, worksheets, and lectures should never be used. They serve as excellent channels for effectively imparting certain kinds of information. But they are only *one small part* of a vast repertoire of teaching strategies— and not necessarily the most important part. Though used extensively in schools all over the United States, this trio of teaching techniques most easily reaches only a segment of the learning population: the most "book-oriented" and "lecture-gifted" students. The five strategies described below are accessible to a broader range of learners because they emphasize open-ended language activities that bring out the linguistic intelligence in *every* learner.

Storytelling

Storytelling has traditionally been seen as entertainment for children in the public library or during special enrichment times in the classroom. However, it should be viewed as a vital teaching tool, for so it has been in cultures all over the world for thousands of years. When using storytelling in the classroom, you weave essential concepts, ideas, and instructional goals into a story that you tell directly to students. Although storytelling is usually thought of as a means of conveying knowledge in the humanities, it can be applied in mathematics and science as well. For example, to teach the idea of multiplication, you can tell students the story of brothers and sisters who have magical powers: whatever they touch multiplies (e.g., for the first child, it doubles; for the second, it triples; and so on). To convey the notion of centrifugal force, you can take students on a mythical journey to a land where everything spins around very rapidly from the center outward.

Prepare for storytelling by listing the essential elements you'd like to include in the story. Then use your imagination to create a special land, a group of colorful characters, or a whimsical plot to carry the message home. It may help to visualize the story at first and then practice telling it to a spouse or to a mirror. Stories needn't be especially original or fabulous for children to benefit from them. Students are often impressed simply by a teacher's willingness to be creative and speak from the heart about a subject.

Brainstorming

Russian psychologist Lev Vygotsky once said that a thought is like a cloud shedding a shower of words. During brainstorming, students produce a torrent of verbal thoughts that can be collected and put on the board or an overhead projector or entered into computer software such as Inspiration or Kidspiration. The brainstorming can be about anything: words for a class poem, ideas for developing a group project, thoughts about material in a lesson being taught, suggestions for a class picnic, and so forth. The general rules for brainstorming are: participants share whatever comes to mind that is relevant, no put-downs or criticisms of any idea are allowed, and *every* idea counts. You can place ideas at random on the board or screen or use a special system such as an outline, a mind-map, or a Venn diagram for organizing them. After everyone has had a chance to share, look for patterns or groupings in the ideas, invite students to reflect on the ideas, or use the ideas in a specific project (such as in a group poem). This strategy allows all students who have an idea to receive special acknowledgment for their original thoughts.

Tape Recording

Tape recorders or other audio recording devices, including some software, are among the most valuable learning tools in any classroom. This is because they offer students a medium through which to learn about their linguistic powers and help them employ verbal skills to communicate, solve problems, and express inner feelings. Students can use tape recorders to "talk out loud" about a problem they are attempting to solve or a project they are planning to do. In this way, they reflect upon their own problem-solving processes or cognitive skills. They can also use tape recorders to prepare for writing, helping to loosen the soil, so to speak, of their topic. Students who are not good writers may also want to record their thoughts on tape as an alternative mode of expression. Some students may use the tape recorder to send "oral letters" to other students in the class, to share personal experiences, and to get feedback about how they are coming across to others in the classroom.

Tape recorders can be used as *collectors* of information (e.g., in interviews) and as *reporters* of information (e.g., talking books). Tape recorders can also be used to provide information. For instance, one can be placed in each activity center so students can listen to information about the topic in that center. Every classroom should have tape recorders available, and teachers should plan on using them regularly to promote the growth of students' minds.

Journal Writing

Keeping a personal journal involves students in making ongoing written records related to a specific domain. The domain can be broad and open-ended ("Write about anything you're thinking about or feeling during the class day") or quite specific ("Use this journal to keep a simulated record of your life as a farmer during the 1800s as part of our history course"). Journals can be kept in math ("Write down your strategy for solving this problem"), science ("Keep a record of the experiments you do, hypotheses you're testing, and new ideas that emerge from your work"), literature ("Keep an ongoing record of your responses to the books you're reading"), or other subjects. They can be kept entirely private, shared only between teacher and student, or regularly read to the class. They can also incorporate multiple intelligences by allowing drawings, sketches, photos, dialogues, and other nonverbal data. (Note that this strategy also draws heavily upon intrapersonal intelligence insofar as students work individually and use the journal to reflect upon their lives.)

Publishing

In traditional classrooms, students complete papers that are turned in, graded, and then often thrown away. Many students exposed to this kind of routine begin to see writing as the dreary process of fulfilling an assignment. Educators ought to be sending students a different message: that writing is a powerful tool for communicating ideas and influencing people. By providing students with opportunities to publish and distribute their work, you can make this point in a strong way.

Publishing takes many forms. Students can submit their writing to a class or school newspaper, a city newspaper, a children's magazine, or some other publishing source that accepts student work. Students' writing can also be published using desktop publishing software such as Microsoft Publisher, Print Shop, or Print Explosion and then bound in book form and made available in a special section of the class or school library.

After publication, encourage interaction between the authors and the readers. You might even have special student autographing parties and book circles to discuss students' writings. When children see that others care enough about their writing to reproduce it, discuss it, and even argue about it, they become linguistically empowered and are motivated to continue developing their writing craft.

Teaching Strategies for Logical-Mathematical Intelligence

Typically, logical-mathematical thinking is restricted to math and science courses. There are components of this intelligence, however, that are applicable throughout the curriculum. The emergence of the critical-thinking movement certainly suggests one broad way in which logical-mathematical intelligence has affected the social sciences and humanities. Similarly, the call for "numeracy" (the logical-mathematical equivalent of "literacy") in our schools and, in particular, the recommendation that mathematics be applied to an interdisciplinary curriculum point to the wide application of this form of thinking to every part of the school day. The following are five major strategies for developing logical-mathematical intelligence that can be employed in all school subjects.

Calculations and Quantifications

In line with school reform efforts, teachers are being encouraged to discover opportunities to talk about numbers both inside and outside the math and science arena. In subjects such as history and geography, you may focus regularly on important statistics: lives lost in wars, populations of countries, and so forth. But how do you accomplish the same aim in literature? You shouldn't force connections that simply aren't there. It's surprising, however, how many novels, short stories, and other literary works make reference to numbers. In a novel by Virginia Woolf, *To the Lighthouse,* there is a mention of 50 pounds to fix a greenhouse roof. How does that figure translate into U.S. dollars? In a short story by Doris Lessing, "Through the Tunnel," a boy must count to see how long he can stay underwater and then compare that to the amount of time it takes experienced divers to swim through a submerged tunnel. Each of these passages provides the basis for mathematical thinking. Of course, you shouldn't feel compelled to make word problems out of great works of art—that would be stifling to say the least. It is a good idea, however, to keep alert for interesting numbers and intriguing math problems wherever they may be found. By tuning into the numbers in the midst of nonmathematical subjects, you can better engage highly logical students, and other students can learn to see that math belongs not just in math class but in life.

Classifications and Categorizations

The logical mind can be stimulated anytime information is put into some kind of rational framework, whether the data be linguistic, logical-mathematical, spatial, or any other kind. For example, in a unit on the effects of climate on culture, students might brainstorm a random list of geographic locations and then classify them by type of climate (e.g., desert, mountain, plains, or tropical). Or, in a science unit on states of matter, the instructor might put the names of three categories—gas, liquid, solid—at the top of columns on the blackboard and then ask students to list examples of things belonging to each category. Other examples of logical frameworks include

Venn diagrams, time lines, attribute webs (listing the attributes of a person, place, or thing as spokes around the subject), 5W organizers (diagrams that answer who, what, when, where, and why questions), and mind-maps. Most of these frameworks are also spatial in nature. The value of this approach is that disparate fragments of information can be organized around central ideas or themes, making them easier to remember, discuss, and think about.

Socratic Questioning

The critical-thinking movement has provided an important alternative to the traditional image of the teacher as knowledge dispenser. In Socratic questioning, the teacher serves as a questioner of students' points of view. The Greek sage Socrates is the model for this type of instruction. Instead of talking *at* students, the teacher participates in dialogues *with* them, aiming to uncover the rightness or wrongness of their beliefs. Students share their hypotheses about how the world works, and the teacher guides the "testing" of these hypotheses for clarity, precision, accuracy, logical coherence, or relevance through artful questioning. A history student who declares that World War II never would have happened if soldiers had actively resisted military service has his point of view subjected to rigorous scrutiny in this approach to teaching. A student defending the motives of a character in *Huckleberry Finn* is carefully questioned to see if her stand is supported by the facts in the novel. The purpose is not to humiliate students or put them in the wrong but, rather, to help them sharpen their own critical thinking skills so that they no longer form opinions simply out of strong emotion or the passion of the moment (see Paul, 1992).

Heuristics

The field of heuristics refers to a loose collection of strategies, rules of thumb, guidelines, and suggestions for logical problem solving. In terms of this book's goals, however, heuristics can be regarded as a major teaching/ learning strategy. Examples of heuristic principles include finding analogies to the problem you wish to solve, separating the various parts of the problem, proposing a possible solution to the problem and then working backward, and finding a problem related to yours and then solving it. While the most obvious applications of heuristics are in the math and science fields, heuristic principles can also be used in subjects other than these. In trying to envision solutions to the problems of government waste, for example, a student might look for analogies by asking himself what other entities create waste. While looking for the main idea in a reading passage, a student might separate out each part of the passage (into sentences) and subject each part to qualifying "tests" of a key point. Heuristics provides students with logical maps, so to speak, to help them find their way around unfamiliar academic terrain (see Polya, 1957).

Science Thinking

Just as you should look for mathematics in every part of the curriculum, so too should you seek out scientific ideas in areas other than science. This strategy is especially important given research showing that up to 70 percent of adults lack a fundamental understanding of the scientific process (Recer, 2002). There are ways to spread science thinking across the curriculum. For instance, students can study the influence important scientific ideas have had on history (e.g., how the development of the atomic bomb influenced the outcome of World War II). They can study science fiction with an eye toward discovering if the ideas described are feasible. They can learn about global issues such as AIDS, overpopulation, and the greenhouse effect that require some science background to be well understood. In each part of the curriculum, science provides another point of view that can considerably enrich students' perspective.

Teaching Strategies for Spatial Intelligence

The cave drawings of prehistoric man are evidence that spatial learning has long been important to human beings. Unfortunately, in today's schools the "sensory-channels" model of presenting information to students through visual as well as auditory modes sometimes translates into simply writing on the board, a practice that is linguistic in nature. Spatial intelligence has to do with *pictures*—either the pictures in one's mind or the pictures in the external world, such as photos, movies, drawings, graphic symbols, ideographic languages, and so forth. Here are five teaching strategies designed to use students' spatial intelligence for academic purposes.

Visualization

One of the easiest ways to help students translate book and lecture material into pictures and images is to have them close their eyes and picture whatever is being studied. An application of this strategy involves having students create their own "inner blackboard" (or movie or video screen) in their mind's eye. They can then place on this mental blackboard any material they need to remember: spelling words, math formulas, history facts, or other data. When asked to recall a specific body of information, students then need only call up their mental blackboard and "see" the data inscribed on it.

A more open-ended application of this strategy involves having students close their eyes and see pictures of what they've just read or studied (e.g., a story or a chapter in a textbook). Afterward, they can draw or talk about their experiences. Teachers can also lead students through more formal "guided imagery" sessions as a way of introducing them to new concepts or material (e.g., leading them on a "guided tour" through the circulatory system to learn anatomy). Students may experience nonspatial content as well during these activities (e.g., kinesthetic images, verbal images, or musical images).

Color Cues

Highly spatial students are often sensitive to color. Unfortunately, the school day is usually filled with black-and-white texts, copy books, worksheets, and chalkboards. There are, however, many creative ways to put color into the classroom as a learning tool. Use a variety of colors of chalk, markers, and transparencies when writing in front of the class. Provide students with colored pencils and pens and colored paper on which to write assignments. Students can learn to use different colored markers to "color code" material they are studying (e.g., mark all the key points in red, all the supporting data in green, all the unclear passages in orange). Use color to emphasize patterns, rules, or classifications during instruction (e.g., coloring all *th*'s red in a phonics lesson, using different colors to write about distinct historical stages in Greek history). Finally, students can use their favorite colors as a stress reducer when coping with difficult problems (e.g., "If you run into a word, problem, or idea you don't understand, imagine your favorite color filling your head; this can help you find the right answer or clarify things for yourself").

Picture Metaphors

A metaphor involves comparing one idea to another, seemingly unrelated idea. A picture metaphor expresses this concept in a visual image. Developmental psychologists suggest that young children are masters of metaphor (Gardner, 1979). Sadly, this capacity often diminishes as children grow older. However, educators can tap this underground stream (to use a metaphor!) to help students master new material. The educational value of using metaphors lies in establishing connections between what a student already knows and what is being presented. Think of the key point or main concept you want students to learn. Then, link that idea to a visual image. Construct the complete metaphor yourself (e.g., "How is the development of the colonies during early American history like the growth of an amoeba?") or have students develop their own (e.g., "If the major organs in the body were animals, which ones would they be?").

Idea Sketching

A review of some of the notebooks of eminent individuals in history, including Thomas Edison, Henry Ford, and Charles Darwin, reveals that these individuals used simple drawings in developing many of their powerful ideas. Teachers should recognize the value that this kind of visual thinking can have in helping students articulate their understanding of subject matter. The Idea Sketching strategy involves asking students to draw the key point, main idea, central theme, or core concept being taught. Neatness and realism should be de-emphasized in favor of a succession of quick sketches that help articulate an idea.

To prepare students for this kind of drawing, it may be helpful to play the game Pictionary (or Pictionary Jr.) so students get used to the notion of making rapid drawings to convey central ideas. Then, begin to ask students to draw the concept or idea you want to focus on in a lesson. This strategy can be used to evaluate a student's understanding of an idea, to emphasize a concept, or to give students ample opportunity to explore an idea in greater depth. Here are some examples of subjects or concepts you might have students choose to illustrate: the Great Depression, gravity, probability (in math), fractions, democracy, pathos (in a literary work), ecosystem, and continental drift. Following up the drawing activity with a discussion of the relationship between the drawings and the subject matter is important.

Do not evaluate the artistic quality of the drawings themselves; instead, seek to "draw out" students' understanding from the sketches (see McKim, 1980).

Graphic Symbols

One of the most traditional teaching strategies involves writing words on a blackboard. Less common, especially after primary school, is *drawing pictures* on the board, even though pictures may be extremely important to the understanding of the spatially inclined student. Consequently, teachers who can support their teaching with drawings and graphic symbols, as well as words, may be reaching a wider range of learners. This strategy, then, requires you to practice *drawing* at least some part of your lessons—for instance, by creating graphic symbols that depict the concepts to be learned. Here are some examples:

- Showing the three states of matter by drawing a solid mass (heavy chalk marks), a liquid mass (lighter curvy marks), and a gaseous mass (little dots)
- Indicating "root words" by putting little roots at the base of those words on the board
- Drawing a time line for a novel's plot or historical event and marking the line not only with dates and names but also with pictures that symbolize events

You do not need superior drawing skills to use this strategy. Roughly drawn graphic symbols will suffice in most cases. Your willingness to model imperfect drawing can actually serve as an example for students who feel shy about sharing their own drawing with the class.

Teaching Strategies for Bodily-Kinesthetic Intelligence

Students may leave their textbooks and folders behind when they leave school, but they take their bodies with them wherever they go. Consequently, finding ways to help students integrate learning at a "gut" level can be very important to increasing their retention, understanding, and interest. Traditionally, physical learning has been considered the province of physical education and vocational education. The following strategies, however, show how easy it is to integrate hands-on and kinesthetic learning activities into traditional academic subjects like reading, math, and science.

Body Answers

Ask students to respond to instruction by using their bodies as a medium of expression. The simplest and most overused example of this strategy is asking students to raise their hands to indicate understanding. This strategy can be varied in any number of ways, however. Instead of raising hands, students could smile, blink one eye, hold up fingers (one finger to indicate just a little understanding, five fingers to show complete understanding), make flying motions with their arms, and so forth. Students can provide "body answers" during a lecture ("If you understand what I've just said, put your finger on your temple; if you don't understand, scratch your head"), while going through a textbook ("Anytime you come to something in the text that seems outdated, I want you to frown"), or in answering questions that have a limited number of answers ("If you think this sentence has parallel construction, I want you to raise your two hands high like a referee indicating a touchdown; if you think it's not parallel, put your hands together over your head like the peak of a house").

Classroom Theater

To bring out the actor in each of your students, ask them to enact the texts, problems, or other material to be learned by dramatizing or role-playing the content. For example, students might dramatize a math problem involving three-step problem solving by putting on a three-act play. Classroom Theater can be as informal as a one-minute improvisation of a reading passage during class or as formal as a one-hour play at the end of the semester that sums up students' understanding of a broad learning theme. It can be done without any materials, or it may involve substantial use of props. Students may themselves act in plays and skits, or they may produce puppet shows or dramatizations in miniature (e.g., showing how a battle was fought by putting miniature soldiers on a plywood battlefield and moving them around to show troop movements). To help older students who may initially feel reluctant to engage in dramatic activities, try some warm-up exercises (see Spolin, 1986).

Kinesthetic Concepts

The game of charades has long been a favorite of partygoers because of the way it challenges participants to express knowledge in unconventional ways. The Kinesthetic Concepts strategy involves introducing students to concepts through physical illustrations or asking students to pantomime specific concepts or terms from the lesson. This strategy requires students to translate information from linguistic or logical symbol systems into purely bodily-kinesthetic expression. The range of subjects is endless. Here are just a few examples of concepts that might be expressed through physical gestures or movements: soil erosion, cell mitosis, political revolution, supply and demand, subtraction (of numbers), the epiphany (of a novel), and biodiversity in an ecosystem. Simple pantomimes can also be extended into more elaborate creative movement experiences or dances (such as dancing the periodic table of the elements).

Hands-On Thinking

Students who are highly developed in the fine-motor aspect of bodily-kinesthetic intelligence should have opportunities to learn by manipulating objects or by making things with their hands. Many educators have already provided such opportunities by incorporating manipulatives (e.g., Cuisenaire rods) into math instruction and involving students in experiments or lab work in science. In thematic projects, too, students can use hands-on thinking—for instance, in constructing adobe huts for a unit on Native American traditions or in building dioramas of the rain forest for an ecology theme. You can extend this general strategy into many other curricular areas as well. At a rote level, students can study spelling words or new vocabulary words by forming them in clay or with pipe cleaners. At a higher cognitive level, students can express complex concepts by creating clay or wood sculptures, collages, or other assemblages. For example, students could convey an understanding of the term "deficit" (in its economic sense) using only clay (or some other available material) and then share their productions during a class discussion.

Body Maps

The human body provides a convenient pedagogical tool when transformed into a reference point or "map" for specific knowledge domains. One of the most common examples of this approach is the use of fingers in counting and calculating (elaborate finger-counting systems such as Chisan-bop have been adapted for classroom use). We can map out many other domains onto the body. In geography, for example, the body might represent the United States (if the head represents the northern United States, where is Florida located?). The body can also be used to map out a problem-solving strategy in math. For example, in multiplying a two-digit number by a one-digit number, the feet could be the two-digit number, and the right knee could be the one-digit number. Students could then perform the following actions in "solving" the problem: tap the right knee and the right foot to get the first product (indicated by tapping the thighs); tap the right knee and the left foot to get the second product (indicated by tapping the stomach); tap the thighs and the stomach (to indicate adding the two products), and tap the head (to indicate the final product). By repeating physical movements that represent a specific process or idea, students can gradually internalize the process or idea.

Teaching Strategies for Musical Intelligence

For thousands of years, knowledge was imparted from generation to generation through the medium of singing or chanting. In the 20th century, advertisers have discovered that musical jingles help people remember their client's product. Educators, however, have been slower to recognize the importance of music in learning. As a result, most of us have thousands of commercial musical jingles in our long-term memory but relatively few school-related musical pieces. The following strategies will help you begin to integrate music into the core curriculum.

Rhythms, Songs, Raps, and Chants

Take the essence of whatever you are teaching and put it into a rhythmic format that can be either sung, rapped, or chanted. At a rote level, this can mean spelling words to the rhythm of a metronome or singing the times tables to the tune of a popular song. You can also identify the main point you want to emphasize in a lecture, the main idea of a story, or the central theme of a concept and then place it in a rhythmic format. For example, to teach John Locke's concept of Natural Law, one-half of the class can chant "natural law, natural law, natural law, natural law . . . ," while the other half repeats: "life, li-ber-ty, happ-i-ness, life, li-ber-ty, happ-i-ness . . . ." Inviting students themselves to create songs, raps, or chants that summarize, synthesize, or apply meanings from subjects they are studying moves students to an even higher level of learning. This strategy can also be enhanced through the addition of percussion or other musical instruments.

Discographies

Supplement your bibliographies for the curriculum with lists of recorded musical selections—tapes, compact discs, MP3 files, and other audio formats—that illustrate, embody, or amplify the content you want to convey. For example, in developing a unit about the Civil War, you could collect songs related to that period in history, including "When Johnny Comes Marching Home Again," "Tenting Tonight," "The Battle Hymn of the Republic," and the more contemporary "The Night They Drove Old Dixie Down." After listening to the recordings, the class can discuss the content of the songs in relation to the themes of the unit.

Additionally, you can find recorded musical phrases, songs, or pieces that sum up in a compelling way the key point or main message of a lesson or unit. For example, to illustrate Newton's first law of motion (a body remains in its state of rest unless it is compelled to change that state by a force impressed on it), you could play the first few lines of Sammy Davis Jr.'s version of "Something's Gotta Give" ("When an irresistible force such as you . . ."). Such "musical concepts" are often effective openers (providing an anticipatory set or "hook") to a lesson.

Supermemory Music

Twenty-five years ago, educational researchers in eastern Europe discovered that students could more easily commit information to memory if they listened to the teacher's instruction against a musical background. Baroque and classical musical selections in 4/4 time were found to be particularly effective (e.g., Pachelbel's Canon in D and the Largo movements of concertos by Handel, Bach, Telemann, and Corelli). Students should be in a relaxed state (putting heads on desks or lying on the floor) while the teacher rhythmically gives the information to be learned (e.g., spelling or vocabulary words, history facts, science terms) against the musical background (see Rose, 1987).

Musical Concepts

Musical tones can be used as a creative tool for expressing concepts, patterns, or schemas in many subjects. For example, to convey musically the idea of a circle, begin humming at a certain tone, drop the tone gradually (indicating the gradual slope of the circle) to a low note, and then gradually move up toward the original tone. You can use similar techniques to express cosines, ellipses, and other mathematical shapes. You can also use rhythms to express ideas. For example, in a lesson on Shakespeare's *Romeo and Juliet*, you can pit the rhythms of the Montagues and the Capulets against each other to suggest the two families in conflict, while in the midst of those rhythms, two quieter musical patterns can be heard coming into harmony with each other (Romeo and Juliet). This strategy offers ample opportunity for creative expression from both teachers and students.

Mood Music

Locate recorded music that creates an appropriate mood or emotional atmosphere for a particular lesson or unit. Such music can even include sound effects (nonverbal sounds are processed through the musical intellect), nature sounds, or classical or contemporary pieces that facilitate specific emotional states. For example, just before students are about to read a story that takes place near the sea, play a recording of sea sounds (waves crashing up against the shore, sea gulls crying, etc.) or *La Mer* (The Sea) by Claude Debussy. (See Bonny & Savary, 1990, for more information on music and the mind.)

Teaching Strategies for Interpersonal Intelligence

Some students need time to bounce their ideas off other people if they are to function optimally in the classroom. These social learners have benefited most from the emergence of cooperative learning. But since all children have interpersonal intelligence to one degree or another, every educator should be aware of teaching approaches that incorporate interaction with and among people. The following strategies can help tap each student's need for belonging and connection to others.

Peer Sharing

Sharing is perhaps the easiest of the MI strategies to implement. All you need to do is say to students, "Turn to a person near you and share _____." The blank space can be filled with virtually any topic. You might want students to process material just covered in class ("Share a question you have about what I just presented"). Or you might want to begin a lesson or unit with peer sharing to unlock students' existing knowledge about the topic under study ("Share three things that you know about the early settlers in America"). You may want to set up a "buddy system" so each student shares with the same person each time. Or you may want to encourage students to share with different members of the class so that by the end of the year, each person has formed a sharing partnership with every student in the classroom. Sharing periods can be short (30 seconds) or extended (up to an hour or more). Peer sharing can also evolve into peer tutoring (one student coaching or teaching specific material to another student) or cross-age tutoring (an older student working with a younger student in a different class).

People Sculptures

Anytime students are brought together to collectively represent in physical form an idea, a concept, or some other specific learning goal, there is the possibility for a *people sculpture to exist*. If students are studying the skeletal system, they can build a people sculpture of a skeleton in which each person represents a bone or group of bones. For a unit on inventions, students can create people sculptures of different inventions, complete with moving parts. In algebra class, students can create people sculptures of different equations, each person representing either a number or a function in the equation. Similarly, in language arts, students can build people sculptures to represent spelling words (each person holding up a letter), sentences (each student representing a word), or whole paragraphs (each person taking responsibility for a complete sentence). Assign a student to help "direct" the activity, or let the components of the sculpture organize themselves. The beauty of this approach is in having people represent things that were formerly represented only in books or lectures. People sculptures raise learning out of its remote theoretical context and put it into an immediately accessible social setting.

Cooperative Groups

The use of small groups working toward common instructional goals is the core component of the cooperative learning model. Such groups generally work most effectively when they have three to eight members. Students in cooperative groups can tackle a learning assignment in a variety of ways. The group may work collectively on a written assignment, for example, with each member contributing ideas—much as screenwriters work when preparing a television episode or as scientists do in preparing a scientific paper. The group may also divide its responsibilities in a number of ways. In one case, the group may assign activities based upon the structure of the assignment, with one member doing the introduction, another taking care of the middle section, and another contributing the conclusion. Or groups may use a "jigsaw" strategy and assign each student responsibility for a particular book or subtopic. Alternatively, they may assign different roles among group members, so that one person does the writing, a second reviews the writing for spelling and punctuation errors, a third reads the report to the class, and a fourth leads the ensuing discussion.

Cooperative groups are particularly suitable for MI teaching because they can be structured to include students who represent the full spectrum of intelligences. For instance, a group charged with the task of creating a videotaped presentation might include a socially developed student to help organize the group, a linguistically inclined member to do the writing, a spatially oriented student to do the drawing, a bodily-kinesthetically disposed student to create props or be a leading actor, and so forth. Cooperative groups provide students with a chance to operate as a social unit—an important prerequisite for successful functioning in real-life work environments.

Board Games

Board games are a fun way for students to learn in the context of an informal social setting. On one level, students are chatting, discussing rules, throwing dice, and laughing. On another level, however, they are engaged in learning whatever skill or subject happens to be the focus of the game. Board games can be easily made using manila file folders, magic markers (to create the typical winding road or path), a pair of dice, and miniature cars, people, or colored cubes (available at toy stores or at teacher supply stores) to serve as game pieces. Topics can include a wide range of subjects, from math facts and phonics skills to rain forest data and history questions. The information to be learned can be placed on the individual squares of the winding road (e.g., the math fact 5×7) or on cards made from tag board or thick construction paper. Answers can be provided in a number of ways: on a separate answer key, from a specially designated "answer person," or on the board squares or cards themselves (glue a tiny piece of folded paper to each square; on the top flap write the question or problem and on the bottom flap, the answer; players then simply open the flap to read the answer).

You can also design board games that involve quick open-ended or activity-oriented tasks. Simply place the directions or activities on each square or card (e.g., "Explain what you would do to control pollution if you were president of the United States" or "Look up the word *threshold* in the dictionary").

Simulations

A simulation involves a group of people coming together to create an "as-if" environment. This temporary setting becomes the context for getting into more immediate contact with the material to be learned. For example, students studying a historical period might actually dress up in costumes of that era, turn the classroom into a place that might have existed then, and begin acting *as if* they were living in that time. Similarly, in learning about geographical regions or ecosystems, students could turn the classroom into a simulated jungle or rain forest.

Simulations can be quick and improvisational in nature, with the teacher providing an instant scenario to act out: "Okay, you've just gotten off the boat from your trip to the New World and you're all standing around together. Begin the action!" Or they can be ongoing and require substantial preparation, such as props, costumes, and other paraphernalia to support the illusion of a particular era or region of the world.

Although this strategy involves several intelligences (including bodily-kinesthetic, linguistic, and spatial), it is included in the interpersonal section because the human interactions that take place help students develop a new level of understanding. Through conversation and other interactions, students begin to get an insider's view of the topic they are studying.

Teaching Strategies for Intrapersonal Intelligence

Most students spend about six hours a day, five days a week in a classroom with 25 to 35 other people. For individuals with strongly developed intrapersonal intelligence and an introverted personality, this intensely social atmosphere can be somewhat claustrophobic. Hence, teachers need to build in frequent opportunities during the day for students to experience themselves as autonomous beings with unique life histories and a sense of deep individuality. Each of the following strategies helps accomplish this aim in a slightly different way.

One-Minute Reflection Periods

During lectures, discussions, project work, or other activities, students should have frequent "time outs" for introspection or focused thinking. One-minute reflection periods offer students time to digest the information presented or to connect it to happenings in their own lives. They also provide a refreshing change of pace that helps students stay alert and ready for the next activity.

A one-minute reflection period can occur anytime during the school day, but it may be particularly useful after the presentation of information that is especially challenging or central to the curriculum. During this one-minute period (which can be extended or shortened to accommodate differing attention spans), there is to be no talking and students are to simply think about what has been presented in any way they'd like. Silence is usually the best environment for reflection, but you occasionally might try using background "thinking" music as an option. Also, students should not feel compelled to "share" what they thought about, but this activity can be combined with Peer Sharing to make it both an intra- and interpersonal activity.

Personal Connections

The big question that accompanies strongly intrapersonal students through their school career is: "What does all this have to do with *my* life?" Most students have probably asked this question in one way or another during their time in school. It's up to teachers to help answer this question by continually making connections between what is being taught and the personal lives of their students. This strategy, then, asks you to weave students' personal associations, feelings, and experiences into your instruction. You may do so through questions ("How many of you have ever. . . ?"), statements ("You may wonder what this has to do with your lives. Well, if you ever plan on . . ."), or requests ("I'd like you to think back in your life to a time when . . ."). For instance, to introduce a lesson on the skeletal system, you might ask, "How many people here have ever broken a bone?" Students then share stories and experiences before going on to the anatomy lesson itself. Or, for a lesson on world geography, you might ask, "Has anybody ever been to another country? What country?" Students then identify the countries they've visited and locate them on the map.

Choice Time

Giving students choices is as much a fundamental principle of good teaching as it is a specific intrapersonal teaching strategy. Essentially, choice time consists of building in opportunities for students to make decisions about their learning experiences. Making choices is like lifting weights. The more frequently students choose from a group of options, the thicker their "responsibility muscles" become. The choices may be small and limited ("You can choose to work on the problems on page 12 or 14"), or they may be significant and open-ended ("Select the kind of project you'd like to do this semester"). Choices may be related to content ("Decide which topic you'd like to explore") or to process ("Choose from this list a method of presenting your final project"). Choices may be informal and spur of the moment ("Okay, would you rather stop now or continue talking about this?"), or they may be carefully developed and highly structured (as in the use of a learning contract for each student). How do you currently provide for choice in your classroom? Think of ways to expand the choice-making experiences your students have in school.

Feeling-Toned Moments

One of the sadder findings of John Goodlad's "A Study of Schooling" (2004) was that most of the 1,000 classrooms observed had few experiences of true feeling—that is, expressions of excitement, amazement, anger, joy, or caring. All too often, teachers present information to students in an emotionally neutral way. Yet we know that human beings possess an "emotional brain" consisting of several subcortical structures (see Goleman, 2006). To feed that emotional brain, educators need to teach with feeling. This strategy suggests that educators are responsible for creating moments in teaching where students laugh, feel angry, express strong opinions, get excited about a topic, or feel a wide range of other emotions. You can help create feeling-toned moments in a number of ways: first, by modeling those emotions yourself as you teach; second, by making it safe for students to have feelings in the classroom (giving permission, discouraging criticism, and acknowledging feelings when they occur); and finally, by providing experiences (such as movies, books, and controversial ideas) that evoke feeling-toned reactions.

Goal-Setting Sessions

One of the characteristics of highly developed intrapersonal learners is their capacity to set realistic goals for themselves. This ability certainly has to be among the most important skills necessary for leading a successful life. Consequently, educators help students immeasurably in their preparation for life when they provide opportunities for setting goals. These goals may be short-term ("I want everybody to list three things they'd like to learn today") or long-term ("Tell me what you see yourself doing 25 years from now"). The goal-setting sessions may last only a few minutes, or they may involve in-depth planning over several months' time. The goals themselves can relate to academic outcomes ("What grades are you setting for yourself this term?"), wider learning outcomes ("What do you want to know how to do by the time you graduate?"), or life goals ("What kind of occupation do you see yourself involved with after you leave school?"). Try to allow time *every day* for students to set goals for themselves. You may also want to show students different ways of representing those goals (through words, pictures, etc.) and methods for charting their progress along the way (through graphs, charts, journals, and time lines).

Teaching Strategies for Naturalist Intelligence

Most of classroom instruction takes place inside of a school building. For children who learn best through nature, this arrangement cuts them off from their most valued source of learning. There are two primary solutions to this dilemma. First, more learning needs to take place for these kids outside in natural settings. Second, more of the natural world needs to be brought into the classroom and other areas of the school building, so that naturalistically inclined students might have greater access to developing their naturalist intelligence while inside of the school building. The strategies that have been selected for inclusion here are all drawn from one or both of these approaches.

Nature Walks

The Nobel Prize–winning physicist Richard Feynman once wrote that he got his start along the path of science by taking walks in nature with his father. It was from the kind of questions that his father would ask him as they walked along (e.g., "What animal do you think made that hole over there?") that his own scientific questioning attitude was formed. In similar fashion, teachers might consider the benefit of "a walk in the woods" (or whatever other natural features are available within walking distance of your school) as a way of reinforcing material being learned inside of the classroom. Virtually any subject lends itself to a nature walk. Science and math, of course, can be examined in the various principles at work in the growth of plants, the weather above, the earth below, and the animals that scurry or fly about. If you're teaching a piece of literature or a history lesson that involves any kind of natural setting (and most do at least somewhere along the way), then you might use a nature walk as an opportunity to reconstruct a scene or two from the story or period of history ("Imagine that this is the meadow where the Pickwick Club had their ridiculous duel in Dickens's *Pickwick Papers*" or "Picture this as the setting of the Battle of Hastings just before the troops arrived on the scene"). Also, nature walks make a superb preparation for getting your class ready to do creative writing, drawing, or other activities.

Windows onto Learning

One of the classic images of an "inattentive" student in the classroom is of a child sitting at a desk looking wistfully out the window while, presumably, fantasizing about what she'd rather be doing! Why do kids want to look out the window? All too often, it's because what they see out there is more interesting than what is going on in the classroom. If this is true, then why not use this "off-task" tendency in students as a positive classroom strategy? In other words, "looking out the window" is a technique that instructors can use to further the curriculum. What can be accomplished, pedagogically speaking, by looking out a window? There are many possibilities, including weather study (have a class weather station to make measurements), bird watching (have binoculars handy), understanding time (study the seasons' effects on the trees, grass, plants, etc.), and creative writing (have students create metaphors based on nature in their writing). In fact, looking out a window can be used as a strategy for just about any subject. As with nature walks, looking out a window can be used to set a scene for literature or history or for scientific observation. Other subjects can take what's beyond the window as a starting point, a place to briefly stop during a lesson, or a final stopping point. Examples include geology or geography ("What nature features do you see in the earth or along the horizon?"), economics ("Investigate the cost of planting the trees just outside the window"), social studies ("How well designed is the area just outside the window for human beings?"), and literature ("As we finish this story, I want you to look out the window and imagine our protagonist walking between the trees there into the distance").

Of course, if you don't have windows in your classroom or your windows look out onto other classrooms or expanses of concrete (a lamentable consequence of using architects who have little of the naturalist in them), then it's not possible to fully realize the possibilities of this strategy. However, even then, you might use the Visualization strategy from spatial intelligence to help your students imagine that they *do* have imaginary windows that they can look out of to gain at least some semblance of connection to the natural world!

Plants as Props

If you can't go out of the classroom on nature walks and don't have windows in your classroom through which to look at nature, then the next viable alternative is to bring nature into your classroom. Many teachers have adorned their windowsills or shelves with house plants simply to create a positive ambiance for learning. However, it is also useful to consider the practical advantage of using plants as learning tools. The fact that the petals of flowers in bloom, for example, often come in multiples is an opportunity to examine the concept of multiplication in a natural setting. Plants can make useful "props" as background scenery for the Classroom Theater and People Sculpture strategies described earlier in this chapter. In teaching about the branches of government, you can use a nearby branching plant as a naturalistic metaphor to illustrate the concept. In science and math, the growth of classroom plants can be measured. In history, their function or usefulness as herbal medicines, foods, or even poisons might be considered. Assigning a particularly difficult child with a naturalistic bent the job of taking care of a plant in the classroom can be a useful way to redirect his or her energies. Finally, I love the idea of using the image of plant growth as a metaphor for the learning that is going on in the classroom—at the beginning of the year, bring in a sprout of a plant, and at the end of the year, point out to the class how much both the plant and the students have grown during the year!

Pet-in-the-Classroom

Many elementary school classrooms already have a "class pet" kept in a gerbil cage, a rabbit hutch, or some other species-appropriate container. This strategy underlines how important this particular addition to the classroom is in terms of sheer instructional value. First of all, having a pet in the classroom automatically creates for many naturalistically inclined students a "safe place" where they can go to have a relationship to the natural world and to feel a sense of caring for nature's beings (some of these kids may be our future veterinarians!). Second, many specific instructional uses can come from having a pet in the classroom. The scientific skill of observation can be developed by having kids keep notes on a pet's behavior. (The naturalist Jane Goodall traces her own love of animals back to an incident at 5 years old where she stayed in a chicken coop for five hours just to see how chickens lay eggs!) Kids can keep math records on their pet's food intake, weight, and other vital statistics. For high school classrooms, teachers can use a class pet as a kind of "alter ego" for the classroom in posing instructional questions (e.g., "How do you think our rabbit Albert would feel about the problem of world hunger?"). Students who relate best to the world through their love of animals might well use Albert's persona in giving voice to their own thinking on the matter. Having a pet in the classroom creates a sort of "reality check" for teachers and students alike, reminding us of our own connection to the animal world and our need sometimes to learn from the wisdom of our pets!

Eco-study

Implied in the concluding statement of the last strategy is the importance of having a sense of respect for the natural world. This is the core idea behind the next strategy: Eco-study. This strategy essentially means that whatever we are teaching, whether it is history, science, math, literature, geography, social studies, art, music, or any other subject, we should keep in mind its relevance to the ecology of the earth. In essence, what I'm suggesting here is that "ecology" shouldn't just be a unit, course, or topic isolated from the rest of the curriculum but that it be integrated into every part of the school day. So, for example, if the topic is fractions or percentages, the teacher can ask students to investigate the fraction of a particular endangered species that exists today as opposed to, say, 50 years ago or the percentage of rain forest left in Brazil compared to what it was in 1900. If the subject is how a bill goes through Congress, students might consider an actual bill having an ecological focus that went through each stage of the process. Or, if a teacher has the option of choosing literature, then a dramatic work like Ibsen's *An Enemy of the People*—an ecological play written before its time—might be assigned or even acted out by the students. For students who are humanity's "earth angels" (those with a particular sensitivity to ecological issues), this sort of strategy can help draw them into the curriculum and at the same time stimulate all students to take a deeper interest in the welfare of our planet's diminishing natural resources.

For Further Study

1. Select three strategies from this chapter that intrigue you and that you haven't already used in your classroom. Do background reading or consult with colleagues as needed, and develop specific lesson plans that describe exactly how you will apply the strategies. Try out your lessons and then evaluate the results. What worked, and what didn't work? How would you modify each strategy in the future to make it more successful?

2. Choose an intelligence that you usually don't address in your instruction and research additional strategies (not mentioned above) to use in your teaching (consult the list of strategies in Chapter 5 and the resources list in Appendix B for more sources of ideas).

3. Develop a broad learning experience for your students that incorporates at least one of the strategies for each intelligence in this chapter. For instance, develop a unit that involves body sculptures, mood music, feeling-toned moments, peer sharing, brainstorming, color coding, and quantifications and calculations. Work alone or as part of an interdisciplinary team.

7

MI Theory and the Classroom Environment

Nowhere else [but in schools] are large groups of individuals packed so closely together for so many hours, yet expected to perform at peak efficiency on difficult learning tasks and to interact harmoniously.

—*Carol Weinstein*

For most Americans, the word "classroom" conjures up an image of students sitting in neat rows of desks facing the front of the room, where a teacher either sits at a large desk correcting papers or stands near a blackboard lecturing to students. This is certainly one way to organize a classroom, but it is by no means the only way or the best way. The theory of multiple intelligences suggests that the classroom environment—or classroom *ecology*, if you will—may need to be fundamentally restructured to accommodate the needs of different kinds of learners.

MI and Ecological Factors in Learning

At a minimum, MI theory provides a template through which educators can view some of the critical ecological factors in learning. Each intelligence, in fact, provides a context for asking some searching questions about those factors in the classroom that promote or interfere with learning and those elements absent from the room that could be incorporated to facilitate student progress. A review of the eight intelligences reveals some of the following questions:

Linguistic

- How are spoken words used in the classroom? Are the words used by the teacher too complex or too simple for the students' level of understanding, or is there a good match?
- How are students exposed to the written word? Are words represented on the walls (through posters, quotations, etc.)? Are written words presented through primary sources (e.g., novels, newspapers, historical documents) or through textbooks and workbooks written by committees?
- Is there too much "linguistic pollution" in class (endless exposure to dittos and busy work), or are students being empowered to develop their own linguistic materials?

Logical-Mathematical

- How is time structured in the classroom? Do students have opportunities to work on long-term projects without being interrupted, or must they continually break off their activities to move on to a new topic?
- Is the school day sequenced to make optimum use of students' attention spans (morning best for focused academic work, afternoon best for more open-ended activities), or do students have to perform under conditions that don't match changes in their attention span?
- Is there some consistency to students' school days (e.g., routines, rituals, rules, effective transitions to new activities), or is there a sense of chaos or of reinventing the wheel with the start of each new school day?

Spatial

- How is the classroom furniture arranged? Are there different spatial configurations to accommodate different learning needs (e.g., desks for written work, tables for discussion or hands-on work, carrels for independent study), or is there only one arrangement (e.g., straight rows of desks)?

- Is the room attractive to the eye (e.g., artwork on the walls), or is it visually boring or disturbing?
- Are students exposed to a variety of visual experiences (e.g., optical illusions, cartoons, illustrations, movies, great art), or does the classroom environment function as a visual desert?
- Do the colors of the room (walls, floors, ceiling) stimulate or deaden students' interest in learning?
- What kinds of illumination are used (fluorescent, incandescent, natural)? Do the sources of light refresh students or leave them feeling distracted and drained?
- Is there a feeling of spaciousness in the learning environment, or do students feel stressed in part due to overcrowding and lack of privacy?

Bodily-Kinesthetic

- Do students spend most of their time sitting at their desks with little opportunity for movement, or do they have frequent opportunities to get up and move around (e.g., through exercise breaks, hands-on activities, role-play, etc.)?
- Do students receive healthy snacks and a well-designed breakfast or lunch during the day to keep their bodies active and their minds alert, or do they eat junk food during recess and have high-fat, low-nutrition cafeteria meals?
- Are there materials in the classroom that allow students to manipulate, build, be tactile, or in other ways gain hands-on experience, or does a "don't touch" ethos pervade the room?

Musical

- Does the auditory environment promote learning (e.g., background music, white noise, pleasant environmental sounds, silence), or do disturbing noises frequently interfere with learning (e.g., loud buzzers or bells, aircraft overhead, car and truck noises outside, industrial machines)?
- How does the teacher use his or her voice? Does it vary in intensity, inflection, and emphasis, or does it have a dull monotone quality that

puts students to sleep (like Ben Stein's voice in the movie *Ferris Bueller's Day Off*)?

Interpersonal

- Does an atmosphere of belonging and trust permeate the classroom, or do students feel alienated, distant, or mistrustful of one another?
- Are there established procedures for mediating conflict between class members, or must problems often be referred to a higher authority (e.g., the principal) for resolution?
- Do students have frequent opportunities to interact in positive ways (e.g., peer teaching, discussions, group projects, cooperative learning, parties), or are students relatively isolated from one another?

Intrapersonal

- Do students have opportunities to work independently, develop self-paced projects, and find time and space for privacy during the day, or are they continually interacting?
- Are students exposed to experiences that heighten their self-concept (e.g., self-esteem exercises, genuine praise and other positive reinforcement, frequent success experiences in their school work), or are they subjected to put-downs, failures, and other negative emotional experiences?
- Do students have the opportunity to share feelings in the classroom, or is the inner life of a student considered off limits?
- Are students with emotional difficulties referred to mental health professionals for support, or are they simply left to fend for themselves?
- Are students given authentic choices in how they are to learn, or do they have only two choices: "My way or the highway"?

Naturalist

- Are students given an opportunity to do some of their learning outside of the school building in natural settings (e.g., field trips, gardening, having class on the lawn), or do they remain isolated from the natural world during most of their school day?

- Does the classroom contain any living things (e.g., pets, fish, gerbils, plants), or is the occasional fly the only nonhuman living thing to enter its portals?
- Does the classroom provide windows that look out onto the sky, clouds, trees, lawns, or other natural phenomena, or is it windowless and shut off from any contact with the world of nature?

The answers to the above questions will provide a telling commentary on the quality of the learning environment available to students in school. If answers consistently tilt toward the negative side of the ecology ledger, then learning is apt to be significantly impaired, even if students come into the classroom able, willing, and excited to learn. On the other hand, answers that tend toward the positive factors listed above will enhance a classroom environment to the point where even students who enter the room with significant academic, emotional, or cognitive difficulties will have an opportunity to feel stimulated toward making great strides in their learning.

MI Activity Centers

In addition to the kinds of general ecological factors described above, there are more specific applications of MI theory to the classroom environment. These focus upon organizing the classroom in such a way that areas of the room are dedicated to specific intelligences. Although students can certainly engage in MI activities while seated at their desks, the use of long periods of seat time places significant limits on the kinds of MI experiences they can have. Restructuring the classroom to create "intelligence-friendly" areas or activity centers can greatly expand the parameters for student exploration in each domain.* Activity centers can take a variety of forms, as illustrated in Figure 7.1. This figure shows MI activity centers existing along two axes, from permanent to temporary centers (Axis A) and from open-ended to topic-specific centers (Axis B).

---

*Write Project Zero (Harvard Graduate School of Education, 321 Longfellow Hall, 13 Appian Way, Cambridge, MA 02138; Web address: http://www.pz.harvard.edu; e-mail: info@pz.harvard.edu) for information about Project Spectrum's use of activity centers for preschool children, and visit the New Horizons for Learning Web site (http://www.newhorizons.org) for information about Bruce Campbell's use of MI activity centers at the elementary school level (see also Campbell & Campbell, 2000).

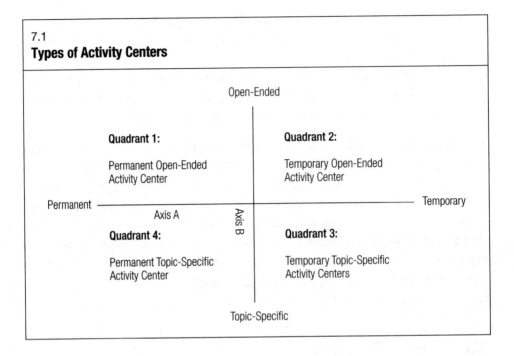

7.1
Types of Activity Centers

Permanent Open-Ended Activity Centers

Quadrant 1 of Figure 7.1 represents permanent (usually year-long) centers designed to provide students with a wide range of open-ended experiences in each intelligence. Here are some examples of such centers for each intelligence (with a very partial list of suggested items):

Linguistic

- Book nook or library area (with comfortable seating)
- Language lab (audio files, earphones, talking books)
- Writing center (typewriters, word processing software, paper)

Logical-Mathematical

- Math lab (calculators, manipulatives)
- Science center (chemistry set, microscope, measurement materials)

Spatial

- Art area (paints, collage materials, draw and paint software)
- Visual media center (videos, animation software, videocams)
- Visual-thinking area (maps, graphs, visual puzzles, picture library, three-dimensional building materials)

Bodily-Kinesthetic

- Open space for creative movement (mini-trampoline, juggling equipment)
- Hands-on center (clay, carpentry, blocks)
- Tactile-learning area (relief maps, samples of different textures, sandpaper letters)
- Drama center (stage for performances, puppet theater)

Musical

- Music lab (audio files of sound effects, earphones, music library)
- Music performance center (percussion instruments, audio recorder, metronome)
- Listening lab (stethoscope, walkie-talkies, small bottles containing different "mystery sounds" when shaken)

Interpersonal

- Round table for group discussions
- Desks paired together for peer teaching
- Social area (board games, comfortable furniture for informal social gatherings)

Intrapersonal

- Study carrels for individual work
- Loft (with nooks and crannies for privacy)
- Computer hutch (for self-paced study)

Naturalist

- Plant center with gardening tools and supplies
- Animal center with a gerbil or rabbit cage, a terrarium, or an ant farm
- Aquatic center with an aquarium and tools for measuring and observing marine life

Clear labeling of each of these activity centers with explicit MI nomenclature (e.g., "Linguistic Intelligence Center," "Picture Smart Center," "Naturalists' Corner") will reinforce students' understanding of MI theory. You may want to explain that the centers are named for the intelligence that is used *most often* in each center. Remember from Chapter 1 that intelligences are always interacting, so students don't have to switch activity centers if, for example, they want to add a picture to the writing they're doing in the Word Smart Center.

Temporary Topic-Specific Activity Centers

In Quadrant 3 of Figure 7.1, diagonally across from Quadrant 1, are topic-specific activity centers that change frequently and are geared toward a particular theme or subject. For example, if students are studying a unit on housing, you may create eight different centers that involve students in meaningful activities within each intelligence. The activities for the housing unit might include the following:

- *Linguistic*—A "Reading Center" where students read books on houses and write about what they've read
- *Logical-mathematical*—A "Computing Center" where students compare the costs, square footage, or other statistical measurements of different houses
- *Spatial*—A "Drawing Center" where students can design a futuristic house
- *Bodily-kinesthetic*—A "Building Center" where students create a model of a house using balsa wood and glue
- *Musical*—A "Music Center" where students listen to songs about dwellings (e.g., "This Old House," "Yellow Submarine") and make up their own songs

- *Interpersonal*—An "Interaction Center" where students "play house" (simulate a home environment with peers)
- *Intrapersonal*—An "Experience Center" where students think, write, draw, and act out their personal experiences with the homes they've lived in or with an image of their own dream house
- *Naturalist*—A "Landscape Architecture Center" where students can design natural features to complement the house (e.g., lawn, bonsai garden, fountain, plants, aquarium, etc.)

Temporary Open-Ended Activity Centers

Quadrant 2 of Figure 7.1 represents activity centers for open-ended exploration that can be set up and taken down quickly by a classroom teacher. This type of center can be as simple as eight tables scattered around the classroom, each clearly labeled with an intelligence and holding intelligence-specific materials that invite students into open-ended activities. Games lend themselves particularly well to temporary open-ended activity centers. Here are some examples:

- *Linguistic*—Scrabble
- *Logical-mathematical*—Monopoly
- *Spatial*—Pictionary
- *Bodily-kinesthetic*—Twister
- *Musical*—Encore
- *Interpersonal*—Family Feud
- *Intrapersonal*—The Ungame
- *Naturalist*—Frank's Zoo

Temporary open-ended activity centers are especially useful for introducing students to the idea of multiple intelligences and for giving them quick experiences that illustrate the intelligences.

Permanent Topic-Specific (Shifting) Activity Centers

Finally, Quadrant 4 of Figure 7.1 represents activity centers that are essentially a combination of Quadrant 1 (ongoing and permanent) and Quadrant 3 (topic-specific and temporary) activity centers. Permanent topic-specific activity centers are most appropriate for teachers working with year-long themes along the lines of Susan Kovalik's (1993, 2001) Highly

Effective Teaching (HET) model (formerly known as Integrated Thematic Instruction [ITI]). Each center exists year-round and has a number of materials and resources that never change (e.g., art supplies in the Spatial Center, hands-on materials in the Bodily-Kinesthetic Center). Within each center, however, are revolving "explorations" that change with every monthly component or weekly topic of the year-long theme. So, for example, if the year-long theme is "Change" (more appealingly titled "Does Everything Change?"), a monthlong component might deal with the seasons, and weekly topics might focus on individual seasons. The activity centers, then, might focus on winter for one week and then shift to spring the next week and to summer and fall in subsequent weeks. Every center might have activity cards posted that tell students what kinds of things they can work on either alone or cooperatively. For example, the activity cards for the topic of "summer" might read as follows:

- *Linguistic*—"Write a poem about what you plan to do during the summer. If this is a cooperative group activity, first choose a scribe to write down the poem. Then each person contributes a line to the poem. Finally, choose someone to read the poem to the class."
- *Logical-mathematical*—"First find out how many days there are in your summer vacation. Then figure how out many minutes are in that number of days. Finally, calculate the number of seconds in your summer vacation. If this is a group activity, collaborate with the other members of your group on your answers."
- *Spatial*—"Make a drawing of some of the things you plan to do during the summer. If this is a group activity, do a group drawing on a long sheet of mural paper."
- *Bodily-kinesthetic*—"Create your own representation of 'summer' out of a piece of clay. If this is a group activity, cooperate with the other members of your group to create a clay sculpture or quickly improvise a short play that includes the group's favorite summer activities."
- *Musical*—"Make up a rap or song about summer. If this is a group activity, collaborate on a group song to sing to the class, or brainstorm all the songs you can think of that have to do with summer and be prepared to sing some of them to the class."
- *Interpersonal*—"Have a group discussion about what you think makes for a *great* summer and select a spokesperson to summarize your conclusions in front of the class."

- *Intrapersonal*—"Make a list or a series of sketches of all the things you like about summer." (*Note:* Students work alone in this center.)
- *Naturalist*—"Close your eyes and picture all the types of animals and plants you are likely to see this summer. Then open your eyes and either draw them or create a story (or list) where they are all mentioned."

Student Choice and Activity Centers

Should students be able to choose which activity centers they work in? The answer to this question may depend upon the type of activity center (i.e., which quadrant the center is in) and the purpose of each center. Generally speaking, Quadrant 1 and 2 activity centers (those involving open-ended experiences) are best structured as "choice" activities. In other words, you can make them available to students during break times, recess, or special "choice times" after students have completed their other schoolwork. When used in this way, activity centers provide excellent assessment information about students' "proclivities" in the eight intelligences. Students usually gravitate toward activity centers based on intelligences in which they feel most competent. For example, students who repeatedly go to the "Picture Smart" area and engage in drawing activities are sending a strong message to the teacher about the importance of spatial intelligence in their lives.

Quadrant 3 and Quadrant 4 activity centers emphasize directed study. Consequently, when using these types of centers, you may want to let students choose the activity center they would like to *start* with but then have them rotate center by center in a clockwise manner until everyone has had experience in all eight centers. Using this rotation system from time to time with Quadrant 1 and 2 activity centers as well will ensure that students have experiences across the wide spectrum of intelligences.

Activity centers provide students with the opportunity to engage in "active" learning. They serve as oases in the desert for many students who are thirsting for something other than boring worksheets and individual work at their desks. MI theory allows you to structure activity centers in ways that activate a wide range of learning potentials in students. Though the descriptions above have been limited to centers based on individual intelligences, there is no reason that centers can't be structured to combine intelligences in different ways. In this sense, virtually any activity center that goes beyond simple reading, writing, or calculation activities qualifies as an MI center. A "Mechanic's Corner" combining logical-mathematical, spatial, and bodily-kinesthetic intelligences and a "Composer's Cabaret" combining linguistic and musical intelligences are just two examples of MI centers that might combine intelligences.

For Further Study

1. Survey your classroom environment using the questions on pages 100–103 as a guide. List the changes you would like to make in the ecology of your classroom. Prioritize them, putting those items that you'd like to change, but can't, on a separate list. Then set about making those changes that you *can* make, one at a time.

2. Set up MI activity centers in your classroom. First, decide which type of activity center you'd like to start out with (i.e., Quadrant 1, 2, 3, or 4). Then list the materials you need and create a schedule for setting up the centers. Enlist the help of parent volunteers, students, or colleagues as necessary.

If you have established permanent centers, assess the project after two or three weeks of use. If you have established temporary centers, assess their success immediately after students experience them. Use your evaluation to guide the design of future centers.

3. To introduce the idea of activity centers to your class, select a topic that has an emotional charge and that everyone has had some experience with—for instance, fast food. Put up eight signs at various points around the room, each bearing the symbol for an intelligence. Under each sign, tape an activity card. Then signal students to move toward the intelligence that they feel most comfortable with (make sure they've been introduced to MI in some way before this activity; see Chapter 3 for ideas). Alternatively, randomly hand out slips of paper on which have been inscribed symbols for each of the eight intelligences (one symbol per slip) and have students go to the center that corresponds with their individual slips of paper. Students then read the activity for their area and cooperatively begin working on it. Set a time to reconvene so the groups can present their findings. Here are some suggestions for activities related to the topic of fast food:

- *Linguistic*—"Create a manifesto (statement of basic principles) concerning student attitudes about fast food."
- *Logical-mathematical*—"Using the nutritional charts provided by the fast-food outlets you see here, develop a fast-food breakfast, lunch, or dinner that is as low in fat as possible; then put together a fast-food breakfast, lunch, or dinner that is as high in fat as possible."
- *Spatial*—"Create a mural that concerns itself with people's fast-food eating habits."
- *Bodily-kinesthetic*—"Rehearse a role-play or commercial (with or without words) about people's fast-food eating habits and then present it to the class."
- *Musical*—"Write a jingle or a rap about people's fast-food eating habits and then sing it together."
- *Interpersonal*—"Discuss among yourselves the fast-food eating habits of your small group, and then go out and canvass the rest of the class about their fast-food eating habits. Select a scribe to record and report the results."
- *Intrapersonal*—"Think about these questions: If you could be any fast food, which would you be? Why? Choose a method for recording your thoughts (e.g., drawing, writing, or pantomime). You may work alone or as a group."
- *Naturalist*—"Make a list of all the plants and animals used in creating the food at a fast-food restaurant. Discuss the potential impact of their consumption upon the world's ecosystems (e.g., oxygen-producing rain forests may be cleared for raising the cattle used for meat in hamburgers)."

8

MI Theory and Classroom Management

Nature endows a child with a sensitiveness to order. It is a kind of inner sense that distinguishes the relationships between various objects rather than the objects themselves. It thus makes a whole of an environment in which the several parts are mutually dependent. When a person is oriented in such an environment, he can direct his activity to the attainment of specific goals. Such an environment provides the foundation for an integrated life.

—Maria Montessori

A classroom is a microsociety complete with student citizens, many of whom have competing needs and interests. Consequently, rules, routines, regulations, and procedures—elements of *order*—are a fundamental part of the classroom infrastructure. MI theory, while not providing a classroom management scheme per se, offers beleaguered teachers a new perspective on the many kinds of management strategies that they have used or might use to "keep order" and ensure a smoothly running learning environment.

Gaining Students' Attention

Perhaps the best illustration of MI theory's utility in the area of classroom management can be seen in the ways in which teachers have sought to gain their students' attention at the beginning of a class or a new learning activity. A comedy record some years ago humorously recounted one teacher's attempts to bring her class to order. Against the loud hum of student noise, the teacher loudly said: "Class!" This not working, she upped the voltage somewhat: "Class!!" And once more, even more loudly: "Class!!!" Seeing her ineffectiveness, she finally screamed: "SHUT UP!!!!" And the class became quiet. But then the talking started again, the noise began to grow, and again she started the same sequence: "Class! Class!! Class!!! SHUT UP!!!!" And once again quiet. The teacher repeated this process several times until the ultimate futility of her attempts became painfully (and laughably) obvious.

Teachers can laugh at this situation because many have had the same experience. From a multiple intelligence perspective, however, the use of mere words to quiet a class—a *linguistic* approach—might be seen as the *least* effective way to gain the class's attention. Often, the teacher's linguistic requests or commands (as "figure") dissolve in the students' linguistic utterances (as "ground"). Students do not readily differentiate the teacher's voice from the other voices surrounding them. As a result, they fail to attend to directions. This phenomenon is particularly evident among students who have been labeled as having attention deficit hyperactivity disorder (ADHD), but it exists to a certain extent among most students.

A look at some of the more effective techniques used by teachers to grab attention suggests the need to move to other intelligences. So, for example, the kindergarten teacher's playing a piano chord to ask for silence (musical intelligence), the 4th grade teacher's flicking the lights on and off to call the class to attention (spatial intelligence), and the high school teacher's use of silence as an injunction to self-responsibility (intrapersonal intelligence) all demonstrate an understanding of the need to find a nonlinguistic way of gaining students' attention. Here are several other strategies for getting students' attention in the classroom:

- *Linguistic*—Write the words "Silence, please!" on the blackboard.
- *Musical*—Clap a short rhythmic phrase and have students clap it back.
- *Bodily-kinesthetic*—Put your finger against your lips to suggest silence while holding your other arm up. Have students mirror your gestures.
- *Spatial*—Put a blown-up photo of an attentive classroom on the board (perhaps a photo of the actual students involved).

- *Logical-mathematical*—Use a stopwatch to keep track of the time being wasted and write on the blackboard the number of seconds lost at 30-second intervals.
- *Interpersonal*—Whisper in the ear of a student, "It's time to start—pass it on," and then wait while students pass the message around the room.
- *Intrapersonal*—Start teaching the lesson and allow students to take charge of their own behavior.
- *Naturalist*—Play a recording of a shrill bird whistle, or (even better) bring a live animal into the classroom. Generally speaking, whenever there is an animal visitor in a classroom, that's where the attention will be!

By looking at these "tricks of the trade" in terms of the theory of multiple intelligences, we discover a fundamental methodology that can be used in structuring other types of classroom routines, such as preparing students for transitions, initiating activities, giving instructions, and forming small groups. Essentially, the underlying mechanism of each of these routines involves cueing students in such a way as to link symbols from one or more of the eight intelligences to specific commands and behaviors. In other words, teachers need to discover ways of cueing students not simply through the spoken word but through pictures or graphic symbols (spatial), gestures and physical movements (bodily-kinesthetic), musical phrases (musical), logical patterns (logical-mathematical), social signals (interpersonal), emotions (intrapersonal), and living things (naturalist).

Preparing for Transitions

To help prepare students for transitions, you can teach the class specific cues and provide a different cue for each type of transition. When focusing on musical intelligence, for example, you could explain that you will use different selections of music to cue different transitions:

- *Recess*—Beethoven's Pastoral Symphony (Symphony No. 6)
- *Lunch*—"Food, Glorious Food" from *Oliver!*
- *Dismissal*—"Goin' Home" movement from Dvořák's New World Symphony (Symphony No. 9)

If spatial intelligence is your focus, you might use graphic symbols or pictures to signal that it's time to get ready for an event. You can use photographs or images of the students themselves:

- *Recess*—Picture of kids playing
- *Lunch*—Kids eating in cafeteria
- *Dismissal*—Students getting on the school bus or walking home from school

For bodily-kinesthetic intelligence, you might use specific gestures or body movements to signal the coming event. With this type of strategy, you begin the gesture and students then make the gesture, indicating that they have "received" the message:

- *Recess*—Stretching and yawning (signifying "time for a break")
- *Lunch*—Rubbing stomach and licking lips
- *Dismissal*—Putting hand above eyes and peering outside of the classroom (signifying looking in a homeward direction)

For logical-mathematical intelligence, you could display a large digital "countdown" clock that students can see from anywhere in the classroom, set it for the time left until the transition, and then let students keep track of the time left until the transition occurs. For interpersonal intelligence, you could use a telephone-tree model; simply give the cue to one student, who then tells *two* students, who themselves each tell two students, and so forth, until all students are personally informed.

Communicating Class Rules

You can communicate the school or classroom rules for proper conduct through a multiple intelligence approach. Some possibilities include

- *Linguistic*—Rules are written and posted in the classroom (this is the most conventional approach).
- *Logical-mathematical*—Rules are numbered and later referred to by number (e.g., "You're doing a great job of following rule #4").
- *Spatial*—Next to the written rules are graphic symbols of what to do and what not do to (e.g., "respect for others" might be symbolized by an image of two people holding hands).

- *Bodily-kinesthetic*—Each rule has a specific gesture; students show they know the rules by going through the different gestures (e.g., "respect for others" might be symbolized by hugging oneself).
- *Musical*—The rules are set to a song (either written by students or set to the melody of an existing song), or each rule is associated with a relevant song (e.g., "respect for others" might be connected to Aretha Franklin's song "Respect")
- *Interpersonal*—Each rule is assigned to a small group of students who then have responsibility for knowing its ins and outs, interpreting it, and even enforcing it.
- *Intrapersonal*—Students are responsible for creating the class rules at the beginning of the year and developing their own unique ways of communicating them to others.
- *Naturalist*—An animal is assigned to each of the rules (e.g., "Respectful Rabbit"). Students learn the rules by imitating the movements of the animals.

Asking students to help create classroom rules is a common way of gaining their support of the rules. Similarly, asking students to help develop their own MI strategies or cues for classroom procedures is a useful way to establish effective cues. Students may want to provide their own music, create their own gestures, draw their own graphic symbols, or come up with their own animals to signal the class for different activities, transitions, rules, or procedures.

Forming Groups

Another application of MI theory to classroom management is in the forming of small groups. Although groups are often formed on the basis of arbitrary commands ("you, you, and you are in a group") or intrinsic factors (e.g., interest/ability groups), educators have increasingly seen the value of heterogeneous groups working cooperatively. MI theory provides a wide range of techniques for creating heterogeneous groups based on incidental features related to each intelligence. Some of the following ideas have been adapted from the book *Playfair: Everybody's Guide to Noncompetitive Play* by Joel Goodman and Matt Weinstein (1980):

- *Linguistic*—"Think of a vowel sound in your first name. Now make that vowel sound out loud. Go around the room and find three or four people who are making the same vowel sound."
- *Logical-mathematical*—"When I give the signal, I want you to raise between one and five fingers. Go! Now keep those fingers raised and find three or four people whose raised fingers combined with yours total an odd number."
- *Spatial*—"Find three or four people who are wearing the same color clothes as you are wearing."
- *Bodily-kinesthetic*—"Start hopping on one foot. . . . Now find three or four people who are hopping on the same foot."
- *Musical*—"What are some songs that everybody knows?" The teacher writes on the board four or five of them (e.g., "Row, Row, Row Your Boat," "Happy Birthday to You," etc.). "Okay, I'd like you to file past me while I whisper in your ear one of these songs. Remember which one it is, and when I give the signal, I'd like you to sing your song and find all the others in the class who are singing the same song. . . . Go!"
- *Naturalist*—"Visualize a sheep, a pig, and a cow in a pasture. Suddenly, there is a loud noise and two of them run off. There is only one animal left. Start making the sound of that animal out loud, and then find three or four people who are making the same animal sound!"

You need not address *all* intelligences when developing a classroom management scheme. But by reaching beyond the traditional linguistic approach and using some of the other intelligences (two or three at a minimum), you will be providing students with more opportunities for internalizing classroom routines.

Managing Individual Behaviors

Regardless of how effectively you communicate class rules, routines, and procedures, there will always be students who—because of biological, emotional, or cognitive differences or difficulties—fail to abide by them. These few students may well take up much of your classroom time as you remind them (through several intelligences!) to sit down, stop throwing things, quit hitting, and start behaving. Although MI theory has no magical answer to their problems, it can provide a context for looking at a range of discipline systems that have proved effective with difficult behaviors. Naturally, MI theory suggests that *no one discipline approach is best for all kids*. In fact, the theory suggests that teachers may need to match different discipline approaches to different kinds of learners. What follows is a broad range of discipline methods matched to the eight intelligences:

- *Linguistic*—Talk with the student; provide books for the student that refer to the problem and point to solutions; help the student use "self-talk" strategies for gaining control.
- *Logical-mathematical*—Use Dreikurs's (1993) logical-consequences approach; have the student quantify and chart the occurrence of negative or positive behaviors.
- *Spatial*—Have the student draw or visualize appropriate behaviors; provide the student with a metaphor to use in working with the difficulty (e.g., "If people say bad things to you, see the bad things as arrows that you can dodge"); show the student videos that deal with the issue or that model the appropriate behaviors.
- *Bodily-kinesthetic*—Have the student role-play the inappropriate and appropriate behaviors and discuss the differences; teach the student to use physical cues to deal with stressful situations (e.g., taking a deep breath, tightening and relaxing muscles).
- *Musical*—Find musical selections that deal with the issue the student is facing; provide music that helps create the appropriate behavior (e.g., calming music for tantrums, stimulating music—"Musical Ritalin"—to help children labeled ADHD focus); teach the student to "play" his favorite music in his mind whenever he feels out of control.
- *Interpersonal*—Provide peer group counseling; buddy up the student with a role model; have the student teach or look after a younger child; give the student other social outlets for her energies (e.g., leading a group).
- *Intrapersonal*—Teach the student to voluntarily go to a nonpunitive "time-out" area to gain control (see Nelsen, 1999); provide one-to-one counseling; develop a behavior contract (that the student has input in creating); give the student the opportunity to work on high-interest projects; provide self-esteem activities.

- *Naturalist*—Tell animal stories that teach about improper and proper behavior (e.g., "The Boy Who Cried Wolf" for a persistent fibber); use animal metaphors in working with difficult behavior (e.g., ask an aggressive student what sort of animal he feels like and how he can learn to "tame" it); use "animal-assisted therapy" to help with social, emotional, and cognitive functioning.

Behavioral strategies can be further tailored to the needs of students with specific kinds of difficulties. Figure 8.1 suggests what some of these interventions might look like.

8.1 **MI Strategies for Managing Individual Behaviors**			
Intelligence	**Aggressive Student**	**Withdrawn Student**	**Hyperactive Student**
Linguistic	Bibliotherapy on theme of anger management	Taking up debate, oratory, or storytelling	Books on theme of hyperactivity (e.g., *The Boy Who Burned Too Brightly*)
Logical-Mathematical	Dreikurs's logical-consequences system	Interactive computer network, chess club	Quantification of time on task
Spatial	Visualizing ways of managing conflict	Movies on theme of withdrawn child who meets a friend	Video games that help develop focus and control (neurofeedback)
Bodily-Kinesthetic	Role-play aggressive behavior and try out alternatives	Pairing with trusted person for walks, sports, games	Progressive relaxation, yoga, hands-on learning, strenuous exercise
Musical	Songs promoting social skills	Discography encouraging connection with others	Stimulating music ("Musical Ritalin")
Interpersonal	Taking group class in martial arts	Group counseling	Leadership role in cooperative learning group
Intrapersonal	Time out, contracting	One-to-one counseling/ psychotherapy	Focusing exercises
Naturalist	Identifying with an animal that can then learn how to "tame itself"	Introspective book about nature involving friendship (e.g., *The Secret Garden*)	Time in nature

Taking a Broader Perspective

The above strategies, of course, are no substitute for a comprehensive professional team approach to a student's emotional problems or behavioral difficulties. MI theory is valuable, however, because it provides teachers with the means to sort through a broad range of behavioral strategies and discipline systems and offers guidelines for selecting a limited number of interventions to try out based upon the student's individual differences.

Sometimes the best strategy for a student may be one matched to a poorly developed intelligence. For example, if a student has behavior problems because of an underdeveloped interpersonal intelligence, then he may benefit most from activities that seek to develop his social skills. In other cases, however, the best strategies will be in a student's areas of strength. For example, you probably would not want to assign reading to a student who has problems with both reading and "acting out" his frustrations. This strategy might only aggravate the situation. On the other hand, helping a student *master* a reading problem may be an important ingredient in improving his classroom behavior. For a student who acquires knowledge easily through the printed word, providing behavioral strategies geared to this strength would, generally speaking, be among the most appropriate choices.

Ultimately, MI theory used in conjunction with classroom management goes far beyond the provision of specific behavioral strategies and techniques. MI theory can greatly affect students' behavior in the classroom simply by creating an environment where individual needs are recognized and attended to throughout the school day. Students are less likely to be confused, frustrated, or stressed out in such an environment. As a result, there is likely far less need for behavioral "tricks" or elaborate discipline systems, which often are initiated only when the learning environment has broken down. As Leslie Hart (1981) points out, "Classroom management, discipline, teacher burnout, student 'failures'—these are all problems inherent in the teacher-does-everything approach. Permit and encourage students to use their brains actively to learn, and the results can be astonishing" (p. 40).

For Further Study

1. Select a classroom routine that students are currently having trouble adapting to (e.g., moving from one activity to another, learning class rules) and experiment with different intelligence-specific cues for helping them master it.

2. Try out nonverbal ways of getting students' attention through musical, spatial, bodily-kinesthetic, interpersonal, logical-mathematical, naturalist, or intrapersonal intelligences. Develop alternative cues from those mentioned in this chapter.

3. Choose a student who has been particularly disruptive in class or whose behavior in some other way has proved difficult to handle. Determine his or her most developed intelligences (using identification strategies from Chapter 3). Then select behavioral strategies that match the student's most developed intelligences. Consider also strategies in less developed intelligences that would help develop skills in areas of need. Evaluate the results.

4. Review the behavioral systems currently used in your classroom or school. Identify which specific intelligences are addressed and how they match or do not match the learning strengths of your students.

5. Identify classroom management issues not specifically discussed in this chapter and relate MI theory to them in some tangible way. What are the advantages of using MI theory in handling classroom management problems? What are its limitations?

9

The MI School

The school we envision commits itself to fostering students' deep understanding in several core disciplines. It encourages students' use of that knowledge to solve the problems and complete the tasks that they may confront in the wider community. At the same time, the school seeks to encourage the unique blend of intelligences in each of its students, assessing their development regularly in intelligence-fair ways.

—Howard Gardner

The implications of MI theory extend far beyond classroom instruction. At heart, the theory of multiple intelligences calls for nothing short of a fundamental change in the way schools are structured. It delivers to educators everywhere the strong message that students who show up for school at the beginning of each day have the right to be provided with experiences that activate and develop all of their intelligences. During the typical school day, every student should be exposed to courses, projects, or programs that focus on developing each of their intelligences, not just the standard verbal and logical abilities that for decades have been exalted above every form of human potential.

MI and the Traditional School

In most U.S. schools today, programs that concentrate on the neglected intelligences (musical, spatial, bodily-kinesthetic, naturalist, interpersonal, intrapersonal) tend to be considered "frill" subjects or at least subjects peripheral to the "core" academic courses. When a school district has a budget crisis, fiscal managers usually don't turn first to the reading and math programs for ways to save money. They begin by eliminating the music program, the art program, and the physical education program (see Viadero, 1991). Even when these programs are still operating, they often show the subtle influence of verbal and logical demands. John Goodlad (2004), commenting on observations of schools from his monumental "A Study of Schooling," writes: "I am disappointed with the degree to which arts classes appear to be dominated by the ambience of English, mathematics, and other academic subjects. . . . They did not convey the picture of individual expression and artistic creativity toward which one is led by the rhetoric of forward-looking practice in the field" (pp. 219–220). Goodlad found the physical education classes similarly flawed: "Anything that might be called a program was virtually nonexistent. Physical education appeared to be a teacher-monitored recess . . . " (p. 222).

Administrators and others who help structure programs in schools can use MI theory as a framework for making sure that each student has the opportunity *every day* to experience direct interaction with each of the eight intelligences in the specific domains where they figure most prominently (e.g., art, music, physical education). Figure 9.1 suggests some of the programmatic features that span the eight intelligences in school, including traditional courses, supplementary programs, and extracurricular offerings.

The Components of an MI School

Simply providing students with access to a diverse range of school subjects, however, does not necessarily constitute a multiple intelligence school. In his book *Multiple Intelligences: New Horizons in Theory and Practice*, Gardner (2006a) sets up one vision of the ideal multiple intelligence school. In particular, Gardner draws upon two nonschool models in suggesting how MI

9.1

MI in Traditional School Programs

Intelligence	Subjects	Supplementary Program	Extracurricular Activities
Linguistic	Reading Language arts Literature English History Most foreign languages Speech	Creative writing lab Communication skills	Debate School newspaper Yearbook Language clubs Honor society
Logical-Mathematical	Sciences Mathematics Economics	Thinking skills Computer programming	Science clubs Honor society
Spatial	Shop Drafting Art	Visual-thinking lab Architecture club Animation Computer-assisted design	Photography club Audiovisual staff Chess club
Bodily-Kinesthetic	Physical education	Theater games Martial arts Walking program	Sports teams Drama Cheerleading
Musical	Music	Orff Schulwerk programs Kodaly method Suzuki training	Band Orchestra Chorus
Interpersonal	Social Sciences	Social skills training Prevention programs (e.g., drugs) Diversity training Counseling	Glee club Student government
Intrapersonal	Psychology	Self-esteem development programs Counseling	Special-interest clubs
Naturalist	Biology Zoology Botany Ecology	Ecological awareness in other school subjects Gardening program Camping trips	Future Farmers of America Future Homemakers of America Naturalist clubs (e.g., gardening, bird watching)

schools might be structured. First, he sees MI schools as based in part on the example of contemporary children's museums. According to Gardner, these environments provide a setting for learning that is hands-on, interdisciplinary, based on real-life contexts, and set in an informal atmosphere that promotes free inquiry into novel materials and situations. Second, he looks to the age-old model of apprenticeships, whereby masters of a trade oversee ongoing projects undertaken by their youthful protégés.

Gardner suggests that in an MI school, students might spend their mornings working on traditional subjects in nontraditional ways. In particular, Gardner recommends the use of project-centered instruction. Students look in depth at a particular area of inquiry (a historical conflict, a scientific principle, a literary genre) and develop a project (photo essay, experiment, journal) that reflects an ongoing process of coming to grips with the many dimensions of the topic. Students then go into the community during the second part of the day and further extend their understanding of the topics they are studying in school. Younger students, according to Gardner, might regularly go to children's museums, art or science museums, or other places where hands-on exploratory learning and play are encouraged and where interaction with docents and other expert guides takes place. Older students (past 3rd grade) could choose apprenticeships based upon an assessment of their intellectual proclivities, interests, and available resources. They could then spend their afternoons studying with experts in the community in specific arts, skills, crafts, physical activities, or other real-life endeavors.

Fundamental to Gardner's vision of an MI school are the activities of three key members of the school staff, representing functions that are currently absent from most schools. In Gardner's model, every MI school would have staff in the following roles:

Assessment specialist: This staff member is responsible for developing an ongoing "picture" or record of each child's strengths, limitations, and interests in all eight intelligences. Using intelligence-fair assessments, the assessment specialist documents each child's school experience in many ways (through observation, informal assessments, and multimedia documentation) and provides parents, teachers, administrators, and students themselves with an overview of their proclivities in each of the eight intelligences. (See Chapter 10 for an MI perspective on testing and assessment.)

Student–curriculum broker: This person serves as a bridge between the student's gifts and abilities in the eight intelligences and the available resources in the school. The student–curriculum broker matches students to specific courses and electives and provides teachers with information about how particular subjects might best be presented to a student (e.g., through video, hands-on experiences, books, music). This staff member is responsible for maximizing the student's learning potentials, given the particular kinds of materials, methods, and human resources available in the school.

School–community broker: This staff person is the link between the student's intellectual proclivities and the resources available in the wider community. A school–community broker should possess a wealth of information about the kinds of apprenticeships, organizations, mentorships, tutorials, community courses, and other learning experiences available in the surrounding geographic area. This person then attempts to match a student's interests, skills, and abilities to appropriate experiences beyond the school walls (e.g., finding an expert cellist to guide a student's burgeoning interest in playing the cello).

Gardner suggests that the creation of such an MI school is far from utopian. Instead, it depends upon the confluence of several factors, including assessment practices that engage students in the actual materials and symbols of each intelligence, curriculum development that reflects real-life skills and experiences, teacher training programs that reflect sound educational principles and that have master teachers working with students committed to the field, and finally, a high level of community involvement from parents, business leaders, museums, and other learning institutions.

A Model MI School: The Key Learning Community

Efforts toward building an MI school have already been under way for several years. One school in particular has been singled out by the media and other educators for recognition: the Key Learning Community in Indianapolis, Indiana. In 1984, a group of eight Indianapolis public school teachers contacted Howard Gardner for assistance in helping start a new school in the district. Out of their collaboration (as well as the infusion of new educational ideas from the likes of Mihaly Csikszentmihalyi, Elliot Eisner, Ernest Boyer, James MacDonald, and John Goodlad), the Key School was officially born in September 1987 (Fiske, 1988; Olson, 1988). Over the past 20 years, the school has expanded from an elementary school to a K–12 institution.

The Key Learning Community combines several different features of multiple intelligence education to create a total learning experience, including the following:

Regular instruction in all eight intelligences: Students at the Key Learning Community middle school take classes in traditional subjects (e.g., math, science, language arts, history, geography, German) but also receive an equal amount of instruction in physical education, art, and music. Compared with schools nationally, students at Key receive double the exposure to art, music, and physical education than does the average student in the United States. Each child learns to play a musical instrument, starting with the violin in kindergarten.

Schoolwide themes: Each year, the school staff selects two themes, one each semester, to help focus curricular activity. Themes used in past years include Connections, Animal Patterns, Changes in Time and Space, Let's Make a Difference—Environmental Focus, Heritage, and Renaissance—Then and Now. During the development of a theme, whole areas of the school may reflect the learning that is going on. For example, during the environmental theme, part of the school was turned into a simulated tropical rain forest. Students select and develop projects for each theme, which they then present to their teachers and peers during special sessions that are videotaped.

"Pods": These are special learning groups that students individually select based upon their interests. Pods are formed around specific disciplines (e.g., gardening, architecture, acting) or cognitive pursuits (e.g., mathematical thinking, problem solving, "the mind and movement"). Students work with a teacher possessing special competence in the selected area in an apprenticeship-like context that emphasizes mastering real-world skills and knowledge. In the architecture pod, for example, students "adopted" nine houses in the surrounding area and studied the designs of the houses through walking tours and other activities.

The "flow room": Students visit the flow room in the school several times each week to engage in activities designed to activate their intelligences in open-ended and playful ways (Cohen, 1991). Named after Mihaly Csikszentmihalyi's (1990) concept of "flow" (referring to a positive state of intense absorption in an activity), the "flow room" is stocked with scores of board games, puzzles, computer software programs, and other learning materials. Students can choose to participate in any activity available in the room (either alone or with others). A teacher helps facilitate their experience and also observes how individual students interact with the materials (each of which is keyed to a specific intelligence; for instance, the game Othello is linked to spatial intelligence, whereas Twister is seen primarily as a bodily-kinesthetic activity).

Heterogeneous mixed-aged grouping: Students who attend the Key Learning Community are chosen randomly by a lottery system. Although some students had previously been labeled "learning disabled" and "gifted" and placed in special education programs, no such programs are currently in place at the Key Learning Community. Students in any one class have a wide range of ability levels, a factor that is seen to enrich the program through diversity. (See Chapter 11 for a discussion of MI theory and special education.)

Although the Key Learning Community is only one of a number of schoolwide and districtwide efforts to implement the theory of multiple intelligences, it clearly provides evidence that systemwide restructuring based on MI theory can become reality—and that successful restructuring can be a grassroots effort. The Key Learning Community was not mandated at an administrative level; it is a product of the energy and commitment of eight public school teachers who had a dream about what education could be for their students.

MI Schools of the Future

The Key Learning Community experience should by no means be taken as the only way, or even the preferred way, to develop a multiple intelligence school (for another example, see Hoerr, 2000). There may be as many possible types of MI schools as there are groups of educators, parents, administrators, and community leaders committed to putting MI principles into action. Regardless of how they are structured, MI schools of the future will undoubtedly continue expanding the possibilities for unleashing children's potentials in all intelligences. Perhaps MI schools of the future will look less like schools and more like the real world, with traditional school buildings serving as temporary conduits through which students move on their way to meaningful experiences in the community. Possibly, programs will arise that specialize in the development of one or more of the intelligences—although we must be quick to guard against a "brave new world" of multiple intelligences that could seek to identify individual students' strongest intelligences early in life so as to exploit them and channel them prematurely into a small niche that would serve a narrowly segmented society.

Ultimately, what will enrich the development of MI theory is its implementation in interdisciplinary ways that reflect the ever-changing demands of an increasingly complex society. As society changes—and perhaps as we discover new intelligences to help us cope with these changes—MI schools of the future may reflect features that are right now beyond our wildest dreams.

For Further Study

1. Evaluate your school in terms of multiple intelligence theory. During the course of a school day, does each student have the opportunity to develop each of the eight intelligences for its own sake? Specify programs, courses, activities, and experiences that develop the intelligences. How could the school's programs be modified to better incorporate the broad spectrum of intelligences?

2. Assuming you had an unlimited amount of money and resources available to you, develop your version of the "ideal" MI school. What will the physical plant look like? Draw a floor plan of the school to illustrate. What kinds of courses will be offered? What will the function of teachers be? What kinds of experiences will students have? Develop a scenario of a typical student going through a typical day at such a school.

3. Contact schools that are now using multiple intelligence theory as an overall framework or philosophy and compare and contrast their different ways of applying the model (use an online search engine and put in the search terms "schools" and "multiple intelligences"). Which aspects of each program are applicable to your own school or classroom? Which components are not?

4. Discuss some of the problems that schools might have in implementing MI theory as part of a broader reform movement. How can MI theory best fit into a school's restructuring process? What elements can be included in staff development to improve the chances for this model's success?

10

MI Theory and Assessment

I believe that we should get away altogether from tests and correlations among tests, and look instead at more naturalistic sources of information about how peoples around the world develop skills important to their way of life.

—Howard Gardner

The kinds of changes in instructional practice described in the previous nine chapters require an equivalent adjustment in the manner of assessment used to evaluate learning progress. It would certainly be the height of hypocrisy to ask students to participate in a wide range of multispectrum experiences in all eight intelligences and then require them to show what they've learned through standardized tests that focus narrowly on linguistic or logical-mathematical intelligences. Educators would clearly be sending a double message to students and to the wider community: "Learning in eight ways is fun, but when it comes to our bottom line—evaluating students' learning progress—we've got to get serious again and test the way we've always tested." Thus, MI theory proposes a fundamental restructuring of the way in which educators assess their students' learning progress. It suggests a system that relies far less on formal standardized or norm-referenced tests and much more on authentic measures that are criterion-referenced, benchmarked, or *ipsative* (i.e., that compare a student to his or her own past performances).

The multiple intelligence philosophy of assessment is closely in line with the perspective of a growing number of leading educators who have argued that authentic measures of assessment probe students' understanding of material far more thoroughly than multiple-choice or fill-in-the-blank tests (see Gardner 1993b, 2006a; Herman, Aschbacher, & Winters, 1992; Popham, 2008; and Wolf, LeMahieu, & Eresh, 1992). In particular, authentic measures allow students to show what they've learned *in context*—in other words, in a setting that closely matches the environment in which they would be expected to show that learning in real life. Standardized measures, on the other hand, almost always assess students in artificial settings far removed from the real world. Figure 10.1 lists a number of other ways in which authentic measures prove superior to standardized testing in promoting educational quality.

Varieties of Assessment Experience

Authentic assessment covers a wide range of instruments, measures, and methods. The most important prerequisite to authentic assessment is *observation*. Howard Gardner (1993a, 1993b, 2006a) has pointed out that we can best assess students' multiple intelligences by observing students manipulating the symbol systems of each intelligence. For instance, you might notice how students play a logical board game, how they interact with a machine, how they dance, or how they cope with a dispute in a cooperative learning group. Observing students solving problems or fashioning products in real-life contexts provides the best picture of student competencies in the range of subjects taught in school.

The next most important component in implementing authentic assessment is the documentation of student products and problem-solving processes. You can document student performance in a variety of ways, including the following:

Anecdotal records: Keep a journal with a section for each child, and record important academic and nonacademic accomplishments, interactions

---

10.1

Standardized Testing Versus Authentic Assessment

Standardized Testing
- Reduces children's rich and complex lives to a collection of scores, percentiles, or grades
- Creates stresses that negatively affect a child's performance
- Creates a mythical standard or norm that requires that a certain percentage of children fail
- Pressures teachers to narrow their curriculum to only what is tested on an exam
- Emphasizes one-shot exams that assess knowledge residing in a single mind at a single moment in time
- Tends to place the focus of interpretation on errors, mistakes, low scores, and other things that children *can't* do
- Focuses too much importance on single sets of data (i.e., test scores) in making educational decisions
- Treats all students in a uniform way
- Discriminates against some students because of cultural background and learning style
- Judges the child without providing suggestions for improvement
- Regards testing and instruction as separate activities

Authentic Assessment
- Gives the teacher a "felt sense" of the child's unique experience as a learner
- Provides interesting, active, lively, and exciting experiences
- Establishes an environment where every child has the opportunity to succeed
- Allows teachers to develop meaningful curricula and assess within the context of that program
- Assesses on an *ongoing* basis in a way that provides a more accurate picture of a student's achievement
- Puts the emphasis on a student's *strengths;* tells what they *can* do and what they're *trying* to do
- Provides *multiple* sources of evaluation that give a more accurate view of a student's progress
- Treats each student as a unique human being
- Provides a *culture-fair* assessment of a student's performance; gives everyone an equal chance to succeed
- Provides information that is *useful* to the learning process
- Regards assessment and teaching as two sides of the same coin

---

with peers and learning materials, and other relevant information about each child.

Work samples: Have a file for each child that contains samples of the student's work in language arts, math, art, or other areas for which you are responsible. The samples can be photocopies if the child wishes to keep the original.

Audio files: Record reading samples (have the student read into a recorder and also tell back the story at the end) and a student's jokes, stories, riddles, memories, opinions, and other samples of oral language; also use audio files to document a child's musical ability (singing, rapping, or playing an instrument).

Video: Use video to record a child's abilities in areas that are hard to document in any other way (e.g., acting out a role in a school play, catching a pass in a football game, demonstrating how she fixed a machine, introducing an ecology project) and to record students presenting projects they've completed.

Photography: Have a digital camera on hand to snap pictures of things kids have made that might not be preserved (e.g., three-dimensional constructions, inventions, science and art projects).

Student journals: Students can keep an ongoing journal of their experiences in school, including writing entries, diagrams, doodles, and drawings.

Student-kept charts: Students can keep their own records of academic progress on charts and graphs (e.g., number of books read, progress toward an educational objective).

Sociograms: Keep a visual record of student interactions in class, using symbols to indicate affiliations, negative interactions, and neutral contacts between class members.

Informal assessments: Create nonstandardized tests to elicit information about a child's ability in a specific area. Focus on building a qualitative picture of the student's understanding of the material rather than devising a method to expose the student's ignorance in a subject.

Informal use of standardized tests: Give standardized tests to individual students, but don't follow the strict administration guidelines. Relax time limits, read instructions to the student, ask the student to clarify responses, and provide opportunities to demonstrate answers in pictures, three-dimensional constructions, music, or other ways. Find out what the student really knows; probe errors to find out how the student is thinking. Use the test as a stimulus to engage the student in a dialogue about the material.

Student interviews: Periodically meet with students to discuss their school progress, their broader interests and goals, and other relevant issues. Keep a record of each meeting in a student's file.

Criterion-referenced assessments: Use measures that evaluate students not on the basis of a norm but with respect to a given set of skills—that is, use assessments that tell in concrete terms what the student can and cannot do (e.g., add two-digit numbers with regrouping, write a three-page story on a subject that interests the student).

Checklists: Develop an informal criterion-referenced assessment system by simply keeping a checklist of important skills or content areas used in your classroom and then checking off competencies when students have achieved them (as well as indicating progress toward each goal).

Classroom maps: Draw up a classroom map (a bird's-eye view of the classroom with all desks, tables, and activity areas indicated) and make copies of it. Each day indicate patterns of movement, activity, and interaction in different parts of the room, writing on the map the names of the students involved.

Calendar records: Have students keep records of their activities during the day by recording them on a monthly calendar. You can collect the calendars at the end of every month.

MI Assessment Projects

Several assessment projects have been initiated nationwide that are congruent with the fundamental philosophy of MI theory, many of them under the direction of Howard Gardner and his colleagues at Harvard University's Project Zero. These include projects at the preschool, elementary, middle school, and high school levels (see Gardner 1993b, 2006a).

Project Spectrum: This was a preschool program piloted at the Eliot Pearson Children's School at Tufts University in Medford, Massachusetts. The program used several assessment instruments that are themselves rich and engaging activities forming an integral part of the Spectrum curriculum. They included creative movement experiences (bodily-kinesthetic/musical); a dinosaur board game involving rolling dice, counting moves, and calculating strategies (logical-mathematical); and a storyboard activity that required students to create a miniature three-dimensional world and then tell a story about it (spatial/linguistic). The program also made use of art portfolios and teachers' observations of children engaged in activities in the different centers (e.g., the storytelling area, the building center, the naturalist's corner). In addition to looking for "proclivities" in the eight intelligences, teachers assessed each student's characteristic "working styles," looking, for example, at whether students were confident or tentative, playful or serious, or reflective or impulsive in their way of approaching different learning settings. (For more information, see Gardner, Feldman, & Krechevsky, 1998a, 1998b, 1998c).

Key Learning Community: This is a K–12 program that is part of the Indianapolis Public Schools in Indiana. In this program, educators use video extensively in their assessment of learning progress. Students are video-taped at two points during the year as they are presenting their learning projects. These video portfolios accompany a student through the grades, providing valuable assessment information to parents, teachers, administrators, and the students themselves. (See Chapter 9 for more information on the Key Learning Community.)

Practical Intelligence for School Units: This program was a middle school infusion curriculum that sought to help students develop metacognitive skills and understandings in school-related activities; units included "Choosing a Project," "Finding the Right Mathematical Tools," "Note Taking," and "Why Go to School." Students were evaluated on these units through contextually rich performance-based assessments. For the unit called "Choosing a Project," the assessment tasks included critiquing three proposal plans and providing suggestions for improving the least promising one. For the unit called "Mathematical Tools," the assessment tasks included solving a problem with limited resources and generating other options for developing solutions (see Williams et al., 1996).

Arts PROPEL: This was a five-year high school arts project piloted in the Pittsburgh Public Schools in Pennsylvania. The focus was on two elements: (1) *domain projects,* which were a series of exercises, activities, and productions in the visual arts, music, and creative writing designed to develop student sensitivity to compositional features; and (2) *processfolios,* which were ongoing collections of students' artistic productions, such as drawings, paintings, musical compositions, and creative writing, from initial idea through rough drafts to final product. Evaluation procedures included self-assessments (requiring student reflection) and teacher assessments that probed students' technical and imaginative skills and their ability to benefit from self-reflection and critique from others (see Scripp, 1990).

Assessment in Eight Ways

MI theory provides its greatest contribution to assessment in suggesting multiple ways to evaluate students. The biggest shortcoming of standardized tests is that they require students to show in a narrowly defined way what they've learned during the year. Standardized tests usually demand that students be seated at a desk, that they complete the test within a specific amount of time, and that they speak to no one during the test. The tests themselves usually contain largely linguistic questions or test items that students must answer by filling in bubbles on computer-coded forms. MI theory, however, supports the belief that students should be able to show competence in a specific skill, subject, content area, or domain in any one of a variety of ways. And just as the theory of multiple intelligences suggests that any instructional objective can be taught in at least eight different ways, so too does it imply that any subject can be *assessed* in at least eight different ways.

If, for example, the objective is for students to demonstrate an understanding of the character of Huck Finn in the Mark Twain novel *Huckleberry Finn*, a standardized test might require students to complete the following task on a testing form:

Choose the word that best describes Huck Finn in the novel:

a.) Sensitive
b.) Jealous
c.) Erudite
d.) Fidgety

Such an item demands that students know the meanings of each of the four words and that every student's interpretation of Huck Finn coincides with that of the test maker. For instance, although "fidgety" might be the answer the testers are looking for, "sensitive" might actually be closer to the truth, because it touches on Huck's openness to a wide range of social issues. But a standardized test provides no opportunity to explore or discuss this interpretation. Students who are not particularly word-sensitive may know a great deal about Huck Finn, yet not be able to show their knowledge on this test item.

On the other hand, MI theory suggests a variety of ways in which students could demonstrate their understanding:

- *Linguistic*—"Describe Huck Finn in your own words, either orally or in an open-ended written format."
- *Logical-mathematical*—"If Huck Finn were a scientific principle, law, or theorem, which one would he be?"

- *Spatial*—"Draw a quick sketch showing something that you think Huck Finn would enjoy doing that's not indicated in the novel."
- *Bodily-kinesthetic*—"Pantomime how you think Huck Finn would act in a classroom."
- *Musical*—"If Huck Finn were a musical phrase, what would he sound like or what song would he be?"
- *Interpersonal*—"Who does Huck Finn remind you of in your own life (friends, family, other students, TV characters)?"
- *Intrapersonal*—"Describe in a few words your personal feelings toward Huck Finn."
- *Naturalist*—"If Huck Finn were an animal, which one would he be?"

By linking Huck Finn to pictures, physical actions, musical phrases, scientific formulas, social connections, personal feelings, or animals, students have more opportunities to use their multiple intelligences to help articulate their understanding. Implied here is the fundamental notion that many students who have mastered the material taught in school may not have the means to show what they've learned if the only setting available for demonstrating competency is a narrowly focused linguistic testing arena. Figure 10.2 shows other examples of how students can show competence in specific academic subjects.

Using the "eight ways" context described above, students might be assessed in any number of ways, including

- Through exposure to all eight performance tasks in an attempt to discover the area(s) in which they were most successful.
- By being assigned a performance task based upon the teacher's understanding of their most developed intelligence.
- By choosing the manner in which they'd like to be assessed themselves. Figure 10.3 contains a sample form that suggests how students might "contract" to be assessed in a specific subject area.

Assessment in Context

MI theory expands the assessment arena considerably to include a wide range of possible contexts within which a student can express competence in a specific area. It suggests that both the manner of presentation and the

10.2

Examples of the Eight Ways Students Can Show Their Knowledge About Specific Topics

Intelligence	Factors Associated with the South Losing the Civil War	Development of a Character in a Novel	Principles of Molecular Bonding
Linguistic	Give an oral or written report	Do oral interpretation from the novel with commentary	Explain concept verbally or in writing
Logical-Mathematical	Present statistics on dead, wounded, supplies	Present sequential cause-effect chart of character's development	Write down chemical formulas and show how derived
Spatial	Draw maps of important battles	Develop flow chart or series of sketches showing rise/fall of character	Draw diagrams that show different bonding patterns
Bodily-Kinesthetic	Create 3-D maps of important battles and act them out with miniature soldiers	Pantomime the role from beginning of novel to end, showing changes	Build several molecular structures with multicolored pop-beads
Musical	Assemble Civil War songs that point to causal factors	Present development of character as a musical score	Orchestrate a dance showing different bonding patterns (see below)
Interpersonal	Design class simulation of important battles	Discuss underlying motives and moods relating to development	Demonstrate molecular bonding using classmates as atoms
Intrapersonal	Develop one's own unique way of demonstrating competency	Relate character's development to one's own life history	Create scrapbook demonstrating competency
Naturalist	Examine how the geographical features of North and South contributed to result	Compare development of character to the evolution of a species or the history of an ecosystem	Use animal analogies to explain dynamics of bonding (e.g., animals that attract and don't attract, symbiotic relationships in nature)

10.3
"Celebration of Learning" Student Sign-Up Sheet

To show that I know _____, I would like to:

- Write a report
- Do a photo essay
- Compile a scrapbook
- Build a model
- Put on a live demonstration
- Create a group project
- Do a statistical chart
- Develop an interactive computer presentation
- Keep a journal
- Record interviews
- Design a mural
- Create a discography
- Give a talk
- Develop a simulation
- Create a series of sketches/diagrams
- Set up an experiment
- Engage in a debate or discussion
- Do a mind-map
- Produce a videotape segment
- Create an ecology project
- Develop a musical
- Create a rap or song
- Teach the topic to someone else
- Choreograph a dance
- Other:

Brief description of what I intend to do:

_____   _____
Signature of Student   Date

_____   _____
Signature of Teacher   Date

method of response will be important in determining a student's competence. If a student learns primarily through pictures, yet is exposed only to the printed word when learning new material, then she will probably not be able to show mastery of the subject. Similarly, if a student is physically oriented (bodily-kinesthetic), yet has to demonstrate mastery through a paper-and-pencil test, then he probably will not be able to express what he knows. Figure 10.4 indicates some of the many combinations possible between method of presentation and method of response in structuring assessment contexts.

Typical testing settings for students in U.S. schools take in only one of the 64 contexts shown in Figure 10.4 (the one in the upper left corner: "Read a book, *then write a response*"). Yet even the contexts listed in Figure 10.4 are but a fraction of the potential settings that could be structured for assessment purposes. For example, "Listen to a talking book" could be substituted for "Read a book," and "Tell a story" might replace "Write a response" to structure several other assessment contexts. There are also many opportunities for variety even within each of the combinations shown in Figure 10.4. For example, the experience of a student who chooses to "go on a field trip, *then build a model*" will vary depending on *where* the field trip is taken, *what* kind of mediating experiences are provided during the trip, and *how* the model-building activity is structured. These factors would themselves give rise to a multiplicity of contexts, some of which might be favorable to a student's demonstration of competency (e.g., a field trip to a place the student is interested in or has had prior experience with) and others that might be unfavorable (e.g., the use of modeling materials the student didn't like or had no familiarity with or their use in a setting with peers he didn't get along with).

Of course, you do not need to develop 64 different assessment contexts for everything you need to evaluate. Figure 10.4 suggests, however, the need to provide students with assessment experiences that include access to a variety of methods of presentation (inputs) and means of expression (outputs). The kinds of assessment experiences that MI theory proposes—particularly those that are project-based and thematically oriented—offer students frequent opportunities to be exposed to several of these contexts at one time (as the Project Zero programs described earlier illustrate). For example, if students are developing a video to show their understanding

10.4

64 MI Assessment Contexts

Activity/ Assessment	Linguistic Activity	Logical-Mathematical Activity	Spatial Activity	Musical Activity	Bodily-Kinesthetic Activity	Interpersonal Activity	Intrapersonal Activity	Naturalist Activity
Linguistic Assessment	Read a book, *then write a response.*	Examine a statistical chart, *then write a response.*	Watch a movie, *then write a response.*	Listen to a piece of music, *then write a response.*	Go on a field trip, *then write a response.*	Play a cooperative game, *then write a response.*	Think about a personal experience, *then write a response.*	Observe nature, *then write a response.*
Logical-Mathematical Assessment	Read a book, *then develop a hypothesis.*	Examine a statistical chart, *then develop a hypothesis.*	Watch a movie, *then develop a hypothesis.*	Listen to a piece of music, *then develop a hypothesis.*	Go on a field trip, *then develop a hypothesis.*	Play a cooperative game, *then develop a hypothesis.*	Think about a personal experience, *then develop a hypothesis.*	Observe nature, *then develop a hypothesis.*
Spatial Assessment	Read a book, *then draw a picture.*	Examine a statistical chart, *then draw a picture.*	Watch a movie, *then draw a picture.*	Listen to a piece of music, *then draw a picture.*	Go on a field trip, *then draw a picture.*	Play a cooperative game, *then draw a picture.*	Think about a personal experience, *then draw a picture.*	Observe nature, *then draw a picture.*
Bodily-Kinesthetic Assessment	Read a book, *then build a model.*	Examine a statistical chart, *then build a model.*	Watch a movie, *then build a model.*	Listen to a piece of music, *then build a model.*	Go on a field trip, *then build a model.*	Play a cooperative game, *then build a model.*	Think about a personal experience, *then build a model.*	Observe nature, *then build a model.*
Musical Assessment	Read a book, *then create a song.*	Examine a statistical chart, *then create a song.*	Watch a movie, *then create a song.*	Listen to a piece of music, *then create a song.*	Go on a field trip, *then create a song.*	Play a cooperative game, *then create a song.*	Think about a personal experience, *then create a song.*	Observe nature, *then create a song.*

(continued)

10.4
64 MI Assessment Contexts (continued)

Activity/ Assessment	Linguistic Activity	Logical-Mathematical Activity	Spatial Activity	Musical Activity	Bodily-Kinesthetic Activity	Interpersonal Activity	Intrapersonal Activity	Naturalist Activity
Interpersonal Assessment	Read a book, *then share with a friend.*	Examine a statistical chart, *then share with a friend.*	Watch a movie, *then share with a friend.*	Listen to a piece of music, *then share with a friend.*	Go on a field trip, *then share with a friend.*	Play a cooperative game, *then share with a friend.*	Think about a personal experience, *then share with a friend.*	Observe nature, *then share with a friend.*
Intrapersonal Assessment	Read a book, *then design your own response.*	Examine a statistical chart, *then design your own response.*	Watch a movie, *then design your own response.*	Listen to a piece of music, *then design your own response.*	Go on a field trip, *then design your own response.*	Play a cooperative game, *then design your own response.*	Think about a personal experience, *then design your own response.*	Observe nature, *then design your own response.*
Naturalist Assessment	Read a book, *then do an ecology project.*	Examine a statistical chart, *then do an ecology project.*	Watch a movie, *then do an ecology project.*	Listen to a piece of music, *then do an ecology project.*	Go on a field trip, *then do an ecology project.*	Play a cooperative game, *then do an ecology project.*	Think about a personal experience, *then do an ecology project.*	Observe nature, *then do an ecology project.*

of the effects of pollution on their local community, they may have to read books, do fieldwork, listen to environmental songs, and engage in cooperative activities (inputs) in order to create a video that includes a montage of pictures, music, dialogue, and words (outputs). This complex project provides the teacher with a context-rich document (the video) within which to assess a student's ecological competencies through a variety of intelligences.

MI Portfolios

As students increasingly engage in multiple intelligence projects and activities, the opportunities for documenting their learning process in MI portfolios expands considerably. In the past two decades, portfolio development among reform-minded educators has often been limited to work requiring the linguistic and logical-mathematical intelligences (writing portfolios and math portfolios). MI theory suggests, however, that portfolios ought to be expanded to include, when appropriate, materials from all eight intelligences. Figure 10.5 lists some of the kinds of documents that might be included in an MI portfolio.

Naturally, the kinds of materials placed in an MI portfolio will depend upon the educational purposes and goals of each portfolio. There are at least five basic uses for portfolios. I call them "The Five C's of Portfolio Development":

1. *Celebration*—To acknowledge and validate students' products and accomplishments during the year
2. *Cognition*—To help students reflect upon their own work
3. *Communication*—To let parents, administrators, and other teachers know about students' learning progress
4. *Cooperation*—To provide a means for groups of students to collectively produce and evaluate their own work
5. *Competency*—To establish criteria by which a student's work can be compared to that of other students or to a standard or benchmark

The checklist in Figure 10.6 can help you clarify some of the uses to which portfolios might be put in the classroom.

The process of evaluating MI portfolios and other MI performances presents the most challenging aspect of their development. Reforms in assessment have emphasized the development of benchmarks, rubrics, or

10.5
What to Put in an MI Portfolio

To document linguistic intelligence:
- Prewriting notes
- Preliminary drafts of writing projects
- Best samples of writing
- Written descriptions of investigations
- Audio recording of debates, discussions, problem-solving processes
- Final reports
- Dramatic interpretations
- Reading skills checklists
- Audio recording of reading or storytelling
- Samples of word puzzles solved

To document logical-mathematical intelligence:
- Math skills checklists
- Best samples of math papers
- Rough notes from computations/problem-solving processes
- Final write-ups of science lab experiments
- Documentation of science fair projects (awards, photos)
- Piagetian assessment materials
- Samples of logic puzzles or brainteasers solved
- Samples of computer programs created or learned

To document spatial intelligence:
- Photos of projects
- Three-dimensional mockups
- Diagrams, flow charts, sketches, or mind-maps of thinking
- Samples or photos of collages, drawings, paintings
- Video recordings of projects
- Samples of visual-spatial puzzles solved

To document bodily-kinesthetic intelligence:
- Video recordings of projects and demonstrations
- Samples of projects actually made
- Videos or other records of the "acting out" of thinking processes
- Photos of hands-on projects

To document musical intelligence:
- Audio recordings of musical performances, compositions, collages
- Samples of written scores (performed or composed)
- Lyrics of raps, songs, or rhymes written by student
- Discographies compiled by student

10.5
What to Put in an MI Portfolio (continued)

To document interpersonal intelligence:
- Letters to and from others (e.g., writing to obtain information from someone)
- Group reports
- Written feedback from peers, teachers, and experts
- Teacher–student conference reports (summarized/transcribed)
- Parent–teacher–student conference reports
- Peer-group reports
- Photos, videos, or write-ups of cooperative learning projects
- Documentation of community service projects (certificates, photos)

To document intrapersonal intelligence:
- Journal entries
- Self-assessment essays, checklists, drawings, activities
- Samples of other self-reflection exercises
- Questionnaires
- Transcribed interviews on goals and plans
- Interest inventories
- Samples of outside hobbies or activities
- Student-kept progress charts
- Notes of self-reflection on own work

To document naturalist intelligence:
- Field notes from nature studies
- Records of 4H or similar club participation
- Photos of caring for animals or plants
- Video recordings of demonstration of naturalist project
- Record of volunteer efforts in ecological activities
- Writings about love of nature or pets
- Photos of nature collections (e.g., leaves, insects)

---

other methods by which complex performances and works can be evaluated (see Herman, Aschbacher, & Winters, 1992). In my estimation, these devices are best suited only for the *competency* dimension of portfolio development. For the other four components, emphasis should be placed less on comparison and more on student self-evaluation and on *ipsative* measures (assessment that compares a student to his or her own past performances). Unfortunately, some teachers are using alternative assessment techniques to reduce students' rich and complex works to holistic scores

10.6
MI Portfolio Checklist

How will you use the portfolio?
- For student self-reflection (Cognition)
- As part of regular school evaluation/report card (Competency)
- At parent conferences (Communication, Competency)
- In IEP/SST meetings (Communication, Competency)
- In communicating to next year's teacher(s) (Communication, Competency)
- In curricular planning (Competency)
- In acknowledging students' accomplishments (Celebration)
- In creating cooperative learning activities (Cooperation)
- Other:

How will it be organized?
- Only finished pieces from a variety of subjects
- Different expressions of a specific objective
- Charting of progress from first idea to final realization
- Representative samples of a week's/month's/year's work
- Only "best" work
- Include "group" work
- Other:

What procedures will you use in placing items in the portfolio?
- Select regular times for pulling student work
- Train students to select (e.g., flagging with stickers)
- Pull items that meet preset criteria
- Random approach
- Other:

What will the portfolio look like?
- Two pieces of posterboard stapled or taped together
- Box or other container
- Scrapbook
- Diary or journal
- Manila folder
- Bound volume
- CD or DVD
- Web site or blog
- Other:

Who will evaluate the portfolio?
- Teacher alone
- Teacher working in collaboration with other teachers
- Student self-evaluation

10.6
MI Portfolio Checklist (continued)

- Peer evaluation
- Other:

How will the works in the portfolio be arranged?
- Chronologically
- By student: from "crummy" to "great" (with reasons given)
- By teacher: from poor to superior (with reasons given)
- From birth of an idea to its fruition
- By subject area
- Other:

What factors will go into evaluating the portfolio?
- Number of entries
- Range of entries
- Degree of self-reflection demonstrated
- Improvement from past performances
- Achievement of preset goals (student's, teacher's, school's)
- Interplay of production, perception, and reflection
- Responsiveness to feedback/mediation
- Depth of revision
- Group consensus (among teachers)
- Willingness to take a risk
- Development of themes
- Use of benchmarks or rubrics for comparison
- Other:

---

or rankings like these: Portfolio A is a 1, Portfolio B is a 3; Child C's art project is at a "novice" level, while Child D's project is at a "mastery" level. This reductionism ends up looking very much like standardized testing in some of its worst moments. I suggest that we instead initially focus our attention in MI assessment on looking at individual students' work *in depth* in terms of the unfolding of each student's uniqueness (for appropriate assessment models of this kind, see Armstrong, 1980; Carini, 1977; and Engel, 1979).

Ultimately, MI theory provides an assessment framework within which students can have their rich and complex lives acknowledged, celebrated, and nurtured. Because MI assessment and MI instruction represent flip sides of the same coin, MI approaches to assessment are not likely to take more time to implement as long as they are seen as an integral part of the instructional process. As such, assessment experiences and instructional experiences should begin to appear virtually indistinguishable. Moreover, students engaged in this process should begin to regard the assessment experience not as a gruesome "judgment day" but, rather, as another opportunity to learn.

For Further Study

1. Choose an educational outcome that you are preparing students to reach, and then develop an MI-sensitive assessment measure that will allow students to demonstrate their competency in a number of ways (i.e., through two or more of the eight intelligences).

2. Help students develop "celebration portfolios" that include elements from several intelligences (see Figure 10.5 for examples of what to put in a portfolio). Develop a set of procedures for selecting material (see Figure 10.6) and a setting within which students can reflect on their portfolios and present them to others.

3. Put on a "Celebration of Learning" fair at which students can demonstrate competencies and show products they've made that relate to the eight intelligences.

4. Focus on one method of documentation that you'd like to explore, develop, or refine (including digital photography, video, audio, or electronic duplication of student work) and begin documenting student work using this medium.

5. Keep a daily or weekly diary in which you record your observations of students demonstrating competency in each of the eight intelligences.

6. Experiment with the kinds of inputs (methods of presentation) and outputs (methods of expression) you use in constructing assessments. Use Figure 10.4 as a guide in developing a variety of assessment contexts.

7. Develop an *ipsative* assessment approach (i.e., one that compares a student to his or her own past performance) and compare its usefulness to other methods of assessment and evaluation (e.g., standardized tests, benchmarked performances, holistically scored portfolios, etc.).

11

MI Theory and Special Education

Treat people as if they were what they ought to be, and you help them to become what they are capable of being.

—Goethe

The theory of multiple intelligences has broad implications for special education. By focusing on a wide spectrum of abilities, MI theory places "disabilities" in a broader context. Using MI theory as a backdrop, educators can begin to perceive children with special needs as whole persons possessing strengths in many intelligence areas. Over the history of the special education movement in the United States, educators have had a disturbing tendency (gifted educators excepted) to work from a deficit paradigm—focusing on what students *can't* do—in an attempt to help students succeed in school. As an example of this trend, Mary Poplin stated the following in her farewell address to her readership as editor of the *Learning Disability Quarterly* (LDQ):

> The horrifying truth is that in the four years I have been editor of LDQ, only one article has been submitted that sought to elaborate on the talents of the learning disabled. This is a devastating commentary on a field that is supposed

to be dedicated to the education of students with average and above average intelligence. . . . Why do we not know if our students are talented in art, music, dance, athletics, mechanical repair, computer programming, or are creative in other nontraditional ways? . . . It is because, like regular educators, we care only about competence in its most traditional and bookish sense—reading, writing, spelling, science, social studies and math in basal texts and worksheets. (Poplin, 1984, p. 133)

Similar themes could also be identified in other areas of special education, including speech *pathology,* emotional *disturbance,* and attention deficit hyperactivity *disorder,* where the very terms themselves strongly suggest the operation of a disease paradigm in each case (see Armstrong 1987b, 1997, 1999b).

MI Theory as a Growth Paradigm

We do not have to regard children with special needs primarily in terms of deficit, disorder, and disease. We can instead begin to work within the parameters of a growth paradigm. Figure 11.1 illustrates some of the key differences between deficit and growth paradigms. MI theory provides a growth paradigm for assisting special-needs students in school. It acknowledges difficulties or disabilities but does so within the context of regarding special-needs students as basically healthy, or "neurodiverse," individuals (for information about the emerging concept of neurodiversity and its application to special education programs, see Armstrong, 2005). MI theory suggests that "learning disabilities," for example, may occur in all eight intelligences. That is, in addition to students with *dyslexia* (linguistic deficit) and *dyscalculia* (logical-mathematical deficit), some have *prosopagnosia,* or specific difficulties recognizing faces (a spatial deficit); *ideomotor dyspraxia*, or difficulty executing specific motor commands (bodily-kinesthetic deficit); *dysmusia,* or difficulty carrying a tune (musical deficit); *dysemia,* or difficulty reading nonverbal social signals, as well as specific personality disorders (intrapersonal deficit); and difficulty relating well to pets or working in gardens (nature deficit). These deficits, however, often operate relatively autonomously in the midst of other dimensions of the individual's learning profile that are relatively intact and healthy. MI theory thus provides a model for understanding the autistic savant who cannot communicate clearly with others but plays music at a professional level, the dyslexic who possesses special drawing or designing gifts, the "developmentally disabled"

11.1

The Deficit Paradigm Versus the Growth Paradigm in Special Education

---

The Deficit Paradigm
- Labels the individual in terms of specific impairment(s) (e.g., ADHD, ED, BD, EMR, LD).
- Diagnoses the specific impairment(s) using a battery of standardized tests; focuses on errors, low scores, and weaknesses in general.
- Remediates the impairment(s) using a number of specialized treatment strategies often removed from any real-life context.
- Separates the individual from the mainstream for specialized treatment in a segregated class, group, or program.
- Uses an esoteric collection of terms, tests, programs, kits, materials, and workbooks that are different from those found in a regular classroom.
- Segments the individual's life into specific behavioral/educational objectives that are regularly monitored, measured, and modified.
- Creates special education programs that run on a track parallel with regular education programs; teachers from the two tracks rarely meet, except in IEP meetings.

The Growth Paradigm
- Avoids labels; views the individual as an intact person who happens to have a special need.
- Assesses the needs of an individual using authentic assessment approaches within a naturalistic context; focuses on strengths.
- Assists the person in learning and growing through a rich and varied set of interactions with real-life activities and events.
- Maintains the individual's connections with peers in pursuing as normal a life pattern as possible.
- Uses materials, strategies, and activities that are good for *all* kids.
- Applies the understandings of biodiversity and cultural diversity to the neurodiversity of each student.
- Establishes collaborative models that enable specialists and regular classroom teachers to work hand in hand.

---

student who can act extremely well on the stage, or the student with cerebral palsy who has special linguistic and logical-mathematical genius.

Successful Disabled Individuals as Models for Growth

It may be instructive to study the lives of eminent individuals in history who struggled with disabilities of one kind or another. Such a study reveals, in fact, the existence of people with all types of special needs who are also exceptionally gifted in one or more of the eight intelligences. Figure 11.2 lists some of these creative individuals along with the specific disability they struggled with and the primary intelligence through which they expressed much of their genius.

11.2
High-Achieving People Facing Personal Challenges

Intelligence	LD	CD	ED	PD	HD	SD
Linguistic	Agatha Christie	Demosthenes	Edgar Allan Poe	Alexander Pope	Samuel Johnson	Rudyard Kipling
Logical-Mathematical	Albert Einstein	Michael Faraday	Charles Darwin	Stephen Hawking	Thomas Edison	Johannes Kepler
Spatial	Leonardo da Vinci	Marc Chagall	Vincent Van Gogh	Henri de Toulouse-Lautrec	Granville Redmond	Otto Litzel
Bodily-Kinesthetic	Auguste Rodin	Admiral Peary	Vaslav Nijinsky	Jim Abbott	Marlee Matlin	Tom Sullivan
Musical	Sergei Rachmaninoff	Maurice Ravel	Robert Schumann	Itzhak Perlman	Ludwig van Beethoven	Joaquin Rodrigo
Interpersonal	Nelson Rockefeller	Winston Churchill	Harry Stack Sullivan	Franklin Roosevelt	King Jordan	Harry Truman
Intrapersonal	General George Patton	Aristotle	Friedrich Nietzsche	Joan of Arc	Helen Keller	Aldous Huxley
Naturalist	Linnaeus	Charles Darwin	Gregor Mendel	Jean Jacques Rousseau	Johannes Kepler	E. O. Wilson

Note: LD = learning difficulties; CD = communicative difficulties; ED = emotional difficulties; PD = physical difficulties; HD = hearing difficulties; SD = sight difficulties.

The persons in Figure 11.2 are known primarily for their achievements in life. In some cases, their disabilities were incidental to their accomplishments. In other cases, their disabilities may have helped spur them on to develop their exceptional abilities. MI theory provides a context for discussing these lives and for applying the understanding gained from such study to the lives of students who are struggling with similar problems. For example, a student with dyslexia can begin to understand that his difficulty may directly affect only a small part of one intelligence area (i.e., the reading dimensions of linguistic intelligence), leaving unimpaired vast regions of his learning potential. It's instructive to note, for instance, that many great writers, including Agatha Christie and Hans Christian Andersen, were dyslexic (Fleming, 1984; Goertzel, Goertzel, & Goertzel, 2004; Illingworth & Illingworth, 1966).

By constructing a perspective of special-needs students as whole individuals, MI theory provides a context for envisioning positive channels through which students can learn to deal with their disabilities. Educators who view disabilities against the background of the eight intelligences see that disabilities occur in only part of a student's life; thus, they can begin to focus more attention on the *strengths* of special-needs students as a prerequisite to developing appropriate remedial strategies. Research on the "self-fulfilling prophecy" or "Pygmalion effect" suggests that the ways in which educators view a student can have a subtle but significant effect upon the quality of teaching the student receives and may help to determine the student's ultimate success or failure in school (see Rosenthal & Jacobsen, 2004).

Cognitive Bypassing

Teachers and administrators need to serve as "MI strength detectives" in the lives of students facing difficulties in school. This kind of advocacy can lead the way toward providing positive solutions to their special needs. In particular, MI theory suggests that students who are not succeeding because of limitations in specific intelligence areas can often bypass these obstacles by using an alternative route, so to speak, that exploits their more highly developed intelligences (see Gardner, 1993a).

In some cases, special-needs students can learn to use an *alternative symbol system* in an unimpaired intelligence. It's interesting to note that Braille, for example, has been used successfully with severely dyslexic students who possessed special strengths in tactile sensitivity (McCoy, 1975). Similarly, researchers have reported more success in teaching a group of "reading-disabled" students Chinese characters than in teaching them English sight words (Rozin, Poritsky, & Sotsky, 1971). In this case, an ideographic symbol system (Chinese) worked more successfully with these spatially oriented youngsters than the linguistic (sound-symbol) English code.

In other cases, the empowering strategy may involve an *assistive technology* or special learning tool. For example, the Kurzweil Reader provides individuals who cannot decode the printed word (due to learning or perceptual difficulties) a means of electronically scanning a printed page and having those signals transformed into sound impulses that can be heard and understood. Similarly, mathematical calculators have come to the rescue of individuals with severe dyscalculia and other math-processing difficulties. Sometimes, the empowering strategy is a *human resource,* as in the case of a therapist (for those struggling with difficulties in the personal intelligences), a coach (for those with behavioral problems), or a tutor (for those with special learning difficulties). Figure 11.3 lists other important empowering strategies. It shows how a difficulty in one intelligence can often be successfully overcome by rerouting a task through a more highly developed intelligence.

The same basic approach used to empower special-needs students can also be employed in developing appropriate *instructional strategies.* The underlying procedure involves translating information in the "intelligence language" that students have trouble learning or understanding into an "intelligence language" that *students do understand.* Figure 11.4 provides a few examples.

Essentially, the approach to developing remedial strategies is the same one used in creating eight-way lesson plans and units for the regular classroom (see Chapter 5). This confluence of regular and special education methodology reinforces the fundamental growth-paradigm emphasis inherent in MI theory. In other words, the best learning activities for special-needs students are those that are most successful with *all* students. What may be different, however, is the way in which lessons are specifically tailored to the needs of individual students or small groups of students.

MI Theory in the Development of IEPs

MI theory lends itself particularly well to the development of teaching strategies in individualized educational programs (IEPs) developed as part of a student's special education program. In particular, MI theory can help teachers identify a student's strengths, and this information can serve as a basis for deciding what kinds of interventions are most appropriate for inclusion in the IEP.

All too often a student having problems in a specific area will be given an IEP that neglects his most developed intelligences while concentrating on his weaknesses. For instance, a student with well-developed bodily-kinesthetic and spatial intelligences may be having difficulty learning to read. In many

11.3

Strategies and Tools for Empowering Intelligences in Areas of Difficulty

Area of Difficulty	Linguistic Strategies and Tools	Logical-Mathematical Strategies and Tools	Spatial Strategies and Tools	Musical Strategies and Tools	Bodily-Kinesthetic Strategies and Tools	Interpersonal Strategies and Tools	Intrapersonal Strategies and Tools	Naturalist Strategies and Tools
Linguistic Difficulty	Tape recorder, Kurzweil Reader	Spell/grammar check software	Ideographic languages	Song lyrics	Braille	Human readers or person to take dictation	Open-ended journal	Reading based on nature, plants, and animals
Logical-Mathematical Difficulty	Calculators	Math tutoring software programs	Arts, diagrams, graphs	Exploring music and math connections	Abacus and other manipulatives	Math tutor	Self-paced math or science programs	Using scientific instruments to observe nature
Spatial Difficulty	Talking books and tapes, talking tours	Computer-assisted design (CAD) software	Magnifiers, maps	Walking stick with tone sensor	Relief maps, Mowat sensor	Personal guide	Self-guided tours	Smell gardens/touching zoos
Bodily-Kinesthetic Difficulty	"How-to" books	Virtual reality software	Choreography diagrams	Neurofeedback using tones	Mobility devices (e.g., motorized wheelchair)	Personal companion	Feedback from videotape	Canine companion
Musical Difficulty	Rhythmic poetry	Music software	Machine that translates music into a sequence of colored lights	Tapes, CDs, records	Amplified vibrating musical instruments	Music teacher	Self-paced music lessons	Recordings of the sounds of different kinds of ecosystems
Interpersonal Difficulty	"Talking cure" in psychotherapy	Cognitive therapy	Movies on interpersonal themes	Music groups (e.g., choir)	Outward Bound adventures	Recovery/self-help support groups	Individual psychotherapy	Sierra Club activities
Intrapersonal Difficulty	Self-help books	Personal digital assistant (PDA)	Art therapy	Music therapy	Obstacle courses	Psychotherapist	Retreats, solitude	Vision quest in nature
Naturalist Difficulty	Field guides, *National Geographic* magazine	Taxonomies and classification systems	Nature programs on PBS, TLC, and the Discovery Channel	Recordings of bird songs and other nature/animal sounds	Extensive nature walks	Expert nature guide, volunteer for ecology organization	Taking care of a pet, planting a garden, or other solo nature project	Camping and hiking experiences

11.4

Examples of MI Remedial Strategies for Specific Topics

Strategy	Letter Reversals: "b" and "d"	The Three States of Matter	Understanding Simple Fractions
Linguistic Remedial Strategy	Identify through context in words or sentences	Give verbal descriptions, assign reading matter	Use storytelling, word problems
Logical-Mathematical Remedial Strategy	Play anagrams or other word-pattern games	Classify substances in the classroom	Show math ratios on number line
Spatial Remedial Strategy	Color code b's and d's; use stylistic features unique to each letter; create "pictures" out of letters (e.g., "bed" where the stems are the posts)	Draw pictures of different states; look at pictures of molecules in different states	Look at a diagram of "pies"; draw pictures
Bodily-Kinesthetic Remedial Strategy	Use kinesthetic mnemonic (put fists together, thumbs upraised, palms facing you—this makes a "bed")	Act out the three states in a dance; do hands-on lab experiments; build models of three states	Put together manipulative puzzles divided into fractions
Musical Remedial Strategy	Sing songs with lots of b's and d's in them to help differentiate	Play musical recording at three different speeds	Play a fraction of a song (e.g., one note of a three-note song)
Interpersonal Remedial Strategy	Give letter cards with b's and d's randomly to students; have them find others with their sound (aurally) and then check answers visually with cards	Create the three states as a class (each person as a molecule)	Divide the class into different fraction pies
Intrapersonal Remedial Strategy	List favorite words that begin with b and d	Examine the three states in one's body, home, and neighborhood	Choose a favorite fraction and collect specific instances of it
Naturalist Remedial Strategy	List favorite animals and plants that begin with b and d	Examine the three states as they exist in nature (e.g., clouds, rain, sand)	Divide apples or other food items into segments

schools today, he would be given an IEP that fails to include bodily-kinesthetic and spatial activities as a means of achieving his educational objectives. Frequently, the interventions suggested for such a student will include *more* linguistic tasks, such as reading programs and auditory awareness activities—in other words, more concentrated and controlled doses of the same sorts of tasks the student was failing at in the regular classroom.

MI theory suggests a fundamentally different approach: teaching through intelligences that have been previously neglected by educators working with the child. Figure 11.5 shows examples of IEPs that might be written for students who have had difficulty learning to read yet possess strengths in other intelligence areas. Note that these examples accommodate the student's learning differences at both the instructional level and the assessment level.

The Broad Implications of MI Theory for Special Education

The influence that MI theory can have on special education goes far beyond the development of new remedial strategies and interventions. If MI theory is implemented on a large scale in both the regular and special education programs in a school district, it is likely to have some of the following effects:

Fewer referrals to special education classes: When the regular curriculum includes the full spectrum of intelligences, referrals to special education classes will decline. Most teachers now focus on the linguistic and mathematical intelligences, neglecting the needs of students who learn best through the musical, spatial, bodily-kinesthetic, interpersonal, or intrapersonal intelligences. It is these students who most often fail in regular classrooms and are placed in special settings (Armstrong, 1987a; Schirduan & Case, 2004). Once regular classrooms themselves become more sensitive to the needs of different kinds of learners through MI learning programs, the need for special placement, especially for learning disabilities and behavior problems, will diminish. This model thus supports the full inclusion movement in education (Kluth, 2003).

A changing role for the special education teacher: The special education teacher or learning specialist will begin to function less as a "pullout" or special class teacher and more as a special MI consultant to the regular

---

11.5
Sample MI Plans for Individualized Education Programs

Subject: Reading

Short-Term Instructional Goal: When presented with an unfamiliar piece of children's literature with a readability level of beginning 2nd grade, the student will be able to effectively decode 80 percent of the words and answer four out of five comprehension questions based on its content.

Plan 1: For a Child with Strong Bodily-Kinesthetic and Spatial Intelligences

Student can

- Act out (mime) new words and the content of new stories.
- Make new words into pictures (e.g., hanging lights on the word "street").
- Sculpt new words using clay.
- Draw pictures expressing the content of books.

Assessment: Student is allowed to move his body while reading the book; student can answer content questions by drawing answers rather than (or in addition to) responding orally.

Plan 2: For a Child with Strong Musical and Interpersonal Intelligences

Student can

- Make up songs using new words.
- Play board games or card games that require learning new words.
- Use simple song books as reading material (singing lyrics accompanied by music).
- Read children's literature to another child.
- Teach a younger child to read.

Assessment: Student is allowed to sing while reading a book; student may demonstrate competency by reading a book to another child or answering content questions posed by a peer.

---

classroom teacher. In this new role, MI consultants, perhaps operating like Gardner's student–curriculum brokers (see Chapter 9), can assist regular classroom teachers in some of the following tasks:

- Identifying students' strongest intelligences
- Focusing on the needs of specific students
- Designing MI curricula
- Creating specific MI interventions
- Working with groups using MI activities

All or most of a special-needs/MI teacher's time can be spent in the regular classroom focusing on the individual needs of students and the targeting of special MI activities to achieve educational outcomes.

A greater emphasis on identifying strengths: Teachers assessing special-needs students will likely put more emphasis on identifying the strengths of students. Qualitative and authentic measures (such as those described in Chapters 3 and 10) are likely to have a larger role in special education and may perhaps even begin to supplant standardized diagnostic measures as a means of developing appropriate educational programs.

Increased self-esteem: With more emphasis placed on the strengths and abilities of special-needs children, students' self-esteem and internal locus of control are likely to rise, thus helping to promote success among a broader community of learners.

Increased understanding and appreciation of students: As students use MI theory to make sense of their individual differences, their tolerance, understanding, and appreciation of those with special needs is likely to rise, making their full integration into the regular classroom more likely.

Ultimately, the adoption of MI theory in education will move special education toward a growth paradigm and facilitate a greater level of cooperation between special education and regular education. MI classrooms will then become the least restrictive environment for all special-needs students except the most disruptive.

For Further Study

1. Develop a curriculum unit for use in a regular or special-needs classroom that focuses upon famous individuals who overcame disabilities. Include biographies, videos, posters, and other materials. Discuss with students how a disability accounts for only one part of an individual's life as a total person. Use MI theory as a model for regarding disabilities as glitches in basically whole human beings.

2. Identify a special-needs student who is currently not succeeding in the school system. Using some of the strategies suggested in Chapter 3, identify the student's strengths in terms of the theory of multiple intelligences. Brainstorm as many strengths as possible, including strengths that combine several intelligences. Then discuss with colleagues how this process of strengths assessment can affect their overall view of the student and generate new solutions for helping her.

3. Identify a special-needs student in your program who is having school-related difficulties because of limitations in one particular intelligence. Identify specific empowering tools (e.g., alternative symbol systems, learning materials, assistive technologies, human resources) that can be used to help "reroute" the problem into more developed intelligences. Choose two or three of the most appropriate and available tools to apply to the student's particular need(s). Evaluate the results.

4. Write multiple intelligence strategies into a student's IEP based upon the student's strengths in one or more intelligences.

5. Meet with a regular classroom teacher (if you are a special education teacher) or a specialist (if you are a regular classroom teacher) and discuss ways in which you can collaboratively use MI strategies to help special-needs kids succeed in the mainstream.

6. Work individually with a special-needs child (or a small group of children) and help him (or them) become aware of his (their) special strengths in terms of MI theory (see Armstrong, 2003, and Margulies, 1995).

12

MI Theory and Cognitive Skills

Though man a thinking being is defined,
Few use the grand prerogative of mind.
How few think justly of the thinking few!
How many never think, who think they do!

—*Jane Taylor*

With the advent of cognitive psychology as the predominant paradigm in education, educators have become increasingly interested in helping students develop thinking strategies. *How* students think has become almost more important than *what* they think about. MI theory provides an ideal context for making sense out of students' cognitive skills. The eight intelligences in the model are themselves cognitive capacities. Hence, to develop any or all of them in the ways described in previous chapters is to facilitate the cultivation of students' ability to think. It may be helpful, however, to look more specifically at how MI theory applies to the areas most often emphasized by educators espousing a cognitive approach to learning, memory, problem solving, and other forms of higher-order thinking, including Bloom's levels of cognitive complexity.

Memory

Classroom teachers have always seemed troubled by the problem of students' memories. "They knew it yesterday, but today it's gone" is a familiar refrain. "It's as if I never even taught it. What's the point?" many teachers lament. Helping students retain what they learn appears to be one of education's most pressing and unresolved issues. MI theory provides a helpful perspective on this age-old educational problem. It suggests that the notion of a "pure" memory is flawed. Memory, according to Howard Gardner, is intelligence-specific (Gardner, 2006a, p. 76). There is no such thing as a "good memory" or a "bad memory" until an intelligence is specified. Thus, one may have a good memory for faces (spatial/interpersonal intelligence) but a poor memory for names and dates (linguistic/logical-mathematical intelligence). One may have a superior ability to recall a tune (musical intelligence) but not be able to remember the dance step that accompanies it (bodily-kinesthetic intelligence).

This new perspective on memory suggests that students with "poor memories" may have poor memories in only one or two of the intelligences. The problem, however, may be that their poor memories are in one or both of the intelligence areas most frequently emphasized in school: linguistic and logical-mathematical intelligence. The solution, then, lies in helping these students gain access to their "good" memories in other intelligences (e.g., musical, spatial, and bodily-kinesthetic). Memory training, or work involving memorization of material in any subject, should therefore be taught in such a way that all eight "memories" are activated.

Spelling is an academic area that has typically relied heavily upon memory skills. Unfortunately, most instructional approaches to studying spelling words have involved the use of only linguistic strategies: write the word five times, use the word in a sentence, spell the word out loud, and so forth. MI theory suggests that problem spellers may need to go beyond these auditory, oral, and written strategies (all linguistic) to find success. Here are some examples of how the orthographic structure of linguistic symbols (i.e., the English alphabet) can be linked to other intelligences to enhance the retention of spelling words:

- *Musical*—Spelling words can be sung. For example, any seven-letter word (or multiple of seven) can be sung to the tune of "Twinkle, Twinkle

Little Star," and any six-letter word can be sung to the tune of "Happy Birthday to You."

- *Spatial*—Spelling words can be visualized. Students can be introduced to an "inner blackboard" or other mental screen in their mind's eye. During study, students place words on the mental screen; during test time, students simply refer to their "inner blackboard" for help. Other spatial approaches include color coding spelling patterns, drawing spelling words as pictures (e.g., the word "sun" can be drawn with rays of light emanating from the word), and reducing spelling words to "configurations" or graphic outlines showing spatial placement of stems.

- *Logical-mathematical*—Spelling words can be "digitalized," that is, reduced to a series of 0s and 1s (consonants = 1, vowels = 0); spelling words can also be coded using other sorts of number systems (e.g., assigning a number to a letter depending upon its placement in the alphabet: a = 1, b = 2, etc.).

- *Bodily-kinesthetic*—Spelling words can be translated into whole-body movements (creating postures that mimic each of the letters of the alphabet). Other bodily-kinesthetic approaches include tracing spelling words in sand, molding spelling words in clay, and using body movements to show patterns in words (e.g., stand up on the vowels, sit down on the consonants).

- *Interpersonal*—Words can be spelled by a group of people. For example, each student has a letter, and when a word is called, students who have the letters in the word form the word with the other students.

- *Intrapersonal*—Students can spell words developmentally (i.e., the way they think they're spelled), or students learn to spell words that have a personal emotional charge.

- *Naturalist*—Students can spell words using natural materials (e.g., twigs, leaves, stems, etc.) or do their spelling words in a natural setting (e.g., making their spelling words with a stick on the ground in a nearby field).

The task for the teacher, then, is to help students associate the material to be learned with components of the different intelligences: words, numbers, pictures, physical movements, musical phrases, social interactions, personal feelings and experiences, and natural phenomena. After students have been exposed to memory strategies from all eight intelligences, they will be able to pick out those strategies that work best for them and be able to use them independently during personal study periods.

Problem Solving

Although research studies suggest that over the past few years U.S. students have improved their performance on rote learning tasks such as spelling and arithmetic, they place U.S. students far down the achievement ladder in comparisons with students in other countries on measures of higher-order cognitive processes. In particular, U.S. students' problem-solving abilities have been regarded as in need of significant improvement (Lemke et al., 2004). Consequently, more and more educators are looking for ways to help students *think* more effectively when confronted with academic problems. Unfortunately, the bias in the critical-thinking movement has been in the direction of logical-mathematical reasoning abilities and in the use of self-talk or other linguistic strategies. MI theory suggests that *thinking* can and frequently does go far beyond these two areas. To illustrate what these other forms of problem-solving behavior "look" like, it may be helpful to review the thinking processes of eminent individuals whose discoveries have helped shape the world we live in (see John-Steiner, 1987, and Gardner, 1993b). By studying the "end-states" of specific problem-solving processes in these great people, educators can learn much that can help foster the same sort of processes in their students.

Many thinkers have used imagery and picture language (spatial intelligence) to help them in their work. The physicist John Howarth described his problem-solving processes as follows:

> I make abstract pictures. I just realized that the process of abstraction in the pictures in my head is similar to the abstraction you engage in dealing with physical problems analytically. You reduce the number of variables, simplify and consider what you hope is the essential part of the situation you are dealing with; then you apply your analytical techniques. In making a visual picture it is possible to choose one which contains representations of only the essential elements—a simplified picture, abstracted from a number of other pictures and containing their common elements. (John-Steiner, 1987, pp. 84–85)

Others have used problem-solving strategies that combine visual-spatial images with certain kinetic or bodily-kinesthetic features of the mind. Albert Einstein, for example, frequently performed "thought-experiments" that helped him develop his relativity theory, including a fantasy that involved riding on the end of a beam of light. When asked by a French mathematician to describe his thinking processes, Einstein said they included elements that were of *visual* and *muscular* type (Ghiselin, 1955). Similarly, Henri Poincaré shares the story of how he struggled for days with a vexing mathematical problem:

> For fifteen days I strove to prove that there could not be any functions like those I have since called Fuchsian functions. I was then very ignorant; every day I seated myself at my work table, stayed an hour or two, tried a great number of combinations and reached no results. One evening, contrary to my custom, I drank black coffee and could not sleep. Ideas rose in crowds; *I felt them collide until pairs interlocked* [italics mine], so to speak, making a stable combination. By the next morning, I had established the existence of a class of Fuchsian functions, those which come from the hypergeometric series; I had only to write out the results which took but a few hours. (Ghiselin, 1955, p. 36)

Musicians speak about a very different kind of problem-solving capacity, one that involves access to musical imagery. Mozart explained his own composing process this way: "Nor do I hear in my imagination the parts [of the composition] successively, but I hear them, as it were, all at once. What a delight this is I cannot tell. All this inventing, this producing, takes place in a pleasing lively dream" (Ghiselin, 1955, p. 45). Einstein acknowledged the operation of musical thought in a logical-mathematical/spatial domain when, referring to Nils Bohr's model of the atom, with its orbiting electrons absorbing and releasing energy, he wrote, "This is the highest form of musicality in the sphere of thought" (Clark, 1972, p. 292).

There are even processes unique to the personal intelligences. For example, a commentator reflecting on the interpersonal intelligence of Lyndon B. Johnson said, "Lots of guys can be smiling and deferential. He had something else. No matter what someone thought, Lyndon would agree with him—would be there ahead of him, in fact. He could follow someone's mind around—and figure out where it was going and beat it there" (Caro, 1990, p. 256). In a more intrapersonal fashion, Marcel Proust used simple sensations like the taste of a pastry to evoke inner feelings that swept him back into the days of his childhood—a context that provided the basis for his masterwork, *Remembrance of Things Past* (see Proust, 1928, pp. 54–58). Finally, in the naturalist domain, a study of Charles Darwin's notebooks reveals that he used the image of a tree to help him generate the theory of evolution: "Organized beings represent a tree, irregularly branched, ... as many terminal buds dying as new ones generated" (Gruber, 1977, p. 126).

How these "end-state" cognitive processes translate into classroom practice may seem at first elusive. It is possible, however, to distill certain basic elements from the problem-solving strategies of the geniuses of culture and create strategies that can be learned even by students in the primary grades. For example, students can learn to "visualize" their ideas in much the same way Einstein performed his thought-experiments. They can learn to sketch metaphorical images that relate to problems they are working on much as Darwin worked with natural images in his own notebooks. The following list indicates the wide range of MI problem-solving strategies that could be used by students in academic settings:

- *Linguistic*—Self-talk or thinking out loud (see Perkins, 1981)
- *Logical-mathematical*—Logical heuristics (see Polya, 1957)
- *Spatial*—Visualization, idea sketching, mind-mapping (see Margulies, 1991, and McKim, 1980)
- *Bodily-kinesthetic*—Kinesthetic imagery (see Gordon & Poze, 1966); also, accessing "gut feelings" or using one's hands, fingers, or whole body to solve problems
- *Musical*—Sensing the "rhythm" or "melody" of a problem (e.g., harmony versus dissonance); using music to unlock problem-solving capacities (see Ostrander & Schroeder, 1979)
- *Interpersonal*—Bouncing ideas off other people (see Johnson, Johnson, & Holubec, 1994)
- *Intrapersonal*—Identifying with the problem; accessing dream imagery, personal feelings that relate to the problem; deep introspection (see Harman & Rheingold, 1984)
- *Naturalist*—Using analogies from nature to envision problems and solutions (see Gordon & Poze, 1966)

Once students have been introduced to strategies like these, they can choose from a cognitive menu the approaches that are likely to be successful for them in any given learning situation. This kind of cognitive training can prove far richer than the traditional "thinking skills" program, which all too often consists of worksheets containing games and puzzles detailing the five-step sequence involved in solving a math word problem. In the future, when students are urged by a teacher to "think harder," students will have the luxury of asking, "In which intelligence?"

Promoting Christopherian Encounters

In his book *The Unschooled Mind,* Howard Gardner (1991) addresses the tendency of contemporary schooling to teach students surface-level knowledge without ever affecting their deeper understanding of the world. As a result, students are graduating from high school, college, and even graduate school still holding on to many of the same naive beliefs they held as preschoolers. In one example, 70 percent of college students who had completed a physics course in mechanics said that a coin tossed up in the air has two forces acting upon it, the downward force of gravity and the upward force coming from the hand (the truth is only gravity exerts a force [Gardner, 1991]). Supposedly well-educated students who can spout algorithms, rules, laws, and principles in a variety of domains still harbor, according to Gardner, a minefield of misconceptions, rigidly applied procedures, stereotypes, and simplifications. What is required is an approach to education that challenges naive beliefs, provokes questions, invites multiple perspectives, and ultimately stretches a student's mind to the point where it can apply existing knowledge to new situations and novel contexts.

Gardner suggests that a student's mind can be expanded through the use of "Christopherian encounters." Although Gardner uses the term specifically in reference to exploding misconceptions in the field of science, this phrases can serve as a beautiful metaphor for the expansion in general of a child's multiple intelligences to higher levels of competence and understanding. Just as Christopher Columbus challenged the notion that the earth is flat by sailing "beyond the edge" and thereby demonstrating its curved shape, so, too, Gardner suggests that educators challenge students' limited beliefs by taking them "over the edge" into areas where they must confront the contradictions and disjunctions in their own thinking. It's possible to apply this general approach to multiple intelligences theory by suggesting examples in which students' minds might be stretched in each of the intelligences:

- *Linguistic*—Moving students beyond the literal interpretation of a piece of literature (e.g., the novel *Moby Dick* is more than a sea yarn about a whale)

- *Logical-mathematical*—Devising science experiments that force students to confront contradictions in their thinking about natural phenomena (e.g., asking students to predict how a ball rolled straight from the center of a rotating merry-go-round will move as it reaches the edge and then discussing the outcome)
- *Spatial*—Helping students confront tacit beliefs about art that might, for example, include the prejudice that paintings should use pleasant colors and depict beautiful scenery and attractive people (e.g., showing students Picasso's painting *Guernica,* which does not contain those characteristics)
- *Bodily-kinesthetic*—Moving students beyond stereotypical ways of using their bodies to express certain feelings or ideas in a dance or play (e.g., helping students explore the wide range of body postures and facial expressions for expressing Willy Loman's sense of defeat in Arthur Miller's *Death of a Salesman*)
- *Musical*—Helping students undo stereotypes that might suggest good music should be harmonious and have a regular beat (e.g., playing students Stravinsky's *Rite of Spring*—a piece that caused a riot when first played because it clashed with the listeners' beliefs about what was good music)
- *Interpersonal*—Helping students go beyond the imputation of simplistic motivations in studying fictional or real characters in literature, history, or other fields (e.g., helping students understand that Holden Caulfield's intentions in *Catcher in the Rye* involved more than a desire for a "night on the town" or that Adolf Hitler's rise to power was motivated by more than a "thirst for power")
- *Intrapersonal*—Deepening students' understanding of themselves by relating different parts of the curriculum to their own personal life experiences and backgrounds (e.g., asking students to think of the "Huck Finn" or "Laura Ingalls Wilder" part of themselves)
- *Naturalist*—Challenging students to critically examine the evidence supporting the theory of evolution versus the idea that the earth was created 6,000 years ago

MI theory must be seen as more than simply a process by which students celebrate and begin to activate their many ways of knowing. Educators must help students develop higher levels of understanding through their multiple intelligences. By making certain that "Christopherian encounters" in each intelligence are a regular part of the school day, educators can help ensure that the unschooled mind will truly develop into a powerful and creative thinking force.

MI Theory and Bloom's Levels of Cognitive Complexity

Almost 40 years ago, University of Chicago professor Benjamin S. Bloom (1956) unveiled his famous "taxonomy of educational objectives." This survey included a cognitive domain, and its six levels of complexity have been used over the past four decades as a gauge by which educators can ensure that instruction stimulates and develops students' higher-order thinking capacities. The six levels are

1. *Knowledge*—Rote memory skills (knowing facts, terms, procedures, classification systems)
2. *Comprehension*—The ability to translate, paraphrase, interpret, or extrapolate material
3. *Application*—The capacity to transfer knowledge from one setting to another
4. *Analysis*—Discovering and differentiating the component parts of a larger whole
5. *Synthesis*—Weaving together component parts into a coherent whole
6. *Evaluation*—Judging the value or utility of information using a set of standards

Bloom's taxonomy provides a kind of quality-control mechanism through which one can judge how deeply students' minds have been stirred by a multiple intelligence curriculum. It would be easy to construct MI instructional methods that appeared compelling—owing to the wide range of intelligences addressed—but that kept learning at the knowledge or rote level of cognitive complexity. MI activities for teaching spelling, the times tables, or history facts are prime examples of MI theory in the service of lower-order cognitive skills. MI curricula, however, can be designed to incorporate all of Bloom's levels of cognitive complexity. The curriculum outline presented in Figure 12.1 shows how a teacher can articulate competencies that address all eight intelligences as well as Bloom's six levels of cognitive complexity.

12.1

MI Theory and Bloom's Taxonomy

Ecology Unit: Local environment—trees in your neighborhood

Intelligence	Knowledge	Comprehension	Application	Analysis	Synthesis	Evaluation
			Bloom's Six Levels of Educational Objectives			
Linguistic Intelligence	memorize names of trees	explain how trees receive nutrients	given description of tree diseases, suggest cause of each disease	describe how each part of a tree functions in relation to the whole	write a paper describing the life cycle of a tree from pre-seed to post-seed	rate different methods of controlling tree growth
Logical-Mathematical Intelligence	remember number of points on specific trees' leaves	convert English to metric in calculating height of tree	given height of smaller tree, estimate height of larger tree	analyze materials found in sap residue	given weather, soil, and other information, chart projected growth of a tree	rate different kinds of tree nutrients based on data
Spatial Intelligence	remember basic configurations of specific trees	look at diagrams of trees and tell what stage of growth they are in	use geometric principles to determine height of tree	draw cellular structure of tree root	create a landscaping plan using trees as central feature	evaluate practicality of different landscaping plans
Bodily-Kinesthetic Intelligence	identify tree by the feel of the bark	given array of tree fruits, identify seeds	given type of local tree, find an ideal location for planting it	create different parts of tree from clay	gather all materials needed for planting a tree	evaluate the quality of different kinds of fruit
Musical Intelligence	remember songs that deal with trees	explain how old tree songs came into being	change the lyrics of an old tree song to reflect current issues	classify songs by issue and historical period	create your own tree song based on information in this unit	rate the songs from best to worst and give reasons for your choices
Interpersonal Intelligence	record responses to the question "What is your favorite tree?"	determine the most popular tree in class by interviewing others	use survey results to pick location for field trip to orchard	classify kids into groups according to favorite tree	arrange field trip to orchard by contacting necessary people	rank three methods to ask others about tree preference
Intrapersonal Intelligence	remember a time you climbed a tree	share the primary feeling you had while up in the tree	develop "tree-climbing rules" based on your experience	divide up your experience into "beginning," "middle," and "end"	plan a tree-climbing expedition based on your past experience	explain what you liked "best" and "least" about your experience
Naturalist Intelligence	learn to discriminate different tree leaves by sight	describe how other living beings (e.g., humans, animals) benefit from trees	create a system for classifying different tree leaves	analyze the function of a given tree in terms of the larger ecosystem in which it finds itself	develop an approach for protecting specific types of trees in your neighborhood from damage or disease	evaluate which trees in your neighborhood are most eco-valuable to the surrounding environment

You needn't feel a compulsion to include all of these activities in one unit. In fact, you may at first want to develop a thematic curriculum without reference to MI theory and Bloom's taxonomy. Then, simply use the instructional model displayed in Figure 12.1 as a road map to help you stay on course in your efforts to address a number of intelligences and cognitive levels. It may become apparent, for example, after laying the MI/Bloom template over the curriculum, that some easily incorporated musical experiences are missing from the unit or that there are no opportunities for students to evaluate experiences—something that can be easily remedied. MI theory represents a model that can enable you to move beyond heavily linguistic, lower-order thinking activities (e.g., worksheets) into a broad range of complex cognitive tasks that prepare students for life.

For Further Study

1. Write 10–15 random words on the board (words that are at students' level of decoding and comprehension). Give the class one minute to "memorize" them. Then cover the words and ask students to write all the words from memory (in any order). Provide immediate feedback. Discuss the strategies that students used to remember the words. Then teach them memory strategies using several intelligences:

- *Linguistic*—String the words together in some kind of intelligible story.
- *Spatial*—Visualize the story taking place.
- *Musical*—Sing the story to a set tune or a tune composed on the spot.
- *Bodily-kinesthetic/interpersonal*—Act out the story, emphasizing the body movements involved for each of the words.
- *Intrapersonal*—Associate personal experiences (and accompanying feelings) with each word.

Practice these strategies using another list of words, and then have students write the list from memory. Discuss what was different this time, and have students talk about which strategies seemed most successful to them. After using this procedure with two or three more lists, have students use these memory strategies for curriculum-related material (e.g., history facts, spelling words, vocabulary, etc.).

2. Have students solve a brainteaser or other logical-mathematical problem involving higher-order thinking processes. Allow students 10–15 minutes to use whatever strategies they wish. Let them know they can work with other people, walk around, ask for resources, and so on. Then have students share their particular strategies or problem-solving processes, writing them on the board as they are given. After everyone has had a chance to share, go over the list of strategies and note which intelligences have been tapped. Ask students: Are some strategies more successful than others? Are certain strategies or problem-solving processes more *fun* than others?

Using other types of problems, repeat this activity. Keep a list of problem-solving strategies organized by primary intelligence. Display the list so students can refer to it throughout the year as a resource in guiding their own study habits.

3. Develop a thematic unit, or take a unit that you've already developed, and note which intelligences and levels of cognitive complexity are addressed through the activities in the unit. List additional activities that might enhance the intellectual breadth and cognitive depth of the unit.

4. Create "Christopherian encounters" for materials in your curriculum that will stretch students' minds, challenge existing beliefs, and bring students' multiple intelligences to higher levels of functioning.

13

Other Applications
of MI Theory

At present, the notion of schools devoted to multiple intelligences is still in its infancy, and there are as many plausible recipes as there are educational chefs. I hope that in the next twenty years, a number of efforts will be made to craft an education that takes multiple intelligences seriously; should this be done, we will be in a position to know which of these "thought" and "action experiments" make sense and which prove to be impractical or ill-advised.

—Howard Gardner

In addition to the areas covered in previous chapters, there are many other applications of MI theory to education. Three that deserve mention before ending this book include computer technology, cultural diversity, and career counseling. In each case, MI theory provides a context through which existing understandings and resources can be extended to include a broader perspective. This wider view, in turn, can allow educators to develop educational materials and strategies that meet the needs of a more diverse student population.

Computer Technology

Our first inclination may be to associate computers with logical-mathematical intelligence. This connection arises in large part because of the stereotypical images of "computer nerds" working on spreadsheets or toiling over highly abstract computer programming languages. Computers themselves, however, are intelligence-neutral mechanisms. What activate computers are the software programs used to run them. And these software programs can be designed to interface with any or all of the eight intelligences. Word processing software, for example, calls forth from its users a certain level of linguistic intelligence, whereas draw-and-paint software more often requires spatial intelligence. The list of program types in Figure 13.1 suggests the broad range of software available to activate the multiple intelligences; examples of specific products are provided in parentheses.

You can use MI theory as a basis for selecting and making available software for use in the classroom or in specially designated computer labs in the school. Perhaps the most exciting technology application involving multiple intelligences is emerging in the area of multimedia learning projects. Using multimedia software, a project incorporating text (linguistic), illustrations (spatial), sound (musical or linguistic), and video (bodily-kinesthetic and other intelligences) can be developed. For example, a student could create a learning project on horticulture. The program might begin with a written text describing local flowers (linguistic) accompanied by statistical charts listing the planting requirements of specific flowers (logical-mathematical). By clicking the mouse on specific nouns in the text—the word "rose" perhaps—an illustration of a rose might appear (spatial) along with a song mentioning the rose—for instance, "The Rose" sung by Bette Midler (musical). Clicking on specific verbs—for example, "to plant"—might activate a video presentation of the student planting a flower (bodily-kinesthetic).

The process of putting together such a project requires a great deal of intrapersonal intelligence. If such a project is cooperative in nature (a class gardening project perhaps), then interpersonal intelligence is called into play as well. The completed CDs or DVDs themselves become valuable documents of a student's learning progress. They can serve as "electronic portfolios" that can easily be passed from one teacher to the next as part of an authentic assessment of the student's accomplishments during the year (see McKenzie, 2005).

13.1
Software and Web 2.0 Features that Activate the Multiple Intelligences

Linguistic Intelligence
- Word processing programs (Microsoft Word)
- Typing tutors (Mavis Beacon Teaches Typing!)
- Desktop publishing programs (Adobe Pagemaker)
- Electronic references (Wikipedia)
- Interactive storybooks (The Cat in the Hat)
- Word games (Textris)
- Foreign language instruction and translation software (Power Translator)
- Web site creation software (Front Page)
- Blog authoring (Typepad)
- Dictation software (Kurzweil 3000)

Logical-Mathematical Intelligence
- Math skills tutorials (Intelligent Tutor)
- Computer programming tutors (LOGO)
- Logic games (Where in the World Is Carmen Sandiego?)
- Science programs (I Love Science)
- Critical thinking programs (Building Thinking Skills)
- Database management (Microsoft Access)
- Financial management software (Quicken Deluxe)
- Science reference guides (Encyclopedia of Science)
- Spreadsheets (Mesa)

Spatial Intelligence
- Animation programs (Toon Boom's Flip Boom)
- Draw-and-paint (Corel Paint Shop Pro)
- Electronic chess games (Hiarcs)
- Spatial problem-solving games (Tetris)
- Electronic puzzle kits (B Puzzle)
- Clip-art programs (Art Explosion 800000)
- Geometry programs (Geometer's Sketchpad)
- Geography programs (Google Earth)
- Home and landscape design software (Better Homes and Gardens Home Designer Suite)
- Maps and atlases (Google Maps)
- Computer-aided design programs (TurboCAD)
- Video-editing software (Power Director)

Bodily-Kinesthetic Intelligence
- Hands-on construction kits that interface with computers (Lego Mindstorms NXT)

- Motion-simulation games (Flight Simulator X)
- Virtual-reality system software (Unigine)
- Tools that plug into computers (Model ChemLab)
- Human anatomy and health reference guides (3D Body Adventure)
- Physical fitness software (Crosstrainer)
- Sports software (cSwing)

Musical Intelligence
- Music literature tutors (The History of Music Online Tutor)
- Voice synthesizer (Pb Vocoder)
- Composition software (Finale Songwriter)
- Tone recognition and melody memory enhancers (Music Memory)
- Musical instrument digital interfaces (Sonar Home Studio)
- Music instrument instruction software (eMedia Essential Rock Guitar)
- Musical notation programs (Pizzicato)

Interpersonal Intelligence
- E-mail software (Outlook Express)
- Online forums (MySpace)
- Simulation games (SimCity)
- Genealogy programs (Legacy)
- Electronic board games (Clue Classic)

Intrapersonal Intelligence
- Personal choice software (Oregon Trail)
- Career counseling software (Cambridge Career Counseling System)
- Self-understanding software (Emotional IQ Test)
- Fantasy role-play software (Second Life)
- Personal digital assistant (PDA) software (Handweek)
- Any self-paced software program

Naturalist Intelligence
- Naturalist reference guides (National Geographic)
- Nature simulation programs (Amazon Trail)
- Animal games software (AnimaX)
- Ecology awareness programs (EcoBeaker)
- Gardening programs (3-D Garden Composer)

Similarly, the use of the Internet provides opportunities for the exploration and expansion of a student's multiple intelligences. One might, for example, bookmark Web pages related to each of the intelligences, including math and science sites (logical-mathematical intelligence), sites for downloading music (musical intelligence) or for downloading images (spatial intelligence), sites that specialize in nature (naturalist intelligence), sites that provide chat rooms and other chances for interaction (interpersonal intelligence), and sites that offer opportunities for self-development (intrapersonal intelligence).

Cultural Diversity

Over the past two decades, the United States has seen tremendous demographic changes that have created a student population more racially, ethnically, and culturally diverse than ever before. Such diversity presents a great challenge for educators in designing curriculums that are not only *content*-sensitive to cultural differences (e.g., exposing students to the beliefs, background, and foundations of individual cultures) but also *process*-sensitive (e.g., helping students understand the many "ways of knowing" that different cultures possess). MI theory provides a model that is culturally sensitive to such differences. As such, it provides educators with a valuable tool to help celebrate the ways in which different cultures think.

According to MI theory, an intelligence must be valued by a culture in order to be considered a true intelligence. This criterium automatically disqualifies many of the tasks that have traditionally been associated with intelligence testing in the schools. For example, the ability to repeat random digits backward and forward is a task found on some intelligence tests, even though this feat is not particularly valued by any culture. Nowhere in the world do a culture's elders pass on random digits to the next generation. What cultures do pass on to their younger members are stories, myths, great art and music, scientific discoveries, social mores, political institutions, and number systems, among many other "end-states" of accomplishment.

All cultures in the world possess and make use of the eight intelligences in MI theory; however, the ways in which they do so, and the manner in which individual intelligences are valued, vary considerably. A person growing up in the Puluwat culture in the South Sea Islands, for example, would discover that the spatial and naturalist intelligences are highly prized because of their use in navigating the seas (Gladwin, 1970). Puluwat peoples live on several hundred islands, and the ability to move easily from one island to another has a high cultural value. They train their children from a very early age to recognize the constellations, the various "bumps" (islands) on the horizon, and the different textures on the surface of the water that point to significant geographical information. The chief navigators in that society have more prestige than even the political leaders.

In some cultures, musical intelligence is a capacity that is considered universal among all members rather than the province of an elite group of performers. Children growing up among the Anang in Nigeria are expected to learn hundreds of dances and songs by the time they are 5 years old. In Hungary, because of the pioneering influence of the composer Zoltán Kodály on education, students are exposed to music every day and are expected to learn to read musical notation. There are also cultures that place a greater emphasis upon connectedness between peoples (interpersonal intelligence) than upon the individual going his own way (intrapersonal intelligence [Gardner, 1993a]).

It is important to repeat, however, that *every culture has and uses all eight intelligences.* Educators would be making a great mistake if they began to refer to specific racial, ethnic, or cultural groups only in terms of one intelligence. The history of intelligence testing is filled with such bigotry and narrow-mindedness (see, for example, Gould, 1981). Indiscriminate use of MI theory in discussions of cultural differences might well revive old racist stereotypes (e.g., "blacks are musical," "Asians are logical"). For a list of some of the ways in which cultural groups value each of the eight intelligences, see Figure 1.1 in Chapter 1.

Such a broad perspective on culture can provide a context for exploring in a school setting the tremendous diversity in the ways different cultures express themselves through each of the eight intelligences. You might want to periodically hold multicultural/multiple intelligence fairs in your school to celebrate such differences. You could develop curriculums that integrate MI theory into multicultural units. And you can also introduce students to MI theory through great figures in each culture who have achieved high "end-state" performances in each of the intelligences (see Figure 13.2 for some examples).

13.2 **Prominent Individuals from Minority Cultures**				
Intelligence	**African American**	**Asian and Polynesian American**	**Hispanic American**	**Native American**
Linguistic	Toni Morrison	Amy Tan	Isabel Allende	Vine Deloria Jr.
Logical-Mathematical	Benjamin Banneker	Yuan Lee	Luis Alvarez	Robert Whitman
Spatial	Elizabeth Catlett Mora	I. M. Pei	Frida Kahlo	Oscar Howe
Bodily-Kinesthetic	Jackie Joyner-Kersee	Kristi Yamaguchi	Juan Marichal	Jim Thorpe
Musical	Mahalia Jackson	Midori	Linda Ronstadt	Buffy Saint Marie
Interpersonal	Martin Luther King Jr.	Daniel K. Inouye	Xavier L. Suarez	Russell Means
Intrapersonal	Malcolm X	S. I. Hayakawa	Cesar Chavez	Black Elk
Naturalist	George Washington Carver	Nainoa Thompson	Severo Ochoa	Wilfred Foster Denetclaw Jr.

Career Counseling

Because it emphasizes the broad range of ways in which adults pursue their work in life, MI theory provides an appropriate vehicle for helping young-sters begin to develop vocational aspirations. If students are exposed from a very early age to a wide variety of adults demonstrating real-life skills in all eight intelligences, they will have a firm basis upon which to launch a career once they leave school. In the early grades, students would benefit by having adults come into class to talk about their life's work and by going to visit adults at their places of work. It is important that educators *not* attempt to match children's proclivities to specific careers too early in their development. By seeing the spectrum of occupations related to each of the eight intelligences through these kinds of visits and field trips, children can begin making their own decisions about what feels right and what doesn't fit vocationally. Children also benefit from periodic discussions about "what they'd like to be when they grow up." Plan on using the MI vocabulary in these discussions to help frame some of their aspirations.

At the middle and secondary school levels, students can participate in an ongoing process of self-assessment to determine what they are temperamentally and cognitively suited for in the job marketplace (the MI self-assessment tools may be useful in the process). Here is a list of occupations categorized by primary intelligence:

- *Linguistic*—Librarian, archivist, curator, speech pathologist, writer, radio or TV announcer, journalist, legal assistant, lawyer, secretary, typist, proofreader, English teacher
- *Logical-mathematical*—Auditor, accountant, purchasing agent, underwriter, mathematician, scientist, statistician, actuary, computer analyst, economist, technician, bookkeeper, math or science teacher
- *Spatial*—Engineer, surveyor, architect, urban planner, graphic artist, interior decorator, photographer, art teacher, inventor, cartographer, pilot, fine artist, sculptor
- *Bodily-kinesthetic*—Physical therapist, recreational worker, dancer, actor, mechanic, carpenter, craftsperson, physical education teacher, factory worker, choreographer, professional athlete, jeweler
- *Musical*—Disc jockey, musician, instrument maker, piano tuner, music therapist, instrument salesperson, songwriter, studio engineer, choral director, conductor, singer, music teacher, musical copyist
- *Interpersonal*—Administrator, manager, school principal, personnel worker, arbitrator, sociologist, anthropologist, counselor, psychologist, nurse, public relations person, salesperson, travel agent, social director
- *Intrapersonal*—Psychologist, clergyman, psychology teacher, therapist, counselor, theologian, entrepreneur
- *Naturalist*—Forest ranger, zoologist, naturalist, marine biologist, veterinarian, beekeeper, farmer, nature guide, ecologist, horticulturist, vintner, entomologist, tree surgeon

Of course, virtually every job consists of a variety of responsibilities touching on several intelligences. For example, school administrators must possess interpersonal intelligence to facilitate their work with teachers, parents, students, and the community. But they must also have logical-mathematical capabilities to plan budgets and schedules and linguistic skills to write proposals and grants or to communicate effectively with others. They must also have good intrapersonal intelligence if they are to have enough confidence in themselves to stick by their decisions. When discussing careers with secondary students, it may be helpful to discuss the multiplicity of intelligences required for each job.

For Further Study

1. Assess your classroom's or school's software library. Note which specific intelligences are activated through each program. Identify intelligence areas that appear to have few or no software programs represented. Obtain catalogs of major educational software companies and list software programs that could be purchased to expand the range of intelligences covered in your school. Provide your classroom or lab with at least two or three software programs for each intelligence. Then label software programs by intelligences developed and encourage students to explore a range of programs during special "choice" times. Similarly, create a list of valued Web sites that feature the eight intelligences.

2. Develop expertise in the use of multimedia software. Then use these resources to help students develop special projects or "electronic portfolios" for assessment purposes.

3. Create a multicultural/multiple intelligence unit for your class. If your community is diverse, focus on cultures represented by students in your classroom or school. In the unit, explore how different cultures express themselves through the eight intelligences, examining oral and written traditions, number systems or sciences, music, art, dance, sports, political and social systems, religious and mythic traditions, and taxonomies for classifying nature.

4. Develop a vocational curriculum unit appropriate for your classroom (planning field trips and parent visits at the elementary level,

self-assessments and specific study of careers at the middle school and high school levels).

5. What are some educational applications of MI theory that have not been mentioned in this book? How might these applications best be developed? Select one unexplored area that has particular interest for you and design a unique expression of it in your classroom or school.

14

MI Theory and Existential Intelligence

[Existential intelligence] has been valued in every known human culture. Cultures devise religious, mystical, or metaphysical systems for dealing with existential issues; and in modern times or in secular settings, aesthetic, philosophical, and scientific works and systems also speak to this ensemble of human needs.

—Howard Gardner

Howard Gardner has written about the *possibility* of a ninth intelligence—the existential (Gardner, 1995, 1999)—and so I would like to examine what some of the potential applications of this candidate intelligence might be in the curriculum. Gardner defines existential intelligence as "a concern with ultimate life issues." He describes the core ability of this intelligence as "the capacity to locate oneself with respect to the furthest reaches of the cosmos—the infinite and the infinitesimal—and the related capacity to locate oneself with respect to such existential features of the human condition as the significance of life, the meaning of death, the ultimate fate of the physical and the psychological worlds, and such profound experiences as love of another person or total immersion in a work of art" (Gardner, 1999, p. 60). Gardner explicitly states that he is *not* proposing here a spiritual, religious, or moral intelligence based upon any specific "truths" that have been advanced by different individuals, groups, or institutions (see Gardner, 1999, pp. 53–77, for a fuller discussion of why he has decided not to propose a spiritual or moral intelligence). Instead, he is suggesting that any rendering of the spectrum of human intelligences should probably address humanity's long-standing efforts to come to grips with the ultimate questions of life: "Who are we?" "What's it all about?" "Why is there evil?" "Where is humanity heading?" "Is there meaning in life?" and so forth. There is room in this inclusive definition for explicitly religious or spiritual roles (theologians, pastors, rabbis, shamans, ministers, priests, yogis, lamas, imams), as well as nonreligious or nonspiritual roles (philosophers, writers, artists, scientists, and others who are asking these deeper questions as a part of their creative work).

Gardner has considered this intelligence for inclusion into MI theory (at times he's quipped that he currently has 8½ intelligences) because it appears to fit quite well with most of his criteria for an intelligence:

- *Cultural value*—Virtually all cultures have belief systems, myths, dogmas, rituals, institutions, or other structures that attempt to grapple with ultimate life issues.
- *Developmental history*—A look at the autobiographies of great philosophical, religious, spiritual, scientific, or artistic individuals often shows an increasing progression from inklings of cosmic concerns in childhood through apprenticeship stages to more advanced levels of understanding or comprehension of these issues in adulthood.
- *Symbol systems*—Most societies historically have developed different kinds of symbols, images, or "maps" with which to communicate to their members about existential themes (witness, for example, key symbols used by the world's major religions such as the cross for Christianity, the star and crescent for Islam, the star of David for Judaism, etc.).
- *Exceptional individuals (savants)*—In many parts of the world, there are to be found individuals who are said by the local populace to possess a deeper wisdom or understanding, or capacity to ask existential questions, while at the same time having a low IQ or lacking substantially in the capacities of the other intelligences (the movie figure Forrest Gump is perhaps the best-known representation of this phenomenon in popular culture).

- *Psychometric studies*—Certain personality assessments purport to measure traits of "religiosity" or "spirituality," although there are certain problems inherent in obtaining quantitative measures of experiences that are by definition nonquantitative
- *Evolutionary plausibility*—There is evidence for an awareness of existential themes in the hunting and burying rituals of prehistoric humans and also in the mourning behaviors of elephants.
- *Brain research*—Individuals who have temporal-lobe epilepsy sometimes show signs of "hyperreligiosity," and identical twins reared apart show a strong link in terms of their religious attitudes, suggesting the possibility of heritability; however, there are problems involved in subjecting existential concerns to bioreductionism.

Although the existential intelligence is not a perfect fit in terms of Gardner's criteria (this being the reason why he has still not fully qualified it for entry into MI theory), there are enough points of confluence to warrant this intelligence being taken seriously by educators as a "new intelligence on the block." I would like to explore some of the potential applications of existential intelligence to the curriculum. However, before I do so, I wish to make some preliminary comments.

First, some educators may feel a certain reluctance to address the existential intelligence for fear of running into controversy from the community, abridging constitutional protections of the separation of church and state, or violating their own consciences or belief systems or those of their students with regard to these deeper life issues. However, it is important to point out that this intelligence does not involve promoting religion, spirituality, or any specific belief system. It, rather, is dedicated to examining the ways in which humanity has addressed existential concerns (both religious and nonreligious) in a diversity of ways since the beginning of recorded time. There are clear constitutional protections for teaching *about* religion in public schools (objectively and neutrally) and important pedagogical reasons for doing this regularly across the curriculum (see Nord & Haynes, 1998).

Second, it appears to me that the potential applications of this intelligence to the curriculum will be more selective than they are for any of the other intelligences. I don't see any particular advantage in attempting to apply existential intelligence to every possible educational objective. Notice the absurdity, for example, in trying to teach multiplication, phonics, sentence structure, class rules, state government, or the different food groups through existential intelligence! I think that the existential intelligence—even if fully endorsed by Howard Gardner as an "official" intelligence someday—will always maintain a somewhat special status within MI theory, somewhere on the periphery of the day-to-day workings of the model.

Finally, I believe that attempts to assess existential intelligence in students, or to develop existential methods for assessing regular school topics, are not going to be at all productive or useful in an educational context because they will tend to force educators into creating criteria that are far too limiting and artificial to be of any pedagogical value (and are conversely likely only to incite controversy and confusion). I also believe that attempts to create "existential strategies" to teach curriculum in specific areas (e.g., having students re-create a religious ritual during a multicultural unit or telling them to do a closed-eyes meditation on the significance of death in a biology class) are likely to violate the consciences of some students and possibly be unconstitutional in a public school setting as well. Consequently, I feel that the most appropriate way to integrate existential intelligence into the classroom is by integrating content into the curriculum that helps students think about the existential dimensions of whatever they are studying and that assists them in considering the ways in which scientists, artists, politicians, writers, and others have incorporated existential concerns into their own work. I suggest that educators read the book *Taking Religion Seriously Across the Curriculum* (Nord & Haynes, 1998) for a solidly grounded, legally based, and pedagogically responsible approach to teaching about religious issues in the classroom. For a look at how children are natural philosophers, I would suggest *The Philosophy of Childhood* (Matthews, 1996).

What follows are some of my own suggestions for how existential intelligence can intersect with different areas of the curriculum and how it can be integrated into the classroom in a way that does not violate the Constitution or the belief systems of individual students.

Science

Although its external logical methodologies may seem to preclude the possibility of entertaining existential issues, the inner core of science is very much alive to issues of ultimate concern in life. One should remember that modern science emerged in the 17th century out of philosophy, religion, alchemy, and other fields that dealt with existential issues. Many of the great scientists of the modern era, including Newton, Boyle, and Einstein, have been motivated in part (sometimes in large part) by religious, spiritual, or cosmic concerns (Einstein, for example, rejected the indeterminacy of quantum physics because he did not believe that God would play dice with the universe). Teachers can address science existentially in the classroom by highlighting those areas that involve, as Gardner (1999) puts it, "the furthest reaches of the cosmos—the infinite and the infinitesimal" (p. 60)—that is, theories about the origins of the universe, subatomic physics, and so forth. An excellent book that vividly demonstrates these extreme limits is *Powers of Ten* (Morrison & Morrison, 1994), which takes readers from inside the atom to the edges of the universe by successive powers of ten. In the biological sciences, teachers can similarly approach the origins of life in an existential way by helping students wonder about the distinctions between non-life-forms (rocks and minerals) and life-forms (plants and animals). Many current controversies in science, from human cloning to nuclear weapons research, raise opportunities for deep reflection upon the nature and destiny of humanity. In fact, wherever science is working at its own frontiers with unanswered questions, there is plenty of room for existential concerns to be brought to the fore in the curriculum.

Mathematics

Like science, mathematics has been entwined for thousands of years with existential issues. The first Western mathematician that we know about, the Greek thinker Pythagoras, was a mathematician and a mystic who believed that number patterns revealed the ultimate harmony of the cosmos. Following Pythagoras, Plato believed that mathematical reasoning was closer to ultimate reality than the unreliable data gathered by our mere human senses. The mystic components of Judaism, Islam, and other great religious traditions saw numbers and mathematical reasoning as doorways into the secrets of the mysteries of the universe. In the classroom, teachers can bring together a multicultural emphasis with mathematics to address some of these historical connections. There are also opportunities to touch upon existential themes when discussing math concepts like zero or infinity, very large or very small numbers, negative numbers, irrational numbers, imaginary numbers, and probability and topology.

History

It is simply not possible to discuss human history in any "intelligent" fashion without bringing in factors related to existential concerns, especially those involving religion. Consider U.S. history. The motivation for many settlers to come to North America in the 17th century was to seek freedom from religious oppression. Consequently, it's important for history students to have a sense of what Puritans believed, for example, and how their own beliefs differed from the Church of England (and, similarly, how the Church of England came to split off from Roman Catholicism). Many if not most of the wars in human history have come about at least partially as a result of religious differences, so students need to know something about the nature of those religions in order to understand the causes of those conflicts. At the same time, students need to be familiar with trends in philosophy or other existential domains, in order to appreciate many world events (e.g., the impact of the Enlightenment on the French Revolution). Then there are events, such as the Holocaust, that transcend any particular point of view and cause us to confront the nature of evil, suffering, and death in a way that can shake up our own personal belief system and cause us to think in new ways about human existence.

Literature

The clearest connection in the West between literature and existential intelligence can be seen in the impact of the Hebrew and Christian Bibles on subsequent writers in history. One can't fully understand or appreciate many of the great books of our culture—including most of Shakespeare's plays, Bunyan's *Pilgrim's Progress,* Melville's *Moby Dick,* Faulkner's *Absolom, Absolom,* and many more—without seeing how biblical or religious sources interpenetrate them. I'm willing to make the claim that virtually all great literature deals with issues of ultimate life concern and cannot be understood apart from them: from the existential crisis of Gilgamesh after the death of his friend Enkidu in the several-thousand-year-old Mesopotamian classic to the philosophical musings of Leopold Bloom and Stephen Daedelus in James Joyce's 20th-century masterpiece, *Ulysses.* In the classroom, teachers need to ascertain in advance whether assigned literature contains existential themes and then provide opportunities for students to reflect on and discuss these ideas in relationship to other course objectives.

Geography

The constantly shifting pattern on a world atlas of alliances, city-states, empires, confederations, and nations, from the ancient past to the current day, can be far better understood in a context that includes existential themes. To make sense of the changing map of the former Yugoslavia, for example, requires an understanding of the distinctions between Roman Catholicism, Orthodox Christianity, and Islam. Making sense of the division between India, Pakistan, and Bangladesh requires familiarity with differences between Islamic and Hindu thinking. Teachers can help students better comprehend how the landscape has been formed and re-formed by spending time discussing how differences in attitudes on issues of ultimate life concern can change geographical boundaries dramatically.

The Arts

Howard Gardner has pointed out in his definition of existential intelligence that "total immersion in a work of art" is one way in which individuals can experience and express themselves with respect to ultimate life concerns. A look at the history of music, painting, sculpture, dance, and drama reveals an ongoing concern with the meaning of life, death, suffering, and other existential issues. Seeing Michelangelo's Pieta or attending a performance of Shakespeare's *Merchant of Venice* can cause us to ponder upon ultimate questions of suffering and mercy. Listening to Beethoven's Fifth Symphony or looking at painter Thomas Cole's series "The Voyage of Life" can engender thoughts about human destiny. In the classroom, teachers can help students appreciate these finer dimensions of the arts and also provide the resources and opportunities for students to express their own existential concerns by creating their own works of art.

In sum, there appear to be plenty of opportunities for the exercise of existential intelligence in a classroom setting. The kinds of connections and applications discussed above do not represent a "side trip" or "remote excursion" to a new intelligence. Rather, they take students more deeply into the material being studied, by focusing on how existential concerns intertwine with scientific, mathematical, historical, literary, artistic, and other fields of study and by emphasizing how questions of ultimate concern in life are integral to a fuller understanding of human culture.

For Further Study

1. Dialogue with members of your learning community (parents, teachers, administrators, students, board members) about bringing more of the existential intelligence into your school's curriculum. Freely air all points of view, and then develop a constitutionally sound framework that provides opportunities to teach *about* religious issues, raise philosophical themes, and discuss other existential concerns as they relate to various parts of the curriculum.

2. Research the existential dimensions of an academic discipline, such as science, math, history, literature, social studies, economics, psychology, sociology, or anthropology, and discuss how they can be more fully incorporated into the regular core curriculum.

15

MI Theory and Its Critics

Gardner's theory provides a much needed corrective to the shortcomings of traditional psychometric approaches. Instead of probing the bases of bubble-sheet results, Gardner sought to illuminate the mental abilities underlying the actual range of human accomplishment that are found across cultures.

—*Mindy Kornhaber*

Along with the expanding popularity of multiple intelligences, there has been a growing body of writing critical of the theory. In fact, one of the criticisms lodged against MI theory is that there has not been enough acknowledgment of the critical literature on the part of MI advocates. Willingham (2004), for example, observes: "Textbooks [on MI theory] for teachers in training generally offer extensive coverage of the theory, with little or no criticism" (p. 24). Traub (1998) writes: "Few of the teachers and administrators I talked to were familiar with the critiques of multiple intelligence theory; what they knew was that the theory worked for them. They talked about it almost euphorically" (p. 22). In this chapter, I'd like to review some of the major criticisms of MI, and attempt to clear up what I believe are some key misconceptions about the theory.

Criticism #1: MI Theory Lacks Empirical Support

Most of those making this complaint about MI theory come from the psychometric, or testing, community. Gottfredson (2004), for example, argues that the literature on intelligence testing offers virtually no support for the idea of eight autonomous intelligences but overwhelming support for the concept of an overarching single intelligence, frequently attributed to Spearman (1927) and often referred to as "Spearman's g" or simply "the g factor." (See also Brody, 2006.) Gottfredson (2004) writes:

> The g factor was discovered by the first mental testers, who found that people who scored well on one type of mental test tended to score well on all of them. Regardless of their contents (words, numbers, pictures, shapes), how they are administered (individually or in groups; orally, in writing, or pantomimed), or what they're intended to measure (vocabulary, mathematical reasoning, spatial ability), all mental tests measure mostly the same thing. This common factor, g, can be distilled from scores on any broad set of cognitive tests, and it takes the same form among individuals of every age, race, sex, and nation yet studied. In other words, the g factor exists independently of schooling, paper-and-pencil tests, and culture. (p. 35)

Visser, Ashton, and Vernon (2006) actually put together a battery of 16 tests ostensibly covering the eight intelligences (two tests for each intelligence) and discovered the presence of g running through most of the tests. These researchers argued that what Gardner calls intelligences are actually capacities that are secondary or even tertiary to the g factor. In other words, they exist but are subservient to g. J. B. Carroll (1993), who created his own hierarchy of human cognitive abilities, with g at the top, compares linguistic intelligence to "fluid intelligence" and musical intelligence to "auditory perception" (a mistake on his part, because the multiple intelligences are not dependent upon the senses), while finding no place at all for bodily-kinesthetic intelligence.

Response to Criticism #1

MI theory agrees that the g factor exists. What it disputes, however, is that g is superior to other forms of human cognition. In MI theory, g has its place (primarily in logical-mathematical intelligence) as an equal alongside of the other seven intelligences. It appears that what is most at stake here is a matter of semantics. Most critics in the psychometric community agree that the intelligences in Gardner's model exist and are supported by testing. What they disagree about is whether or not they should be called "intelligences." They want to reserve the word "intelligence" for the g factor, while regarding the other seven intelligences as talents, abilities, capacities, or faculties. Gardner (2003) has written that he intended to be provocative in referring to multiple "intelligences" rather than multiple "talents." He wanted to challenge the sacrosanct nature of "intelligence" as a singular phenomenon and get people to think more deeply about what it means to be intelligent. The fact that he has stirred up so much controversy from the psychometric community suggests that he has accomplished his goal. The reality is that MI theory is supported empirically from a number of sources. In *Frames of Mind* (1993a), Gardner established eight criteria that needed to be met in order for an intelligence to appear in his theory (see Chapter 1). Each of these eight criteria provides a range of empirical data, from studies of brain-damaged individuals and "savant" populations, to evidence from prehistoric humanity and other species, to biographical studies of human development and research on human cultures. As Gardner (2004) notes, nothing substantial has emerged in the past 25 years to seriously challenge his theory. Posner (2004), for example, observes that recent neuroimaging research supports Gardner's idea of separate areas of the brain being related to different intelligences. Ironically, the fact that the psychometric community has stayed within the narrow confines of numbers and standardized testing actually limits its ability to give broad empirical support to the notion of a pure g-factor intelligence (Gottfredson's argument notwithstanding, g appears to measure "school-like" thinking; see Gardner, 2006b). On the other hand, MI's multiple sources of empirical data considerably expand its validity as a theoretical construct.

Criticism #2: No Solid Research Support for MI Exists in the Classroom

This criticism parallels the first one in suggesting that MI has no empirical support (or, to put it in a more contemporary context, "MI is not research-based"). Here we are concerned, however, not with pure theory but, rather, with its practical applications in schools. Collins (1998), for example, writes that "evidence for the specifics of Gardner's theory is weak, and there is no firm research showing that its practical applications have been effective" (p. 95). Willingham (2004) writes:

> ... hard data are scarce. The most comprehensive study was a three-year examination of 41 schools that claim to use multiple intelligences. It was conducted by Mindy Kornhaber, a longtime Gardner collaborator. The results, unfortunately, are difficult to interpret. They reported that standardized test scores increased in 78 percent of the schools, but they failed to indicate whether the increase in each school was statistically significant. If not, then we would expect scores to increase in half the schools by chance. Moreover, there was no control group, and thus no basis for comparison with other schools in their districts. Furthermore, there is no way of knowing to what extent changes in the school are due to the implementation of ideas of multiple intelligences rather than, for example, the energizing thrill of adopting a new schoolwide program, new statewide standards, or some other unknown factor. (p. 24)

Response to Criticism #2

Perhaps the greatest problem with the argument that MI is not research-based is that it is founded upon a very narrow conception of what constitutes authentic research. In the restrictive climate of the No Child Left Behind law, the idea of "valid research" has been severely limited to highly controlled studies using standardized tests and quantitative tools based on correlation coefficients and levels of statistical significance. One government definition of the "gold standard" in educational research is provided in a "user-friendly guide" published by the U.S. Department of Education (2003):

> For example, suppose you want to test, in a randomized controlled trial, whether a new math curriculum for 3rd graders is more effective than your school's existing math curriculum for 3rd graders. You would randomly assign a large number of 3rd grade students to either an intervention group, which uses the new curriculum, or to a control group, which uses the existing curriculum. You would then measure the math achievement of both groups over time. The difference in math achievement between the two groups would represent the effect of the new curriculum compared to the existing curriculum. (p. 1)

There are many problems, however, with using this type of ostensibly "rigorous" methodology to validate the success of multiple intelligences in the classroom. First, multiple intelligences do not represent a specific program such as, for example, Direct Instruction (Marchand-Martella, Slocum, & Martella, 2003), which is implemented uniformly by all trained teachers. As can be seen from reading the previous chapters of this book, MI represents a wide range of techniques, programs, attitudes, tools, strategies, and methods, and each teacher is encouraged to develop his or her own unique approach to implementing them. Therefore, it is impractical to conduct controlled studies of the kind Willingham demands since multiple intelligences in one classroom could be very different from multiple intelligences in another classroom and because even the "control classroom" would probably be using multiple intelligence strategies to some extent. (In other words, how do you find a "pure" MI classroom and a control group that uses absolutely no MI to compare it with?) Second, to demand a certain level of statistical significance from a study, as Willingham does, is to risk rejecting an educational intervention simply for "missing the cut" (e.g., if the level of statistical significance were .05, then a level of .06 would be considered "insignificant"). McCloskey and Ziliak (2008) suggest that using statistical significance as a quantitative analysis tool is often misguided even in the hard sciences. Third, to reduce the success or failure of a study to mere numbers is to reject other valid sources of a program's effectiveness, including individual case studies of children's learning improvement, parent reports of improved attitudes toward school, and documentation of learning progress through projects, problem solving, and portfolios (see Chapter 10). The demand for quantitative precision in education is an unfortunate nod toward *positivism*—the idea that ultimate truth can be expressed only through numbers or similarly precise scientific formulations (see Comte, 1988). There are many other thinkers in the Western intellectual tradition who argue for the validity of qualitative forms of research (see, for example, Dilthey, 1989; Gadamer, 2005; and Polyani, 1974), and it is methodologies derived from these philosophers that are especially appropriate to use in guiding educational research (see, for example, Denzin & Lincoln, 2005).

The fact is that there are many examples of successful implementation of MI theory in educational programs around the world (see also Chapter 16). In addition to the study mentioned by Willingham (Kornhaber, Fierros, & Veenema, 2003), which also noted increased levels of parent participation, deceased levels of discipline problems, and increased academic performance for students with learning difficulties, there have been a number of research projects initiated by Harvard Project Zero that have won accolades over the years, including Project Spectrum (Gardner, Feldman, & Krechevsky, 1998a, 1998b, 1998c), Practical Intelligences for School (Williams et al., 1996), and Arts Propel (Zessoules & Gardner, 1991), which was called by *Newsweek* magazine one of the two best educational programs in the United States (the other was the graduate school of the California Institute of Technology [Chideya, 1991]). The American Educational Research Association has had a special interest group (MI-SIG) dedicated to multiple intelligences research since 1999, where researchers have presented hundreds of papers providing validation of MI in numerous educational contexts. (MI-SIG hosts an online database of over 200 doctoral dissertation abstracts concerned with multiple intelligences that can be accessed at the following URL: http://209.216.233.245/aerami/dissertation.php.) To celebrate the 20th anniversary of multiple intelligences theory, an entire issue of the prestigious *Teachers College Record* at Columbia University was dedicated to the work of multiple intelligences researchers and theoreticians in 2004 (Shearer, 2004). In addition, the educational literature is replete with examples of individual schools and teachers who have shared in different ways their successes in implementing MI theory (see, for example, Campbell & Campbell, 2000; Greenhawk, 1997; Hoerr, 2000; and Kunkel, 2007). To reject MI theory as not research-based simply because there are no inappropriately precise research studies that attempt to mimic research from the hard sciences is to deprive children of a wealth of positive interventions that can open new doors to the world of knowledge.

Criticism #3: MI Theory Dumbs Down the Curriculum to Make All Students Mistakenly Believe They Are Smart

Some critics have accused MI practitioners of using superficial applications of MI theory—strategies of which even Gardner himself would not approve. Willingham (2004), for example, has criticized previous editions of this very book for its "trivial ideas" (he cites two spelling strategies—singing spelling words and spelling with leaves and twigs—as his examples of trivial applications). Collins (1998) criticizes strategies from another multiple intelligences curriculum guide (not by this author) referring to a unit concerned with learning about the oceans, where students build boats and role-play at being sea creatures. He writes of a child using bodily-kinesthetic intelligence to learn U.S. history: "How deeply can a student comprehend a given topic by relying on his strongest intelligence? Using his hands, Dave may be able to learn about the boats of the settlers, but can a kinesthetic approach help him understand central historical issues, like the reasons the Europeans came to America in the first place?" (p. 96). Similarly, critics have suggested that MI theory promulgates an artificial "feel-good" attitude where every child is told that he or she is smart. Barnett, Ceci, and Williams (2006) write: ". . . mere relabeling may not have a permanent curative effect. . . . Focusing on the label rather than on meaningful performances that demonstrate skill may lead children to become further disillusioned once the first blush passes." They indicate that "the focus must be on displaying meaningful skills and competencies, not simply on feeling that one is smart" (p. 101).

Response to Criticism #3

Willingham was wrong to take two spelling strategies out of a book containing over a thousand ideas and make them represent the whole of *Multiple Intelligences in the Classroom* (this, I believe, is known as a "straw man" argument and is an example of a logical fallacy). If all a teacher did to apply MI theory in the classroom was to use these two spelling strategies, I too would criticize the effort. But the intention of this book (and many others like it, I believe) is to show how MI theory can be used in the service of a wide range of practical pedagogical goals, from lower-order rote skills like spelling (which some teachers actually do care about!) to higher-order thinking strategies such as those used in the Christopherian encounters discussed in Chapter 12 (see also Figure 12.1 for an example of a clear differentiation between levels of cognitive complexity using MI theory).

It is true that during my 22 years of training teachers in MI I have all too often seen teachers take the easy way out—believing, for instance, that "rapping math facts" meant they were doing multiple intelligences. But I have also seen many wonderfully original ideas related to MI theory come out of the minds of experienced teachers over the years. Collins (1998) doubts whether it is possible to use bodily-kinesthetic intelligence to teach the historical factors that led Europeans to come to America. However, a well-designed role-play that imaginatively puts students at Plymouth Rock on November 11, 1620, and has them improvise reasons why they decided to leave England gives the highly dramatic learner an opportunity to think this objective through in a highly physical way.

It is also true that it is not enough merely to tell students that they are smart in eight different ways and expect them to blossom. This has to be followed up with solid academic effort leading to tangible improvements in knowledge of history, math, science, reading, and other basic subjects. The argument of MI theory is that it is not enough to produce this kind of understanding of the disciplines through textbooks, lectures, and standardized tests, but that *something more* is required. Students need to investigate ideas in world history, chemistry, ecology, literature, economics, algebra, and other domains by involving their whole selves (and whole brains), and this includes using their bodies, imagination, social sensibilities, emotions, and naturalistic inclinations, as well as their verbal and reasoning skills.

It is interesting to note that most of the criticisms of MI theory have come from academics and journalists—people who are usually far removed from the classroom. Few criticisms actually come from those who have *applied* the theory in their classrooms and seen it make a difference in their students' lives. This suggests a profound split between generalists, who can find lots of logical holes in MI theory, and practitioners, who are too busy looking for ways to motivate children and for methods to turn their lives around to worry about a few logical inconsistencies or insufficiencies.

MI theory was not originally designed by Howard Gardner as an educational model to be applied in the classroom. He initially wanted to convince academic psychometricians that there was another, broader way of conceiving intelligence. Ironically, despite arousing controversy, he seems to have failed in this effort. And yet, unexpectedly, he found teachers responding enthusiastically to his model because it filled a need that had not been met by an educational establishment too concerned with standardized measures and lock-step textbook approaches to learning. Instead of treating children as colorless denizens of a bell curve, MI theory revealed the positive qualities of each child and provided practical ways for each child to experience success in the classroom. Thus, the most authentic refutation of the critics of MI can be found in the children themselves. Whenever a light goes on in a child's mind in a well-designed MI classroom, the argument supporting MI theory becomes that much stronger and clearer.

For Further Study

1. Read some of the articles critical of multiple intelligences cited in this chapter (e.g., Barnett et al., 2006; Brody, 2006; Collins, 1998; Gottfredson, 2004; Traub, 1998; Visser et al., 2006; Waterhouse, 2006; Willingham, 2004).

Which aspects of their criticism do you agree with? Which aspects do you disagree with? Does your attitude toward MI theory change as a result of reading this critical literature? If so, how?

2. Howard Gardner has provided a number of responses to criticisms of MI theory, including to some of the above-mentioned authors (Gardner, 2006a, 2006b, 2006c; Gardner & Moran, 2006). Read the original critics and then some of his responses to them, and evaluate the success or failure of his defense of MI theory.

3. In other writing (Armstrong, 2006), I have suggested that today's educational climate is characterized by an overemphasis on academic performance as measured by standardized testing and an underemphasis on the education of the whole child. To what extent has this restrictive atmosphere given rise to the criticisms noted above?

4. Using some of the materials discussed above, organize a debate on MI theory, with one individual or team taking a pro-MI stance and the other individual or team taking an anti-MI stance. Afterward, discuss who did the most effective job of defending their position.

5. Interview colleagues and other school personnel about their attitudes toward MI theory and whether they have changed their opinion about it over the past 10 years. If they have a different attitude about it now than previously, ask them to share the reasons for their change in opinion.

16

MI Theory Around the Globe

I have had the opportunity . . . to travel to many other nations. It has been fascinating to discover the ways in which [MI] theory has been interpreted and the activities that it has catalyzed.

—Howard Gardner

One of the most exciting developments of the theory of multiple intelligences has been its international impact. MI theory is now a part of the educational scene to one degree or another in most of the nations of the world. In some cases, its impact has been at the governmental level, with MI incorporated into the national education initiatives of some countries. In other cases, its impact has been more local, with individual schools and teachers taking the theory and applying it to the unique requirements of their own culture. In this chapter, we'll look at several ways in which MI theory has been applied in cultures around the world.

MI Theory at the Policymaking Level

There have been a number of cases in which MI theory has been incorporated at the highest levels of a nation's or international body's policymaking institutions. According to Gardner (2006a), ". . . I have been amazed to learn of jurisdictions in which the terminology of MI has been incorporated into white papers, recommendations by ministries, and even legislation. . . . I have heard from reliable sources that MI approaches are part of the policy landscape in such diverse lands as Australia, Bangladesh, Canada, China, Denmark, Ireland and the Netherlands" (p. 248). In Bangladesh, for example, with support from UNICEF, the government initiated its Intensive District Approach for All Learners project in the 1990s (Chanda, 2001). As part of this effort, tens of thousands of teachers were trained in MI theory through the initiative Multiple Ways of Teaching and Learning (Ellison & Rothenberger, 1999). India's National Curriculum Framework for School Education requires teachers to be familiar with the concepts of multiple intelligences (Saranga-pani, 2000). In Geneva, Switzerland, the prestigious International Baccalaure-ate (IB) Organization, which offers programs to over 600,000 students in 128 countries, has recently acknowledged Gardner's role in influencing its own approach to learning: "Howard Gardner has been influential in changing views about learning and the ways we learn. Access and equity within the IB today is much wider than it was previously. It is acknowledged that all students have strengths and weaknesses which must be supported in a strategic way for them to meet their potential" (Reed, 2007).

MI Theory at the Academic Level

Multiple intelligences theory has been the subject of increasing academic research in universities around the world. I have heard personally by e-mail from scores of individuals who are pursuing their master's theses and doctoral dissertations on MI theory at institutions such as Middle East Technical University in Ankara, Turkey; the University of Jordan in Amman, Jordan; Mulawaram University in Samarinda, Indonesia; and Ferhat Abbes University in Setif, Algeria. A growing number of internationally oriented academic studies on MI theory have been published in peer-reviewed journals. One topic that has been given much attention is the estimation of one's multiple intelligences profile compared to estimations of MI profiles in one's parents, children, and/or partner. Journal articles dedicated to this subject have covered populations from Namibia, Zimbabwe, Zambia, and South Africa

(Furnham & Akanda, 2004), Malaysia (Swami, Furnham, & Kannan, 2006), China (Furnham & Wu, 2008), and Japan (Furnham & Fukumoto, 2008). Other international studies have looked at MI and information literacy education in Singapore (Mohktar, Majid, & Fu, 2007), musical aptitude and multiple intelligences among Chinese gifted students in Hong Kong (Chan, 2007), and improved academic performance in Kuwaiti middle school reading programs using multiple intelligences (Al-Bahan, 2006).

MI Theory at the Individual School Level

Thousands of schools around the world have applied MI theory to their curricula in different ways. A teacher in Argentina, for example, writes about how she taught English as a second language to a group of 1st grade students. Developing a unit on "helpers" (postman, firefighter, doctor, nurse), students visited service-oriented people around town, kept journals, wrote letters, built a model of the community, created a mural, made musical instruments, and reflected orally on their learning while looking in a mirror (Ribot, 2004). In Chile, the Amancay Elementary School of La Florida in Santiago has put on multiple intelligences theme weeks. During the "Week of the Arts," they have a day when children talk with real writers and a day when children paint with painters. They also have a "Scientific Week" that includes students' sharing their own inventions and a "Sea Month" focused on the naturalist intelligence (Gundian & Anrìquez, 1999). In the Philippines, the MI International High School in Quezon City puts MI theory to work in the cause of promoting entrepreneurship among its students. Students are challenged to develop real-world business plans based on ideas that emerge from MI lessons. A linguistic group, for example, developed Flash Range, a media center that creates books for teens that deal with environmental and personal and emotional growth issues. A musical group created a business called Boom Box Music, which offers musical composition and record production services. A group of people-smart students conceptualized their own family restaurant, Pastuchi, featuring a fusion of Italian and Japanese cuisines. The school has an annual bazaar that sells products made by the various businesses and then donates the profits to a charity that helps the poor (*Manila Times,* 2008).

MI Theory at the Community Level

Beyond formal schooling applications, multiple intelligences theory has also had an impact on the popular culture in many countries around the world. In China, for example, the Multiple Intelligences Education Society promotes MI theory through seminars, magazine articles, radio programs, and TV interviews, all coordinated as part of an effort to reform parent education, vocational education, and the formal examination process (Chen, Moran, & Gardner, in press). In Denmark, the industrial manufacturer Danfoss has created a theme park, Danfoss Universe, that incorporates many strategies and ideas from multiple intelligences. They have essentially created an interactive MI museum, where children and adults participate in over 50 activities designed to both test their multiple intelligences and also raise awareness concerning the many different ways of being smart. Activities include turning physical movements into electronic art, negotiating an obstacle course, cooperating with others to move a robot, playing a theremin (an electronic musical instrument played without touching it), unscrambling melodies, being a music producer, putting together tangrams, solving word and visual puzzles, building structures, making predictions about natural phenomena, speaking a foreign language, transmitting images just by thinking, and building a bridge across a lake to an island. Danfoss Universe also contains exhibits for experiencing the primal force of a volcano, a geyser, strong hot winds, and other natural phenomena. As a final example, in the Chinese Special Administrative Region of Macau, multiple intelligences theory appeared in a very unlikely place: the grocery store. Gardner (2006a) writes: "In Macau I received a tour of the island from Mr. U. The next morning he picked me up for my presentation at the Education Ministry. 'Look what my wife picked up at the grocery store,' he said. He showed me a multicolored flyer that depicted each of the intelligences on a separate leaf. The flyer, replete with illustrations, charts, and figures, was an advertisement for Frisogrow processed milk. . . . The consumer was informed, 'If you drink our milk, you will develop each of the different intelligences.' Never before had it occurred to me that the MI in the theory might stand for MIlk!" (p. 245).

What Happens When MI Theory Connects with Another Culture

It's fascinating to study the interaction of MI theory with different cultures around the world. One must keep in mind that MI theory itself is a cultural product emanating from contemporary U.S. culture. As such, it embodies many values and ideals that are considered important in the United States, including pluralism, pragmatism, and egalitarianism. What happens when these U.S. values contact the values of another culture is quite instructive. Often it appears that MI theory gains significantly from its contact with another culture. In Norway, for example, education and the outdoors are given much greater emphasis than they are in the United States. Norwegian education incorporates into its curriculum an important institution called an *utskole,* or "outdoor school." It is part of a larger framework in Norwegian culture referred to as *friluftsliv,* which can be roughly translated as "outdoor nature life" and which encompasses a wide range of physical activities and attitudes regarding nature such as hiking, skiing, ecological awareness, and maritime activities. As part of the *utskole*, most elementary schools in Norway have a structure called a *gapahuk*, which is often just a hut or lean-to structure set apart from the regular school building and situated in a natural setting. Students engage in a variety of curriculum-related activities in the *gapahuk.* In 2005, I had the opportunity to visit a *gapahuk* while speaking in Norway and saw students learning about Norwegian history by making ancient cooking implements from natural sources such as branches and twigs. Every student in elementary school in Norway has the opportunity to spend one day a week outdoors in the *gapahuk*. There are also kindergartens in Norway where children spend all day, every day, engaged in an outdoor setting. This contrasts radically with the United States, where outdoor activities, if they occur at all, are usually short and infrequent. The Norwegian experience offers to MI theory a whole new attitude toward the naturalist intelligence (and to bodily-kinesthetic intelligence as well), suggesting that these neglected intelligences be honored in a serious way by delegating a good part of the school week to their robust development in an outdoor setting.

At other times, the theory of multiple intelligences represents a challenge to certain long-established values of a culture. In South Korea, for example, traditional linguistic and logical-mathematical learning is valued so highly that it is often difficult to change parent attitudes. Two South Korean university professors, who sought to replicate Harvard Project Zero's Project Spectrum for young children there, noted the following: "In Korea, parents believe that high academic achievement means excellent achievement in linguistic and mathematics. Children who have a weakness in linguistic and mathematics consider themselves as helpless at school" (Jung & Kim, 2005, p. 585). These beliefs have deep cultural origins, according to Jung and Kim: "South Korea is a competitive-oriented society with an examination-oriented culture that continues to influence education today. The state examination is considered to be most difficult; one should prepare for it from birth. By tradition, pencils and cotton threads are displayed at a baby's first birthday, which is the grandest celebration. Family members encourage the baby to grab a pencil, which means the baby will study hard and pass the state examination" (pp. 591–592). The Project Spectrum assessment tools (described in Chapter 10) were implemented successfully in this South Korean setting and were viewed as a way to help undo some of these deeply entrenched ideas about learning and human development. As Jung and Kim wrote: "The Project Spectrum approach based on MI theory facilitates a child-oriented education by assuming equality and independence among multiple intelligences. . . . Under such an assessment system, children/students will be able to avoid the 'negative self image' too often experienced in the Korean education system and develop into successful and active learners" (p. 591).

However, even in cultures that have long histories of formal examinations, there are opportunities to witness the goodness of fit between MI theory and many other aspects of those cultures. In Japan, for example, where students attend "cram schools" in an attempt to improve their chances of passing university entrance examinations, there are many different aspects of ancient Japanese culture that are harmonious with MI theory. The ancient temple school of Japan, referred to as *terakoya,* taught traditional literacy and numeracy skills to Japanese citizens from all walks of life (Chen et al., in press). But Japanese culture also provided many other entry points into the multiple intelligences through calligraphy, haiku, the Kabuki theater, the traditional tea ceremony, and a wide range of martial arts traditions including sumo wrestling, judo, and jujutsu. In my own work as an MI consultant, I have been involved in a project to integrate multiple intelligence activities into a group of cram schools in Tokyo, to help combat social problems of youth including school refusal, bullying, and social isolation.

The remarkable thing about multiple intelligences internationally is that it seems to be finding a place for itself in widely diverse cultural contexts, even in cultures that have values that seem to conflict radically with the pluralistic and egalitarian underpinnings of MI theory. The theory of multiple intelligences has found its way into the schools and university systems of Iran and Saudi Arabia; *Multiple Intelligences in the Classroom* has been translated into Farsi, Arabic, and 17 other languages. MI has been taught in the madrassas (or holy Islamic schools) of Pakistan (Schmidle, 2007); and according to Gardner, his book *Frames of Mind* was one of only two books in English found in a library in North Korea (the other book was Michael Moore's *Stupid White Men* [Gardner, 2006a]). I think a big reason for the widespread success of MI theory internationally has been its friendliness to cultural diversity (see Chapter 13). At the core of the model there is the requirement that each intelligence must be *culturally valued* in order to find a place for itself on Gardner's list of intelligences. Implicit in this requirement is the observation that each of the elements of the multiple intelligences—music, words, logic, pictures, social interaction, physical expression, inner reflection, and nature appreciation—*can be found in all cultures*. Thus, each country around the world has the opportunity to see its own indigenous traditions honored and celebrated through MI theory.

For Further Study

1. Choose an indigenous culture from any country in the world (including from within the United States) and describe in detail how each of the eight intelligences is celebrated and honored.

2. Make contact with a school using MI theory in another country (including any of those listed above or those that might be found on the Internet). Initiate a cultural exchange of ideas regarding specific applications of multiple intelligences.

3. Integrate an MI-oriented practice used in another culture into your own school or classroom (e.g., the *utskole* or "outdoor school" from Norway for the naturalist intelligence, judo from Japan for the bodily-kinesthetic intelligence, etc.). Evaluate its effectiveness.

4. To what extent does MI theory reflect the values of late-20th- and early-21st-century U.S. culture? Examine the ways in which those values either connect or collide with the values of another culture.

Appendix A

Related MI Resources

Books

Armstrong, T. (1999). *7 kinds of smart: Discovering and identifying your multiple intelligences—Revised and updated with information on two new kinds of smart.* New York: Plume.

Armstrong, T. (2000). *In their own way: Discovering and encouraging your child's multiple intelligences.* New York: Tarcher/Putnam.

Armstrong, T. (2003). *The multiple intelligences of reading and writing: Making the words come alive.* Alexandria, VA: ASCD.

Armstrong, T. (2003). *You're smarter than you think: A kid's guide to multiple intelligences.* Minneapolis, MN: Free Spirit Publishing.

Baum, S., Viens, J., & Slatin, B. (2005). *Multiple intelligences in the elementary classroom: A teachers toolkit.* New York: Teachers College Press.

Borenson, H. (2007). *The Hands-On Equations home packet.* Allentown, PA: Borenson and Associates Inc.

Bower, B., Lobdell, J., & Swensen, L. (1994). *History alive! Engaging all learners in the diverse classroom.* Menlo Park, CA: Addison-Wesley.

Campbell, B. (1994). *The multiple intelligences handbook.* Tucson, AZ: Zephyr Press.

Campbell, B., & Campbell, L. (2000). *Multiple intelligences and student achievement: Success stories from six schools.* Alexandria, VA: ASCD.

Campbell, L., Campbell, B., & Dickinson, D. (2003). *Teaching and learning through multiple intelligences* (3rd ed.). Upper Saddle River, NJ: Allyn & Bacon.

Carreiro, P. (1998). *Tales of thinking: Multiple intelligences in the classroom.* Portland, ME: Stenhouse Publications.

Faculty of the New City School. (1994). *Celebrating multiple intelligences.* St. Louis, MO: Author.

Faculty of the New City School. (1996). *Succeeding with multiple intelligences: Teaching through the personal intelligences.* St. Louis, MO: Author. (Order from New City School, 5209 Waterman Ave., St. Louis, MO, 63108.)

Fogarty, R., & Bellanca, J. (1995). *Multiple intelligences: A collection.* Thousand Oaks, CA: Corwin Press.

Fogarty, R., & Stoehr, J. (1995). *Integrating the curriculum with multiple intelligences.* Palatine, IL: Skylight Publications.

Gardner, H. (1991). *To open minds.* New York: Basic Books.

Gardner, H. (1993). *Frames of mind: The theory of multiple intelligences—10th anniversary edition.* New York: Basic Books.

Gardner, H. (1994). *Creating minds: An anatomy of creativity seen through the lives of Freud, Einstein, Picasso, Stravinsky, Eliot, Graham, and Gandhi.* New York: Basic Books.

Gardner, H. (1998). *Extraordinary minds.* New York: Basic Books.

Gardner, H. (1999). *The disciplined mind: What all students should understand.* New York: Simon & Schuster.

Gardner, H. (1999). *Intelligence reframed: Multiple intelligences for the 21st century.* New York: Basic Books.

Gardner, H. (2006). *Multiple intelligences: New horizons in theory and practice.* New York: Basic Books.

Gardner, H., Feldman, D. H., & Krechevsky, M. (Eds.). (1998). *Project Zero frameworks for early childhood education, Vol. 1: Building on children's strengths: The experience of Project Spectrum.* New York: Teachers College Press.

Gardner, H., Feldman, D. H., & Krechevsky, M. (Eds.). (1998). *Project Zero frameworks for early childhood education, Vol. 2: Project Spectrum: Early learning activities.* New York: Teachers College Press.

Gardner, H., Feldman, D. H., & Krechevsky, M. (Eds.). (1998). *Project Zero frameworks for early childhood education, Vol. 3: Project Spectrum: Preschool assessment handbook.* New York: Teachers College Press.

Haggerty, B. (1994). *Nurturing intelligences*. Menlo Park, CA: Addison-Wesley.

Hirsch, R. A. (2004). *Early childhood curriculum: Incorporating multiple intelligences, developmentally appropriate practices, and play*. Upper Saddle River, NJ: Pearson/Allyn & Bacon.

Hoerr, T. R. (2000). *Becoming a multiple intelligences school*. Alexandria, VA: ASCD.

Kornhaber, M., Fierros, E., & Veenema, S. (2003). *Multiple intelligences: Best ideas from research and practice*. Upper Saddle River, NJ: Pearson/Allyn & Bacon.

Lazear, D. (1999). *Eight ways of knowing: Teaching for multiple intelligences*. Palatine, IL: Skylight.

Lazear, D. (1999). *The intelligence curriculum: Using MI to develop your students' full potential*. Tucson, AZ: Zephyr Press.

Lazear, D. (1999). *Multiple intelligence approaches to assessment: Solving the assessment conundrum*. Tucson, AZ: Zephyr Press.

Lazear, D. (2001). *Seven pathways of learning: Teaching students and parents about multiple intelligences*. Tucson, AZ: Zephyr Press.

Lazear, D. (2003). *Eight ways of teaching: The artistry of teaching with multiple intelligences*. Thousand Oaks, CA: Corwin Press.

Lazear, D. (2004). *Higher order thinking the multiple intelligences way*. Tucson, AZ: Zephyr Press.

Margulies, N. (1995). *The magic seven: Tools for building multiple intelligences*. Tucson, AZ: Zephyr Press.

McKenzie, W. (2005). *Multiple intelligences and instructional technology* (2nd ed.). Washington, DC: International Society for Technology in Education.

Nelson, K. (1998). *Developing students' multiple intelligences*. New York: Scholastic.

Puchta, H., & Rinvolocri, M. (2007). *Multiple intelligences in EFL: Exercises for secondary and adult students*. Cambridge, UK: Cambridge University Press.

Shearer, B. (1996). *The MIDAS: A guide to assessment and education for the multiple intelligences*. Columbus, OH: Greyden Press.

Silver, H. F., Strong, R. W., & Perini, M. J. (2000). *So each may learn: Integrating learning styles and multiple intelligences*. Alexandria, VA: ASCD.

Stefanakis, E. H. (2002). *Multiple intelligences and portfolios: A window into the learner's mind*. Portsmouth, NH: Heinemann.

Teele, S. (2000). *Rainbows of intelligence: Exploring how students learn*. Thousand Oaks, CA: Corwin Press.

Teele, S. (2004). *Overcoming barricades to reading: A multiple intelligences approach.* Thousand Oaks, CA: Corwin Press.

Viens, J., & Kallenbach, S. (2004). *Multiple intelligences and adult literacy: A sourcebook for practitioners.* New York: Teachers College Press.

Wahl, M. (1997). *Math for humans: Teaching math through 7 intelligences.* Langley, WA: LivnLern Press. (Order from 416 Fourth St., Langley, WA 98260.)

Williams, R. B. (2007). *Multiple intelligences for differentiated learning.* Thousand Oaks, CA: Corwin Press.

Zwiers, J. (2004). *Developing academic thinking skills in grades 6–12: A handbook of multiple intelligences activities.* Newark, DE: International Reading Association.

Videos and DVDs

Videos

Armstrong, T. (1997). *Multiple intelligences: Discovering the giftedness in all.* Port Chester, NY: National Professional Resources, Inc.

Armstrong, T. (2003). *The multiple intelligences of reading and writing: Making the words come alive.* Alexandria, VA: ASCD.

Gardner, H. (1995). *How are kids smart? Multiple intelligences in the classroom.* Port Chester, NY: National Professional Resources, Inc.

Gardner, H., Goleman, D., & Csikszentmihalyi, M. (1998). *Optimizing intelligences: Thinking, emotion, and creativity.* Port Chester, NY: National Professional Resources, Inc.

Hoerr, T. (2000). *Becoming a multiple intelligences school.* Alexandria, VA: ASCD.

Teele, S. (2000). *Rainbows of intelligence: Raising student performance through multiple intelligences.* Port Chester, NY: National Professional Resources, Inc.

DVDs

BBC Worldwide Ltd. (2007). *Battle of the brains: The case for multiple intelligences.* London: Author.

Feinstein, S. (2007). *Multiple intelligences.* Monterey, CA: Coaches Choice.

Appendix B

Related Books on MI Teaching

Linguistic Intelligence

Ashton-Warner, S. (1986). *Teacher.* New York: Simon & Schuster.

Bissex, G. (1980). *Gnys at work: A child learns to write and read.* Cambridge, MA: Harvard University Press.

Graves, D., & Stuart, V. (1987). *Write from the start: Tapping your child's natural writing ability.* New York: New American Library.

Rico, G. L. (2000). *Writing the natural way.* Los Angeles: Jeremy P. Tarcher.

Trelease, J. (2006). *The read-aloud handbook.* Harmondsworth, UK: Penguin.

Logical-Mathematical Intelligence

Allison, L. (1976). *Blood and guts: A working guide to your own insides.* Boston: Little, Brown & Co. (Grades 5–12)

Burns, M. (2006). *The I hate mathematics! book.* Boston: Little, Brown & Co.

Jacobs, H. (1994). *Mathematics: A human endeavor* (3rd ed.). San Francisco: W. H. Freeman. (Grades 9–12)

Lorton, M. B. (1995). *Mathematics their way.* Menlo Park, CA: Addison-Wesley.

Stein, S. (1980). *The science book.* New York: Workman. (Grades 4–7)

Spatial Intelligence

DeMille, R. (1997). *Put your mother on the ceiling: Children's imagination games* (5th ed.). Gouldsboro, ME: Gestalt Journal Press.

Edwards, B. (1999). *The new drawing on the right side of the brain.* Los Angeles: Jeremy P. Tarcher.

McKim, R. H. (2003). *Experiences in visual thinking.* London: Thomson Learning Custom Publishing.

Samples, R. (1993). *The metaphoric mind.* Austin, TX: Jalmar Press.

Warner, S. (1989). *Encouraging the artist in your child.* New York: St. Martin's Press.

Bodily-Kinesthetic Intelligence

Benzwie, T. (1988). *A moving experience: Dance for lovers of children and the child within.* Tucson, AZ: Zephyr Press.

Cobb, V. (1984). *Science experiments you can eat* (rev. ed.). New York: Harper Trophy.

Gilbert, A. G. (2002). *Teaching the 3 Rs through movement experiences.* Silver Spring, MD: National Dance Education Organization.

Schneider, T. (1976). *Everybody's a winner: A kids' guide to new sports and fitness.* Boston: Little, Brown & Co.

Spolin, V. (1986). *Theater games for the classroom.* Evanston, IL: Northwestern University Press.

Musical Intelligence

Bonny, H., & Savary, L. (1990). *Music and your mind.* Barrytown, NY: Station Hill Press.

Brewer, C. B., & Campbell, D. G. (1991). *Rhythms of learning.* Tucson, AZ: Zephyr Press.

Goodkin, D. (2003). *Play, sing, and dance: An introduction to Orff Schulwerk.* New York: European American Music Corporation.

Houlahan, M., & Tacka, P. (2008). *Kodaly today: A cognitive approach to elementary music education.* Oxford, UK: Oxford University Press.

Judy, S. (1990). *Making music for the joy of it.* Los Angeles: Jeremy P. Tarcher.

Merritt, S. (1996). *Mind, music, and imagery: 40 exercises using music to stimulate creativity and self-awareness.* New York: New American Library.

Interpersonal Intelligence

Johnson, D. W., Johnson, R. T., & Holubec, E. J. (1994). *The new circles of learning: Cooperation in the classroom and school.* Alexandria, VA: ASCD.

Orlick, T. (2006). *Cooperative games and sports: Joyful activities for everyone.* Champaign, IL: Human Kinetics Publishers.

Sobel, J. (1984). *Everybody wins: 393 noncompetitive games for young children.* New York: Walker & Co.

Wade, R. C. (1991). *Joining hands: From personal to planetary friendship in the primary classroom.* Tucson, AZ: Zephyr Press.

Weinstein, M., & Goodman, J. (1992). *Playfair: Everybody's guide to noncompetitive play.* San Luis Obispo, CA: Impact.

Intrapersonal Intelligence

Armstrong, T. (2007). *The human odyssey: Navigating the twelve stages of life.* New York: Sterling Publishing.

Desetta, A. (Ed.). (2005). *The courage to be yourself: True stories by teens about cliques, conflicts, and avoiding peer pressure.* Minneapolis, MN: Free Spirit Publishing.

Fox, A., Ruth, K., & Verdick, E. (2005). *Too stressed to think? A teen guide to staying sane when life makes you crazy.* Minneapolis, MN: Free Spirit Publishing.

Gibbons, M. (1991). *How to become an expert: Discover, research, and build a project in your chosen field.* Tucson, AZ: Zephyr Press.

Oaklander, V. (1988). *Windows to our children.* Gouldsboro, ME: Gestalt Journal Press.

Naturalist Intelligence

Beame, R. (2004). *Backyard explorer kit: 3-in-1 collectors kit.* New York: Workman Publications.

Cornell, J. (1998). *Sharing nature with children—20th anniversary edition.* Nevada City, CA: Dawn Publications.

Lingelbach, J. R. (Ed.). (2000). *Hands-on nature: Information and activities for exploring the environment with children* (rev. ed.). Quechee, VT: Vermont Institute of Natural Science.

Louv, R. (2008). *Last child in the woods: Saving our children from nature-deficit disorder.* New York: Algonquin Books/Workman.

Marina, L. (1991). *Teaching kids to love the earth*. Minneapolis, MN: University of Minnesota Press.

Mitchell, A. (2008). *The young naturalist kid kit*. Evelyth, MN: Usborne Books.

Roth, K. (1999). *Naturalist intelligence: An introduction to Gardner's eighth intelligence*. Thousand Oaks, CA: Corwin Press.

Examples of MI Lessons and Programs

The following examples of lessons and programs based upon MI theory are designed for different grade levels. Note that in some cases MI theory is used to provide the basis for the development of a program (e.g., a primary-level reading list); in other cases, MI theory is limited to the development of ideas that can be incorporated into existing curricular frameworks. In some cases, the educational focus is on the development of skills (e.g., learning how to multiply by 7); in other cases, the emphasis is more on concepts (e.g., understanding Boyle's Law). In every lesson, however, activities spanning all eight intelligences have been used to achieve the given instructional objective.

Example One

Level: Preschool
Subject: Shapes
Objective: To teach students to recognize circles

Students will experience different types of circles in the following ways:
- Make a group circle by joining hands. [Interpersonal, Bodily-Kinesthetic]
- Make circles by using their bodies. [Intrapersonal, Bodily-Kinesthetic]
- Look for circles around the classroom. [Spatial]
- Make circles in art projects. [Spatial, Bodily-Kinesthetic]
- Sing "The Circle Game" by Joni Mitchell and other circle songs (including "rounds," which are themselves musically circular). [Musical]
- Make up stories about circles. [Linguistic]
- Compare sizes of circles (from small to large). [Spatial, Logical-Mathematical]
- Find circular forms in nature. [Naturalist]

Example Two

Level: K–1st grade
Subject: Reading
Objective: To help develop a "book positive" attitude in students
Materials: Books that combine linguistic intelligence with one or more other intelligences

A classroom library will be stocked with books of the following types:
- Books with read-along CDs [Linguistic]
- Three-dimensional pop-up books [Spatial]
- Wordless books (pictorial stories) [Spatial]
- Touch-and-feel books [Bodily-Kinesthetic]
- Books with sing-along CDs [Musical]
- Books with computerized keyboards and song lyrics [Musical]
- Science fun books [Logical-Mathematical]
- Counting books [Logical-Mathematical]
- "This is me"–type books [Intrapersonal]
- Books on emotional themes, such as loss or anger [Intrapersonal]
- Interactive books [Interpersonal]
- Books with nature themes [Naturalist]
- Books that come with naturalist tools (e.g., book on insects with magnifying glass) [Naturalist]

Example Three

Level: 2nd–3rd grade
Subject: Math
Objectives: To help students master the multiplication facts for the 7s; to reinforce the concept of what it means to "multiply"

Students will do one of these activities each day during math class:

- Count to 70, standing up and clapping on every seventh number. [Bodily-Kinesthetic]
- Sing the "Multiplication Rock" song for the 7s. [Musical]
- Chant the numbers 1 to 70, placing special emphasis on every seventh number. [Musical]
- Complete a "hundreds chart," coloring in every seventh number. [Spatial]
- Form circles of 10 students, each student wearing a number from 0 to 9. Starting with the 0, participants count off as they go around the circle (the second time around the circle, the 0 becomes a 10, the 1 an 11, and so on; the third time around, the 0 becomes a 20, the 1 a 21, and so on). As they count, participants pass a ball of yarn around the circle, unrolling it as they do so. The first person grasps the end of the yarn, and every seventh person after that also grasps a section before passing the ball of yarn on. On reaching the count of 70, students will see that the yarn creates a geometric design. [Spatial, Bodily-Kinesthetic, Interpersonal]
- Create geometric designs for the 7s on a board with yarn and nails or in a drawing using the strategy described above (i.e., use a circle numbered 0 to 9 and then connect with string or a line every seventh number up to 70). [Spatial]
- Listen to a story about the "As Much" brothers, who can touch things and see them multiply (e.g., when Seven Times As Much touches 3 golden hens, 21 golden hens appear). [Linguistic]
- Create before-and-after drawings based on the "As Much" brothers story (e.g., pictures of Seven Times As Much just before touching the three golden hens and just after touching them). [Spatial]

- Find natural forms that come in sevens (e.g., flowers), and explore math through nature's own multiples ("How many petals are there in six seven-petaled flowers?"). Do this with living forms in a natural setting. [Naturalist]

Example Four

Level: Upper elementary
Subject: History
Objective: To assist students in understanding the conditions that led to the development of Rhode Island in early U.S. history

Students will do one of these activities each day during history:
- Read textbook passages that give reasons for the settling of Rhode Island and discuss the material. [Linguistic]
- Create a time line of the events surrounding the development of Rhode Island. [Logical-Mathematical, Spatial]
- Study maps of the United States during the colonial era showing the progressive development of Rhode Island. [Spatial]
- Compare the settling of Rhode Island with the growth of an amoeba. [Naturalist]
- Act out the events surrounding the settling of Rhode Island. [Bodily-Kinesthetic, Interpersonal]
- Create a song that describes the circumstances leading to the settling of Rhode Island. [Musical]
- Divide into groups representing different colonies; groups then relate to the development of a new group of students that becomes Rhode Island. [Interpersonal, Bodily-Kinesthetic]
- Relate the settling of Rhode Island to students' own need or desire to break away from authority at times (e.g., conflicts with parents/ teachers). [Intrapersonal]

Example Five

Level: Junior high school
Subject: Algebra
Objective: To explain the function of x in an equation

- Students are provided with a verbal description of x ("x is an unknown"). [Linguistic]
- Students are given an equation (e.g., $2x + 1 = 5$) and shown how to solve for x. [Logical-Mathematical]
- Students are told that x is like a masked outlaw that needs to be unmasked and are asked to draw their own version of x. [Spatial]
- Students act out an algebraic equation; a student wearing a mask plays x, and other students represent numbers or functions. A designated student then "solves" the equation by removing students on both sides of the equation in a series of steps. For instance, in the equation $2x + 1 = 5$, one student is removed from the left side, and one from the right, then half the students are removed from the right, and half from the left, revealing x as 2 (who would then unmask himself to reveal the number 2). [Interpersonal, Bodily-Kinesthetic]
- Students perform algebraic equations using manipulatives (numbers and functions on a scale; sides must be kept in balance in order to solve). [Bodily-Kinesthetic]
- Students rhythmically repeat the following lyrics several times:

  x is a mystery
  you've gotta find a way
  to get him all alone
  so that he's gotta say his name

  Students can accompany their chanting with any available percussion instruments. [Musical]

- Students are asked, "What are the mysteries, or *x*s, in your own life?" Discuss how students "solve for *x*" in dealing with personal issues. [Intrapersonal]
- Students are told, "We go hunting for a little animal whose name we don't know, so we call it *x*. When we bag our game we pounce on it and give it its right name." According to Clark (1972), Albert Einstein's uncle used this particular strategy when teaching his nephew math! [Naturalist]

Example Six

Level: High school
Subject: Chemistry
Objective: To teach the concept of Boyle's Law

- Students are provided with a verbal definition of Boyle's Law: "For a fixed mass and temperature of gas, the pressure is inversely proportional to the volume." They discuss the definition. [Linguistic]
- Students are given a formula that describes Boyle's Law: $P \times V = K$. They solve specific problems connected to it. [Logical-Mathematical]
- Students are given a metaphor or visual image for Boyle's Law: "Imagine that you have a boil on your hand that you start to squeeze. As you squeeze it, the pressure builds. The more you squeeze, the higher the pressure, until the boil finally bursts and puss spurts out all over the room!" [Spatial]
- Students do the following experiment: They breathe air into their mouths so that their cheeks puff up slightly and are told not to swallow the air or let it out. Then they put all the air into one side of their mouth (less volume) and indicate whether pressure goes up or down (it goes up); then they're asked to release the air into both sides of their mouth (more volume) and asked to indicate whether pressure has gone up or down (it goes down). [Bodily-Kinesthetic]
- Students rhythmically repeat the following musical mnemonic:

    When the volume goes down
    The pressure goes up

The blood starts to boil
And a scream erupts
"I need more space
Or I'm going to frown"
The volume goes up
And the pressure goes down [Musical]

- Students become "molecules" of air in a "container" (a clearly defined corner of the classroom). They move at a constant rate (temperature) and cannot leave the container (constant mass). Gradually, the size of the container is reduced as two volunteers holding a piece of yarn representing one side of the container start moving it in on the "molecules." The smaller the space, the more pressure (i.e., bumping into each other) is observed; the greater the space, the less pressure. [Interpersonal, Bodily-Kinesthetic]
- Students do lab experiments that measure air pressure in sealed containers and chart pressure against volume. [Logical-Mathematical, Bodily-Kinesthetic]
- Students are asked about times in their lives when they were "under pressure": "Did you feel like you had a lot of space?" (Typical answer: lots of pressure/not much space.) Then students are asked about times when they felt little pressure (little pressure/lots of space). Students' experiences are related to Boyle's law. [Intrapersonal]
- Students are told about scuba diving guidelines that caution divers never to dive down deep with scuba equipment, take a deep breath, hold it, and then go up to the surface. In terms of Boyle's law, diving down deep increases pressure, taking a deep breath increases volume, going up to the surface decreases pressure, and, according to Boyle's law, this increases volume in the lungs; however, lungs have already expanded to maximum capacity. Students are asked to predict what might happen. (Answer: possible life-threatening condition with air embolisms forming in bloodstream). [Naturalist]

References

Al-Bahan, E. M. (2006, Spring). Multiple intelligences styles in relation to improved academic performance in Kuwaiti middle school reading. *Digest of Middle East Studies*, 18–34.

Armstrong, M. (1980). *Closely observed children.* London: Writers and Readers.

Armstrong, T. (1987a). Describing strengths in children identified as "learning disabled" using Howard Gardner's theory of multiple intelligences as an organizing framework. *Dissertation Abstracts International, 48,* 8A. (University Microfilms No. 8725-844)

Armstrong, T. (1987b). *In their own way: Discovering and encouraging your child's personal learning style.* New York: Tarcher/Putnam.

Armstrong, T. (1988). Learning differences—not disabilities. *Principal, 68*(1), 34–36.

Armstrong, T. (1997). *The myth of the ADD child: 50 ways to improve your child's behavior and attention span without drugs, labels, or coercion.* New York: Plume.

Armstrong, T. (1999a). *7 kinds of smart: Discovering and identifying your multiple intelligences—Revised and updated with information on two new kinds of smart.* New York: Plume.

Armstrong, T. (1999b). *ADD/ADHD alternatives in the classroom.* Alexandria, VA: ASCD.

Armstrong, T. (2003). *You're smarter than you think: A kid's guide to multiple intelligences.* Minneapolis, MN: Free Spirit Publishing.

Armstrong, T. (2005, September). Special education and the concept of neurodiversity. *New Horizons for Learning.* Retrieved June 23, 2008, from http://www.newhorizons. org/spneeds/inclusion/information/armstrong.htm

Armstrong, T. (2006). *The best schools: How human development research should inform educational practice.* Alexandria, VA: ASCD.

Armstrong, T. (In press). When cultures connect: Multiple intelligences as a successful American export to other countries. In J. Q. Chen, S. Moran, & H. Gardner (Eds.), *Multiple intelligences theory around the world*. San Francisco: Jossey-Bass.

Associated Press. (1988, October 25). Poll finds Americans are ignorant of science. *New York Times*, p. C10.

Barnett, S. M., Ceci, S. J., & Williams, W. M. (2006). Is the ability to make a bacon sandwich a mark of intelligence? and other issues: Some reflections on Gardner's theory of multiple intelligences. In J. A. Schaler (Ed.), *Howard Gardner under fire: The rebel psychologist faces his critics* (pp. 95–114). Chicago: Open Court.

Bloom, B. (1956). *Taxonomy of educational objectives*. New York: David McKay.

Bonny, H., & Savary, L. (1990). *Music and your mind*. Barrytown, NY: Station Hill Press.

Brody, N. (2006). Geocentric theory: A valid alternative to Gardner's theory of intelligence. In J. A. Schaler (Ed.), *Howard Gardner under fire: The rebel psychologist faces his critics* (pp. 73–94). Chicago: Open Court.

Campbell, L., & Campbell, B. (2000). *Multiple intelligences and student achievement: Success stories from six schools*. Alexandria, VA: ASCD.

Carini, P. (1977). *The art of seeing and the visibility of the person*. Grand Forks, ND: Center for Teaching and Learning, University of North Dakota.

Caro, R. (1990). *Means of ascent: The years of Lyndon Johnson* (Vol. 2). New York: Knopf.

Carroll, J. B. (1993). *Human cognitive abilities: A survey of factor-analytic studies*. Cambridge, UK: Cambridge University Press.

Chan, D. (2007). Musical aptitude and multiple intelligences among Chinese gifted students in Hong Kong: Do self-perceptions predict abilities? *Personality and Individual Differences, 43*(6), 1604–1615.

Chanda, S. (2001, March). Multiple ways of teaching and learning in Bangladesh. *Teachers Forum*. Retrieved June 30, 2008, from http://www.unicef.org/teachers/forum/0301.htm

Chen, J. Q., Moran, S., & Gardner, H. (In press). *Multiple intelligences theory around the world*. San Francisco: Jossey-Bass.

Chideya, A. (1991, December 2). Surely for the spirit, but also for the mind. *Newsweek*, 61.

Clark, R. W. (1972). *Einstein: The life and times*. New York: Avon.

Cohen, D. L. (1991, June 5). "Flow room," testing psychologist's concept, introduces "learning in disguise" at Key School. *Education Week*, 6–7.

Collins, J. (1998, October 19). Seven kinds of smart. *Time*, 94–96.

Comte, A. (1988). *Introduction to positive philosophy*. Indianapolis, IN: Hackett.

Csikszentmihalyi, M. (1990). *Flow: The psychology of optimal experience*. New York: Harper & Row.

Denzin, N., & Lincoln, Y. (Eds.). (2005). *The Sage book of qualitative research* (3rd ed.). Thousand Oaks, CA: Sage.

Diaz-Lefebvre, R., & Finnegan, P. (1997). Coloring outside the lines: Applying the theory of multiple intelligences to the community college setting. *Community College Journal, 68*(2), 28–31.

Dilthey, W. (1989). *Introduction to the human sciences: An attempt to lay a foundation for the study of society and history*. Detroit, MI: Wayne State University Press.

Dreikurs, R. (1993). *Logical consequences: The new approach to discipline.* New York: Plume.

Edwards, B. (1989). *Drawing on the right side of the brain* (Rev. ed.). Los Angeles: Jeremy P. Tarcher.

Ellison, L., & Rothenberger, B. (1999). In Bangladesh: The multiple ways of teaching and learning. *Educational Leadership, 57*(1), 54–57.

Engel, B. S. (1979). *Informal evaluation.* Grand Forks, ND: Center for Teaching and Learning, University of North Dakota.

Feldman, D. H. (1980). *Beyond universals in cognitive development.* Norwood, NJ: Ablex.

Fiske, E. B. (1987, January 11). U.S. pupils lag in math ability, 3 studies find. *New York Times,* pp. A1, A17–A18.

Fiske, E. B. (1988, May 24). In Indiana, public school makes "frills" standard. *New York Times,* pp. A16–A17.

Fleming, E. (1984). *Believe the heart: Our dyslexic days.* San Francisco: Strawberry Hill Press.

Furnham, A., & Akanda, A. (2004). African parents' estimation of their own and their children's multiple intelligences. *Current Psychology, 22*(4), 281–294.

Furnham, A., & Fukumoto, S. (2008). Japanese parents' estimates of their own and their children's multiple intelligences: Cultural modesty and moderate differentiation. *Japanese Psychological Research, 50*(2), 63–76.

Furnham, A., & Wu, J. (2008). Gender differences in estimates of one's own and parental intelligence in China. *Individual Differences Research, 6*(1), 1–12.

Gadamer, H-G. (2005). *Truth and method.* New York: Continuum.

Gardner, H. (1979). The child is father to the metaphor. *Psychology Today, 12*(10), 81–91.

Gardner, H. (1987). Beyond IQ: Education and human development. *Harvard Educational Review, 57*(2), 187–193.

Gardner, H. (1989). *To open minds: Chinese clues to the dilemma of contemporary education.* New York: Basic Books.

Gardner, H. (1991). *The unschooled mind.* New York: Basic Books.

Gardner, H. (1993a). *Frames of mind: The theory of multiple intelligences—10th anniversary edition.* New York: Basic Books.

Gardner, H. (1993b). *Multiple intelligences: The theory in practice.* New York: Basic Books.

Gardner, H. (1993c). *Creating minds.* New York: Basic Books.

Gardner, H. (1995). Reflections on multiple intelligences: Myths and messages. *Phi Delta Kappan, 77*(3), 200–208.

Gardner, H. (1999). *Intelligence reframed: Multiple intelligences for the 21st century.* New York: Basic Books.

Gardner H. (2003, April 21). *Multiple intelligences after twenty years.* Paper presented at the annual meeting of the American Educational Research Association, Chicago.

Gardner, H. (2004). Audiences for the theory of multiple intelligences. *Teachers College Record, 106*(1), 212.

Gardner, H. (2006a). *Multiple intelligences: New horizons in theory and practice.* New York: Basic Books.

Gardner, H. (2006b). On failing to grasp the core of MI theory: A response to Visser et al. *Intelligence, 34*(5), 503–505.

Gardner, H. (2006c). Replies to my critics. In J. A. Schaler (Ed.), *Howard Gardner under fire: The rebel psychologist faces his critics* (pp. 277–307). Chicago: Open Court.

Gardner, H., Feldman, D. H., & Krechevsky, M. (Eds.). (1998a). *Project Zero frameworks for early childhood education, Vol. 1. Building on children's strengths: The experience of Project Spectrum.* New York: Teachers College Press.

Gardner, H., Feldman, D. H., & Krechevsky, M. (Eds.). (1998b). *Project Zero frameworks for early childhood education, Vol. 2. Project Spectrum: Early learning activities.* New York: Teachers College Press.

Gardner, H., Feldman, D. H., & Krechevsky, M. (Eds.). (1998c). *Project Zero frameworks for early childhood education, Vol. 3. Project Spectrum: Preschool assessment handbook.* New York: Teachers College Press.

Gardner, H., & Moran, S. (2006). The science of multiple intelligences theory: A response to Lynn Waterhouse. *Educational Psychologist, 4*(4), 227–232.

Gentile, J. R. (1988). *Instructional improvement: Summary and analysis of Madeline Hunter's essential elements of instruction and supervision.* Oxford, OH: National Staff Development Council.

Ghiselin, B. (1955). *The creative process.* New York: Mentor.

Gladwin, T. (1970). *East is a big bird: Navigation and logic on Puluwat Atoll.* Cambridge, MA: Harvard University Press.

Goertzel, V., Goertzel, M. G., & Goertzel, T. G. (2004). *Cradles of eminence: Childhoods of more than 700 famous men and women.* Scottsdale, AZ: Great Potential Press.

Goleman, D. (2006). *Emotional intelligence: Why it can matter more than IQ.* New York: Bantam.

Goodlad, J. I. (2004). *A place called school—20th anniversary edition.* New York: McGraw-Hill.

Goodman, J., & Weinstein, M. (1980). *Playfair: Everybody's guide to noncompetitive play.* San Luis Obispo, CA: Impact.

Gordon, W. J. J., & Poze, T. (1966). *The metaphorical way of learning and knowing.* Cambridge, MA: Porpoise.

Gottfredson, L. S. (2004). Schools and the "g" factor. *Wilson Quarterly, 28*(3), 35–45.

Gould, S. J. (1981). *The mismeasure of man.* New York: W. W. Norton.

Grandin, T., & Johnson, C. (2006). *Animals in translation: Using the mysteries of autism to decode animal behavior.* New York: Simon & Schuster.

Green, W. (1999, September). *The bourgeois gentleman, multiple intelligences theory, and public law courses.* Paper presented at the annual meeting of the American Political Science Association, Atlanta, GA.

Greenhawk, J. (1997). Multiple intelligences meet standards. *Educational Leadership, 5*(1), 62–64.

Gruber, H. (1977). Darwin's "tree of nature" and other images of wide scope. In J. Wechsler (Ed.), *On aesthetics in science* (pp. 121–142). Cambridge, MA: MIT Press.

Gundian, X., & Anrìquez, C. (1999, September). An innovative project for Chilean education: Colegio Amancay de La Florida. *New Horizons for Learning.* Retrieved June 30, 2008, from http://www.newhorizon.org/trans/international/gundian.htm

Harman, W., & Rheingold, H. (1984). *Higher creativity: Liberating the unconscious for breakthrough insights.* Los Angeles: Jeremy P. Tarcher.

Hart, L. (1981). Don't teach them; help them learn. *Learning, 9*(8), 39–40.

Herman, J. L., Aschbacher, P. R., & Winters, L. (1992). *A practical guide to alternative assessment.* Alexandria, VA: ASCD.

Hoerr, T. R. (2000). *Becoming a multiple intelligences school.* Alexandria, VA: ASCD.

Illingworth, R. S., & Illingworth, C. M. (1966). *Lessons from childhood: Some aspects of the early life of unusual men and women.* London: Livingstone.

Johnson, D., Johnson, R. T., & Holubec, E. (1994). *The new circles of learning: Cooperation in the classroom and school.* Alexandria, VA: ASCD.

John-Steiner, V. (1987). *Notebooks of the mind: Explorations of thinking.* New York: Harper & Row.

Jung, T., & Kim, M-H. (2005). The application of multiple intelligences theory in South Korea: The Project Spectrum approach for young children. *School Psychology International, 26*(5), 581–594.

Kluth, P. (2003). *You're going to love this kid!: Teaching students with autism in the inclusive classroom.* Baltimore: Brookes Publishing Co.

Kornhaber, M., Fierros, E., & Veenema, S. (2003). *Multiple intelligences: Best ideas from research and practice.* Upper Saddle River, NJ: Allyn & Bacon.

Kovalik, S. (1993). *ITI: The model—Integrated Thematic Instruction* (2nd ed.). Black Diamond, WA: Books for Educators.

Kovalik, S. (2001). *Exceeding expectations: A user's guide to implementing brain research in the classroom.* Black Diamond, WA: Books for Educators.

Kunkel, C. (2007). The power of Key: Celebrating 20 years of innovation at the Key Learning Community. *Phi Delta Kappan, 89*(3), 204–209.

Lemke, M., Sen, A., Pahlke, E., Partelow, L., Miller, D., Williams, T., Kastberg, D., & Jocelyn, L. (2004). *International outcomes of learning in mathematics literacy and problem solving: PISA 2003 results from the U.S. perspective.* Washington, DC: U.S. Department of Education, National Center for Education Statistics.

Manila Times. (2008, June 15). Multiple Intelligence High School: A school for future responsible entrepreneurs. Retrieved June 30, 2008, from http://www.manilatimes.net/national/2008/june/15/yehey/weekend/20080615week3.html

Marchand-Martella, N. E., Slocum, T. A., & Martella, R. E. (2003). *An introduction to direct instruction.* Upper Saddle River, NJ: Allyn & Bacon.

Margulies, N. (1991). *Mapping inner space: Learning and teaching mind mapping.* Tucson, AZ: Zephyr Press.

Margulies, N. (1995). *The magic seven: Tools for building multiple intelligences.* Chicago: Zephyr Press.

Marzano, R. J., Brandt, R. S., Hughes, C. S., Jones, B. F., Presseisen, B. Z., & Rankin, S. C. (1988). *Dimensions of thinking: A framework for curriculum and instruction.* Alexandria, VA: ASCD.

Matthews, G. B. (1996). *The philosophy of childhood*. Cambridge, MA: Harvard University Press.

McCloskey, D. N., & Ziliak, S. (2008). *The cult of statistical significance: How standard error costs us jobs, justice, and lives*. Ann Arbor, MI: University of Michigan Press.

McCoy, L. E. (1975). Braille: A language for severe dyslexics. *Journal of Learning Disabilities, 8*(5), 34.

McKenzie, W. (2005). *Multiple intelligences and instructional technology* (2nd ed.). Washington, DC: International Society for Technology in Education.

McKim, R. H. (1980). *Experiences in visual thinking* (2nd ed.). Boston: PWS Engineering.

Merrefield, G. E. (1997). Three billy goats and Gardner. *Educational Leadership, 55*(1), 58–61.

Miller, A. (1981). *The drama of the gifted child*. New York: Basic Books.

Mohktar, I. A., Majid, S., & Fu, S. (2007). Information literacy education through mediated learning and multiple intelligences. *Reference Services Review, 35*(3), 463–486.

Montessori, M. (1972). *The secret of childhood*. New York: Ballantine.

Morrison, P., & Morrison, P. (1994). *Powers of ten*. New York: W. H. Freeman.

Nelsen, J. (1999). *Positive time-out and over 50 ways to avoid power struggles in the home and the classroom*. New York: Prima.

Nord, W. A., & Haynes, C. C. (1998). *Taking religion seriously across the curriculum*. Alexandria, VA: ASCD.

Olson, L. (1988, January 27). Children "flourish" here: 8 teachers and a theory changed a school world. *Education Week*, 18–19.

Ostrander, S., & Schroeder, L. (1979). *Superlearning*. New York: Delta.

Paul, R. (1992). *Critical thinking: What every person needs to survive in a rapidly changing world*. Santa Rosa, CA: Foundation for Critical Thinking.

Perkins, D. N. (1981). *The mind's best work*. Cambridge, MA: Harvard University Press.

Plato. (1952). *The dialogues of Plato* (B. Jowett, Trans.). In R. M. Hutchins (Ed.), *Great books of the Western world* (Vol. 7). Chicago: Encyclopedia Britannica.

Polya, G. (1957). *How to solve it*. New York: Anchor Books.

Polyani, K. (1974). *Personal knowledge: Toward a post-critical philosophy*. Chicago: University of Chicago Press.

Popham, J. (2008). *Transformative assessment*. Alexandria, VA: ASCD.

Poplin, M. (1984). Summary rationalizations, apologies, and farewell: What we don't know about the learning disabled. *Learning Disability Quarterly, 7*(2), 133.

Posner, M. I. (2004). Neural systems and individual differences. *Teachers College Record, 106*(1), 24–30.

Proust, M. (1928). *Swann's way*. New York: Modern Library.

Recer, P. (2002, April 30). Study: Science literacy poor in U.S. *Associated Press*.

Reed, J. (2007, September). Learning with IB. *IB World*. Retrieved June 30, 2008, from http://www.ibo.org/ibworld/sept07/

Ribot, N. (2004, March). My experience using the Multiple intelligences. *New Horizons of Learning*. Retrieved March 17, 2009, from http://www.newhorizons.org/trans/international/ribot.htm

Rose, C. (1987). *Accelerated learning.* New York: Dell.

Rosenthal, R., & Jacobsen, L. (2004). *Pygmalion in the classroom: Teacher expectation and pupils' intellectual development.* New York: Crown House Publishing.

Rozin, P., Poritsky, S., & Sotsky, R. (1971, March 26). American children with reading problems can easily learn to read English represented by Chinese characters. *Science, 171*(3977), 1264–1267.

Sacks, O. (1985). *The man who mistook his wife for a hat.* New York: HarperCollins.

Sacks, O. (1990). *Seeing voices: A journey into the world of the deaf.* New York: Harper Collins.

Sacks, O. (1995). *An anthropologist on Mars.* New York: Vintage.

Sarangapani, P. M. (2000). The great Indian tradition. Retrieved June 30, 2008, from http://www.india-seminar.com/2000/493/493%20padma%20m%20sarangapani.htm

Schirduan, V., & Case, K. (2004). Mindful curriculum leadership for students with attention deficit hyperactivity disorder: Leading in elementary schools using multiple intelligences theory (SUMIT). *Teachers College Record, 106*(1), 87–95.

Schmidle, N. (2007, January 22). Reforming Pakistan's "dens of terror." Retrieved July 10, 2008, from http://www.truthdig.com/report/ item/20070122_nicholas_schmidle_reforming_pakistans_dens_of_terror/

Scripp, L. (1990). *Transforming teaching through arts PROPEL portfolios: A case study of assessing individual student work in the high school ensemble.* Cambridge, MA: Harvard Graduate School of Education.

Shearer, B. (1994). *Multiple Intelligence Developmental Assessment Scales (MIDAS).* Kent, OH: Multiple Intelligences Research and Consulting.

Shearer, B. (2004). Multiple intelligences after 20 years. *Teachers College Record, 106*(1), 2–16.

Silver, H., Strong, R., & Perini, M. (1997). Integrating learning styles and multiple intelligences. *Educational Leadership, 55*(1), 22–29.

Spearman, C. (1927). *The abilities of man: Their nature and measurement.* London: Macmillan.

Spolin, V. (1986). *Theater games for the classroom.* Evanston, IL: Northwestern University Press.

Steiner, R. (1964). *The kingdom of childhood.* London: Rudolf Steiner Press.

Swami, V., Furnham, A., & Kannan, K. (2006). Estimating self, parental, and partner intelligences: A replication in Malaysia. *Journal of Social Psychology, 146*(6), 645–655.

Taylor-King, S. (1997, July 9). *Using multiple intelligences and multisensory reinforcement approaches to enhance literacy skills among homeless adults.* Paper presented at the International Congress on Challenges to Education, Kihei, Hawaii. (ERIC Document Reproduction Service No. ED 417 332)

Teele, S. (1992). *Teele Inventory for Multiple Intelligences (TIMI).* Redlands, CA: Sue Teele & Associates, Inc.

Traub, J. (1998, October 26). Multiple intelligence disorder. *The New Republic, 219*(17), 20–23.

U.S. Department of Education. (2003). *Identifying and implementing educational practices supported by rigorous evidence: A user friendly guide.* Washington, DC: Author.

Viadero, D. (1991, March 13). Music and arts courses disappearing from curriculum, commission warns. *Education Week, 4.*

Visser, B., Ashton, M., & Vernon, P. (2006). Beyond G: Putting multiple intelligences to the test. *Intelligence, 34*(5), 487–502.

Wallis, C. (2008, June 8). No Child Left Behind: Doomed to fail? *Time.* Available: http://www.time.com/time/nation/article/0,8599,1812758,00.html

Walters, J., & Gardner, H. (1986, March 30). *The crystallizing experience: Discovery of an intellectual gift.* (ERIC Document Reproduction Service No. ED 254 544)

Waterhouse, L. (2006). Multiple intelligences, the Mozart effect, and emotional intelligence: A critical review. *Educational Psychologist, 4*(4), 207–225.

Weinreich-Haste, H. (1985). The varieties of intelligence: An interview with Howard Gardner. *New Ideas in Psychology, 3*(4), 47–65.

Weinstein, C. (1979). The physical environment of the school: A review of the research. *Review of Educational Research, 49*(4), 585.

Williams, W., Blythe, T., White, N., Li, J., Sternberg, R., & Gardner, H. (1996). *Practical intelligence for school.* New York: HarperCollins College Publishers.

Willingham, D. (2004). Reframing the mind. *Education Next, 4*(3), 19–24.

Wolf, D., LeMahieu, P., & Eresh, J. (1992). Good measure: Assessment as a tool for educational reform. *Educational Leadership, 49*(8), 8–13.

Zessoules, R., & Gardner, H. (1991). Authentic assessment: Beyond the buzzword and into the classroom. In V. Perrone (Ed.), *Assessment in schools* (pp. 47–71). Washington, DC: ASCD.

Index

Note: page numbers followed by *f* refer to figures. Those followed by n refer to notes.

About the Author

Thomas Armstrong is the author of four other books published by ASCD: *Awakening Genius in the Classroom* (1998), *ADD/ADHD Alternatives in the Classroom* (1999), *The Multiple Intelligences of Reading and Writing* (2003), and *The Best Schools: How Human Development Research Should Inform Educational Practice* (2006). He has also written several trade books, including *In Their Own Way: Discovering and Encouraging Your Child's Personal Learning Style* (Tarcher/Putnam, 1987), *7 Kinds of Smart: Identifying and Developing Your Many Intelligences* (Plume, 1993), *The Myth of the ADD Child: 50 Ways to Improve Your Child's Behavior and Attention Span Without Drugs, Labels, or Coercion* (Plume, 1997), and *The Human Odyssey: Navigating the Twelve Stages of Life* (Sterling, 2007). For further information about his work, visit his Web site at www.thomasarmstrong.com and his blog at www.thehumanodyssey.com. To contact him, write: P.O. Box 548, Cloverdale, CA 95425; phone: 707-894-4646; fax: 707-894-4474; or e-mail: thomas@thomasarmstrong.com.